P9-BJE-778

The Life and Political Times of
TOMMY DOUGLAS

The Life and Political Times of
TOMMY DOUGLAS

Walter Stewart

McArthur & Company
Toronto

First published in Canada in 2003 by McArthur & Company.

McArthur & Company
322 King St. West, Suite 402
Toronto, Ontario
M5V 1J2
www.mcarthur-co.com

Copyright © 2003 Walter Stewart

The use of any part of this publication reproduced, transmitted in any form or by any means, electronic, mechanical, photocopying, recording or otherwise stored in a retrieval system, without the expressed written consent of the publisher, is an infringement of the copyright law.

National Library of Canada Cataloguing in Publication

    Stewart, Walter, 1931-
    Tommy : the life and politics of Tommy Douglas / Walter Stewart.

    Includes index.
    ISBN 1-55278-382-0

    1. Douglas, T. C. (Thomas Clement), 1904-1986. 2. Saskatchewan—Politics and government—1944-1964. 3. Prime ministers—Saskatchewan—Biography. I. Title.

    FC3525.1.D68S74 2003   971.24'03'092   C2003-904056-9

Design & Composition: *Mad Dog Design*
Cover & f/x: *Mad Dog Design*
Cover Image: *The Canadian Press*
Printed in Canada by: *Transcontinental Printing Inc.*

An honest attempt has been made to secure permission for all photographs, and if there are errors or omissions, these are wholly unintentional and the publisher will be grateful to learn of them.

The publisher would like to acknowledge the financial support of the Government of Canada through the Book Publishing Industry Development Program, the Canada Council, and the Ontario Arts Council for our publishing activities. We also acknowledge the Government of Ontario through the Ontario Media Development Corporation Ontario Book Initiative.

10 9 8 7 6 5 4 3 2 1

Contents

Author's Note

I covered Tommy Douglas as a journalist for many years, as Ottawa correspondent for the *Star Weekly*; as Ottawa bureau chief for *Maclean's* magazine, then as associate editor, and later as Washington bureau chief; and as an investigative reporter for the *Toronto Star*. However, I had another and earlier acquaintance with him that should be mentioned here. In 1959, I became the editor of the *Ontario CCF News,* which flourished as the *Ontario New Democrat* when the Co-operative Commonwealth Federation became the New Democratic Party in 1961. I saw him from a closer, albeit less neutral, point of view before the Movement became merely another party.

One odd thing I noted was that he was much more friendly to me when I was a working journalist for the capitalist press than when I was, apparently, another loyal lad. I decided then that he was a much more complex character than the public image seemed to suggest. (When I said so in a profile in the *Star Weekly*, he was not pleased.)

Two first-rate biographies of Tommy have already been written, one by Doris Shackleton, the other by Thomas H. McLeod and Ian McLeod. The careful reader will see in the footnotes that I have leaned heavily on them. My reasons for entering the lists are twofold. The first is to present a look at the man that is essentially a survey of him in the political context of his times. The second is that, at this time when medicare is in crisis (again), it seems to me Canadians might want to know something more about the man without whom, I venture to say, medicare would not exist in Canada today.

A Summer Night in Regina

Probably the greatest speech in his life was in 1983 in Regina at the fiftieth annual convention. The greatness of the thing — with everyone else floundering in uncertainty — it was a very simple speech, nothing complicated.

— Tom McLeod, friend, co-worker, and biographer, 1990

Things were not going well. The New Democratic Party was assembled for its 1983 convention, 2,000 strong, with delegates, alternates, and observers; the bold banners blossomed along the auditorium walls; speeches had been prepared, and made, and received with applause, if not enthusiasm; and there were proposals, resolutions, memos, study notes, and raw ideas stuffed into the delegate kits, handbags, heads, purses, attaché cases throughout the hall. These proposals, resolutions, and ideas, once translated into action — which is always the hard part — would no doubt solve all the nation's ills, just as previous proposals, resolutions, and ideas had promised to do in a long line of party conferences reaching back to the beginning of the NDP's predecessor, the Co-operative Commonwealth Federation, half a century before.

The trouble was that nobody believed that anymore. In 1933, when 131 delegates gathered in the old Regina city hall, not far from here, they were fewer, poorer, and vastly less experienced. They came equipped with notepads and determination, and not much else. There was no sound system worthy of the name, no videos, music, prompters, computers, or consultants. But by God, they believed. And when that 1933 gathering passed the Regina Manifesto, with its ringing peroration that declared "No C.C.F. Government will rest content until it has eradicated capitalism," the delegates rose up on their hind legs and thundered their support.

They didn't understand all the complications this proud period would entail — it had been tacked on at the last moment, to give the thing some zing, and nobody really knew exactly what it meant — they had no doubt that it portended a tough time for the gang in charge, as it was meant to do.

Now, in 1983, what was once a movement had become a party. It had, from time to time and place to place, formed governments, and enacted legislation, and gained respectability. But the fire was gone. It suffered from tired blood and low polls. The NDP government of Saskatchewan, despite the leadership of Allan Blakeney, a man whose high intelligence and transparent decency were recognized from coast to coast, had been soundly trounced by Grant Devine's Conservatives in 1982. Federally, the NDP held 32 seats, exactly one more than its predecessor, the CCF, had held in 1945, its high point thirty-seven years earlier. Its share of the 1980 election vote had come to 18 per cent, 2 percentage points higher than it had been under the 1945 CCF. Moreover, the party was deeply split, by arguments over federal and provincial rights, energy policy, and economic reform. Socialism, the foundation of early CCF policy, was a dark secret whispered only in convention corridors. Capitalism was no longer to be eradicated, but embraced, in an "egalitarian society guaranteeing human freedom and promoting social and economic security,"[1] This wording could have slid smoothly down the gullets of not only every party in Canada, but the Republican Party of the United States. It would be easier to defend on the hustings than the eradication of capitalism, while making it harder to explain why Canada needed another party to pass pious clichés as platforms.

There were still believers, of course, mostly older folks, and a scattering of young ones, but the vast, central core of delegates did not believe, in their heart of hearts, that the NDP would ever form the government of Canada, so what was the point? The usual resolutions were drawn up, the usual speakers rose and moved and seconded, and the usual critics rose and complained and cavilled, but the overwhelming feeling in the steam bath of a hall favoured just getting on with it, and getting out into the soft evening air.

---

[1] This was the wording in the major resolution passed by the convention. Reported in *Leader-Post* (Regina), 2 July 1983, A4.

And then the doors swung open, and in came a golf cart — a golf cart, of all things — bearing a man who had not played golf in years, and trailing a mammoth replica of a birthday cake, with a sign saluting the party's fiftieth anniversary. Which it wasn't, of course; the NDP was formed in 1961, out of the ashes of the CCF, a quite different party. But the man had been around all that time: Tommy Douglas. This was his formal farewell, and the party wanted to show its appreciation for his decades of work with the usual presents, and a nice round of applause, and a chance to make a speech. Tommy was seventy-eight years old, and looked it. He was suffering from the cancer that would finally conquer him in 1986; his face was lined, with pain and weariness and plain old age, and he was drawn and gaunt. Well, he was always drawn and gaunt, come to that. He never weighed more than 135 pounds wringing wet. But the grin was still there, and, as the cart rolled around the hall, and he laughed and pointed, and joked with dear old friends from so many campaigns, so many battles, the mood shifted a little, and lightened.

He was introduced by Allan Blakeney, the convention chairman, and he cracked a few jokes. He was nervous. He didn't show it, but he never did. He had walked to the hall from his hotel, all the way down Victoria Avenue, although his old pal Ed Whelan had wanted to drive him. He told Ed that he wanted to walk because he wanted to be by himself, wanted to think out what he was going to say on this occasion, wanted to get it right.[2]

Which he did. After the jokes, he socked it to them. It was The Speech. He had given it many times before, but like every great speech, it improved with age. He had the timing just right, the pauses in just the right places, the lifted hand, the pointed finger, the long sentences broken by abrupt ones, the jokes interspersed with sombre warnings. It was a sermon, really — not surprising in a man who had trained as a preacher — a political sermon that drew on his experience, and his humanity, and his faith, to lift that crowd for forty-five minutes, and make it believe.

Political commentator Dale Eisler, no friend of the New Democrats, would later write, "It was as if the membership had been reawakened to

---

[2] Ed Whelan, interview by author, Regina, 26 October 2001.

the knowledge that to be a member of the NDP means to be a part of the political conscience of Canada."[3] Given the low state of the party, Eisler observed, "It was the ultimate irony for the NDP" that Tommy Douglas, its most potent personality by far, was able "to reconnect the delegates to their emotional links with the party's past. Suddenly, personalities didn't matter as much anymore."

Tommy told the assembly that they were in tough times, but they had always been in tough times. He told them that they had been beaten, and they would be beaten again. He told them that whenever the party came up with a really good idea, like decent pensions, or hospital insurance, or medicare, their political opponents were bound to steal it, and take it over, and make it less than what it was meant to be. But that didn't matter. What mattered was that the ideas took root, and became part of the culture, part of society, part of Canada.

Medicare was a case in point. Possibly, Canada would have had medicare without Tommy, and without the CCF, but there is much room for doubt. The Liberals began talking about a national health program in 1916, and put it into the official party program in 1919. Twenty-eight years later, in 1947, the government of Saskatchewan — Tommy's government, fed up with federal inaction — brought in the first state-financed, universal hospital insurance. And fourteen years after that, in 1961, the same government passed the nation's first full medicare scheme, in the teeth of the organized opposition of the medical establishment. And the elaborate disinterest, not to say hostility, of the federal government. When the party succeeded, when even the medical establishment agreed that it had succeeded, the Liberals took the program over, adopted it as their own, and began to boast that medicare reflected Canada's unique and caring personality.

At least that's what they said for public consumption. When Tommy rose to speak in Regina in 1983, a federal Liberal government was already beginning the process of what Tommy called "the subtle strangulation" of medicare. But the Liberals could only act so while praising the plan they choked.

---

[3] *Leader-Post* (Regina), 2 July 1983, A4.

Canadians in general knew how good medicare was; and, in general, they didn't care who had brought it in, or who got the credit, as long as it remained part of the national heritage. That was what ought to concern the party, Tommy told them. To defend medicare, "we must fight like we've never fought before." Whether they got credit for it was of less significance than whether the advance held. What was most important was not whether they won the next election, or the one after that, or the one after that, but whether they kept at the work they had begun here fifty years earlier — the building of a productive, caring, and peaceful world. Their concern ought to be not how large the party became, but whether it remained faithful to its founding ideas:

> The growth and development of the New Democratic Party must never allow us to forget our roots. Don't sacrifice conviction for success. Don't ever give up quality for quantity.
>
> In a movement like ours, as socialist movements around the world have demonstrated, we're not just interested in getting votes. We are seeking to get people who are willing to dedicate their lives to build a different kind of society, a society founded on the principles of concern for human well-being and human welfare.[4]

Well, as they say, the crowd went wild. People stood and cheered, waved their arms, banners, delegate kits; they stamped their feet, and hugged each other; and some — both men and women — stood there with arms held out and wept openly. It all came together for them, all the hopes of yesterday, all the dreams of tomorrow, all the triumphs and disappointments, focussed on and through this grey-haired, tired, ailing little man with the lined face and large grin. They wouldn't shut up. After five minutes, Allan Blakeney moved to the microphone where Tommy still stood, and he waved his arms, feebly and forlornly, at the crowd. Then they began to sing. Tommy and Allan both sat down, but

---

[4] Quoted in Thomas H. McLeod and Ian McLeod, *Tommy Douglas: The Road to Jerusalem* (Edmonton: Hurtig, 1987), 308. Tom McLeod was a close friend and co-worker of Tommy's; Ian was his son; together they produced a biography Tommy would have been proud of.

the roar, if anything, grew louder. Tommy leaned over to Allan and said, "Shut 'em down, Al; for Pete's sake, shut 'em down!"[5]

So Allan got up and waved at the crowd again, but they wouldn't stop. Then Tommy climbed up on a table and tried to hush them so the meeting could go on, but that just made them holler all the louder.

It went on for twenty-three minutes, and nobody who was there will ever forget it, as the party said goodbye to Tommy and all he meant, in hopes and dreams, not only to the people there but to the entire nation. It was hard to know whether they were moved more by sorrow, because Tommy was leaving them, or by renewed faith; what was clear was that they were moved, and that they would go on.

That was Tommy Douglas. He was a little man, but he cast a long shadow. There was no one like him.

Chapter ONE

The Spotted Kirk

Health enthusiasts might try Thomas Lyon's "crebanus borax and eucalyptus soap," visit Alexander McDonald, the "tonsorial artist," where the "hair brushing is done by machinery," or even pass an hour or two at the new Waverley Public Wash-House and Baths in the Howgate, described as "a much desiderated convenience, and a marvel of moderation in respect of tariff."
— Ian Scott, *The Life and Times of Falkirk,* 1994

Thomas Clement Douglas was born on October 20, 1904, in Falkirk, Scotland, a town about thirty kilometres east of Glasgow, on the railway line between that city and Edinburgh. At that time, Falkirk was noted for its glorious history and dirty iron foundries, and not much else. Because of its advantageous position in the valley of the River Forth, and the surrounding flat and fertile lands, it has been inhabited since at least 4000 BC by fishing families and primitive farmers. It was also occupied, and then abandoned, by Roman legions, who built a section of the Antonine Wall right through the centre of town, as well as erecting a scattering of forts nearby. The wall, nearly sixty kilometres long, three metres high, and five metres across in spots, does not seem to have kept anybody out, but it must have impressed the lurking tribes in the area, and it provided a splendid two-year burst of activity for the legions from AD 142 to 144. It is all gone now, with Nineveh and Tyre, but parts of the ditch that bordered it can still be seen in Callendar Park, on the edge of the modern city.

Demons with Ox Goads Required

You cannot chuck half a brick in any direction anywhere in Britain without hitting some claim that the legendary King Arthur once passed this way, and Falkirk had its own "Arthur's O'on" (Arthur's Oven), which had absolutely nothing to do with Arthur, except in the minds of the locals. It was, in fact, a Roman monument, and possibly a place of worship. It stood about seven metres high and was round — in drawings, it looks like a stone igloo — with walls more than a metre thick. It was torn down by Sir Michael Bruce in 1743, to provide a cheap supply of dressed stones for a weir on the River Carron.

Not a popular move. A scholar of the time prayed that Sir Michael, the oaf, would be fitted with an iron collar, with two stones from Arthur's O'on suspended therefrom. "Thus accoutered let him wander the banks of the Styx, perpetually agitated by angry demons with ox goads."[1]

I bring this up to let you know that Tommy was born steeped in history and tough attitudes.

The Roman departure led to centuries of not much happening, until, not long after the Norman Conquest, King William sent his son Robert to Scotland, to battle Malcolm (no luck there). Robert visited a settlement known in Gaelic as Egglesbreth, which meant "speckled" or "spotted" church. Later, this became Faukirk or Fawkirk or even Faukirke, take your choice, all of which mean "spotted church" and referred to the odd-coloured stones of the local church's construction. In the early nineteenth century, the church minister dug up what he purported was an inscribed foundation stone that proved the church had been founded by Malcolm III, in 1080. He needed such a proof to help him in a lawsuit; but, as someone had carelessly engraved the date in Arabic numerals, which were not in use in Scotland in the eleventh century, the minister was treated with some skepticism, and lost his case.

William Wallace lost a great battle here — the First Battle of Falkirk — to King Edward I on July 22, 1298, and fled towards the River Carron. One of the prisoners exchanged after the battle was Sir John de

---

[1] Ian Scott, *The Life and Times of Falkirk* (Edinburgh: John McDonald Publishers, 1994), 14.

Livingston, who fought on the English side. After that, the local notables became adept at switching sides whenever the swords came out — and if they later discovered they were on the wrong side, they would switch again.

Mary Queen of Scots often stayed at Callendar House nearby (she was once under the protection of its lord), and the area was much fought over in the days of Cromwell, as the gentry here declared for the Stuart kings (although the kirk shunned them). The notables took off for France to rally around the Stuart cause, leaving their loyal followers to explain things to the swords of the English.

There followed some centuries of dynastic wars, cattle raising, cattle thieving, religious strife, crop failures, and hard times — the usual Scottish fare — which included the Second Battle of Falkirk, won by the Jacobites, with the locals on the winning side for once, almost immediately followed by the Battle of Culloden, just down the road from Falkirk, near Stirling. By the mid-eighteenth century, Falkirk, despite the presence of eighteen bakers, twenty-two grocers, and four watchmakers, was still nothing much. And then, in 1759, the Industrial Revolution came to town, with the establishment of the Carron iron works, followed by the cutting of the great canal from Forth to Clyde.

The Carron Works became the town's principal employer, making stoves, grates, kitchen ranges, pots, kettles, spades, hoes, hinges, bolts, sugar boilers for the West Indies, and cannons for the British army. The word "carronade," describing a short, light iron cannon, salutes this last activity. By the end of the nineteenth century, the town's population had grown to 16,000, with 4 out of 10 men in the burgh employed in the iron industry.

"Men were attracted to the town in large numbers by the prospect of steady employment, no matter how punishing or unpleasant,"[2] historian Ian Scott writes.

> The iron foundries which earned fortunes for their masters offered unremitting, back-breaking labour in the foullest of conditions . . . The people had to survive

---

[2] Ibid., 117–18.

as best they could and, sadly, many found relief from
their labours at the bottom of a whisky glass in any one
of the dozens of Falkirk pubs which stood along the
length of the High Street.[3]

One of these pubs, the Crosskeys, enjoyed the patronage of Robert
Burns, the wicked radical poet whose works were Tommy's lifelong
treasure.

Falkirk had a poorhouse, accommodation for "lunatic paupers," and,
in 1894, when a depression led to layoffs in the iron industry, a soup
kitchen, where the poor were fed with cattle carcasses that had been
condemned because they were infected with tuberculosis, although it
was recognized that "it would be better to say nothing about it, and so
the meat problem was solved."[4]

Tom Douglas, Tommy's paternal grandfather, was an iron moulder at
Falkirk. (I asked my cab driver, who showed me around the present,
pleasant city of 146,000, what an iron moulder was. "Fella who moulds
iron," he replied. The local museum proves this to be true; it has an old
photograph of a man standing on the edge of a huge metal box, pushing
molten iron with a paddle towards forms.) He was a self-taught intellectual — no surprise, the schools were dreadful — a radical Liberal, and an
ardent admirer of Burns, whose poems he recited by the hour to his
grandson.

Tom Douglas, Tommy's father, followed his own father into the
foundry at the age of thirteen, going to school in the morning and
working in the afternoon. The next year, he went to work full-time. The
eldest of eight brothers, he was a tall man, strong and well built, quick of
temper, fond of argument, and full of politics, although he never became
a formal politician. He supported the newly created Scottish Labour
Party, a precursor to the Labour Party in Britain. It was founded by Keir
Hardie, a self-educated working man, like Tom Douglas, and a devout
Christian from a nonconformist sect. Hardie could never get elected in

---

[3] Ibid., 125.
[4] The quote is from the burgh surveyor of the time, David Ronald, in his memoirs.

Scotland, which was dominated by Gladstone's Liberals, and finally got into the House of Commons with the votes of dockside workers in London's east end.

Tom's embrace of the Labour Party, later followed by all seven of his brothers (but not his lone sister), led to tremendous rows with his father, who remained loyal to the Liberals, and the two men did not speak for months as a result. Also as a result of this quarrel, young Tom and his wife, Anne, were evicted from a house that they rented from his father. They moved into another rental house in the Sunnyside district of Falkirk (the place where the house once stood is a cricket field today), and it was here that Tommy was born. One day not long after Tommy's birth, Grandfather Tom appeared at the door, announcing that he had "come to see the boy." The family split was at an end, though not the arguments about politics.

Robbie Burns

Anne Clement, Tom's wife, and Tommy's mother, was the daughter of a Highlander who had come down to Glasgow speaking only Gaelic and got a job working in the huge co-operative wholesale market near the Glasgow waterfront, on the street where Tom and his family were later to live. Her father, Andrew Clement, was Conservative, and Baptist, and had been a Baptist lay preacher, so he, too, was a nonconformist, although on the religious rather than political side. He regarded Robbie Burns as a womanizer, a drunk, and a heretic, all of which was, of course, perfectly true. Tom and Tommy saw only that Burns was a nationalist, and a wonder with a line of poetry.

Anne Clement, a small but vibrant woman, went to work in the cotton mills at Paisley at the age of sixteen. If Tommy knew how his parents met, he didn't say, but he has left vivid descriptions of both of them. Of Anne, he said:

> Certainly, she was the religious influence in our home,
> and in terms of public speaking and elocution, she was

the most influential. Whenever any of us had to say a piece at the Christmas Tree, we would say it before my mother twice a day for a week before, and she would drill us on it . . . She had the Highland strain in there, the imagination. I can remember our main family treat when we were small was Sunday evening, when we would all sit around and she would read to us . . . She read beautifully and with imagination. The characters became alive. She was largely responsible for my great interest in English literature and dramatics.[5]

Tom Douglas, like his father, was a master moulder, which meant that he made a good wage; the family — Tommy had one sister, Nan, at the time; Isobel, another sister, was born soon after the move to Canada — was comfortable, if never rich. Tommy's radicalism was never driven by deprivation, but by background and observation. His grandfathers and parents all taught him, in their various ways, the importance of thinking for oneself, and not being afraid to strike out on new intellectual paths. It is clear from his recollections in *The Making of a Socialist* that Tommy got his imagination and his religion from his mother, his stubborn integrity from his father, and his fire from both.

His father had little patience with organized religion, which he saw as part and parcel of the Liberal establishment, so he left that side of life pretty much to his wife. Of Tom, Tommy said this, in part:

Sometimes he would lean over backwards to make sure nobody would think he was trying to pretend to be something he wasn't. I can still recollect one of the things he used to do when he would come back from working in the foundry. He still had the black sand on him, and although he had had a bit of a wash at the works, he would never be quite cleaned up. When he came into the house, the first thing he did was sit down

[5] T.C. Douglas, interviews by Chris H. Higginbotham, in *The Making of a Socialist: The Recollections of T.C. Douglas*, ed. Lewis H. Thomas (Edmonton: University of Alberta Press, 1982), 21–22. Noted journalist and radio personality Chris Higginbotham conducted a series of taped interviews with Tommy in late 1958, from which this book was produced.

with a bottle of beer. He worked over a 200-degree furnace all day and perspired heavily, and so he'd go and have a bottle of beer and go and have a bath and then he'd come down and have his supper. He came in one day and the minister was in visiting our home. My mother and the rest of us were all on our best behaviour. So the minister wouldn't be under any misapprehension, my father said to him, "I'm going to have a bottle of beer. Would you like one?" This embarrassed my mother and sisters and myself considerably, and undoubtedly the minister, who was a strict Baptist teetotaler. But my father felt he wasn't going to do without the beer, not because he minded doing without the beer, but because he didn't want anyone to get the impression that he was trying to keep the minister from knowing that he had a glass of beer when he came in. This is the sort of thing he did all his life.[6]

It is not easy to form a picture of Tommy's early days by walking around modern Falkirk, a city with a good deal more scrubbing and a good deal less sanctimoniousness than it had at the start of the twentieth century. The Carron Works closed long ago; all that remains is a sort of stone keep, decorated with old cannons and a plaque. No doubt, in time, these will become "Arthur's Cannon," to prod the brisk tourist trade hereabouts. The largest local industries in the area today are a petrochemical complex serving the North Sea oil development and an electronics firm turning out doodads mainly for American defence firms. The town centre houses a splendid new shopping mall, and the old streets with names like Cow's Wynd and Comely Place are lined with chi-chi townhouses cunningly fitted into centuries-old stone edifices. A local history notes with regret that, where once mighty hammers clanged, the sounds today are made by hedge clippers.

---

[6] Ibid.

Plenty of Rats

It is very much to be doubted that Tom or Tom or Tommy Douglas would share in this regret. The Falkirk of Tommy's youth was dirty, depressed, and despairing. Most of its population worked for scarce wages and lived in teeming tenements, some of them dating from the 1600s, whose populations included "immigrant labourers, street entertainers, second hand dealers and public scavengers."[7] And rats, of course. Lots of rats.

> In this Scotland, according to the first manifesto of the Scottish Labour Party, every twentieth inhabitant is a pauper, a million men are out of work, one-fifth of the community is insufficiently clad, what are known as starvation diseases are rife among large classes, and . . . one-third to one-half of the families of the country are huddled together six to a room.[8]

It was a time and place where even such facilities as lights, water, and clean streets were considered less important than low or no taxes (is there an echo of today in here?), and medical care was scant and crude. This became important when at the age of six, Tommy, a small, slight, and sickly boy, fell and cut his right knee on a stone. The knee failed to heal, and osteomyelitis developed in the leg. He was operated on at the kitchen table, with his mother and grandmother on hand to administer chloroform. The operation was not a success, with results, as we shall see, that came to affect a nation.

These were the discontents that were breeding unrest, political dissent, and even backchat against the landlords. The notion that things had to go on as before was becoming shopworn, and the class distinctions that divided Falkirk just as sharply as the railway line were anathema to Tom Douglas. Tommy later recalled:

> I think one of the things that made him want to leave Scotland, one of the things that made me, even as a boy,

---

[7] Scott, *Falkirk,* 129.
[8] Quoted in McLeod and McLeod, *Road to Jerusalem,* 9.

glad to be leaving Scotland, was his hatred of class distinction. The idea of taking off your cap to a squire and touching your cap to the doctor and preacher was foreign to him. He felt that he was as good as any man, and that a man's a man:

> The rank is but the guinea's stamp,
> The man's the gowd for a' that.

If he were honest and upright with God and man, he had as much right to walk the earth with dignity as any lord or knight or king.[9]

Burns's lines, as quoted above, represented nothing more than a vague wish when he wrote them, and things weren't much better in Scotland at this time. For Tom Douglas, there was another unsettling, or, if you prefer, broadening, experience to make him restless. He had joined the British army during the Boer War and had served not only in South Africa but in India and Afghanistan with the Sutherland Highlanders. He caught enteric fever and was invalided back to Scotland, where he worked as head gardener at the hospital while he recovered. In due course, he regained his strength and went back to the foundry. But he was not going to settle down peaceably in the backwater that was then Falkirk, especially at a time when, in the great world outside, there were political changes in the air, led by men like Keir Hardie.

The Labour Party emerged in 1900, then under the name of the Labour Representation Committee, an affiliation of the Independent Labour Party, founded in 1893 by Hardie, the Fabian Society, and the Social Democratic Federation, a Marxist group originated by Henry Mayers Hyndman (who later took his group out to form the British Socialist Party). The founding meeting defeated two motions, one for a party based upon "recognition of class war," another that only "members of the working class" would be accepted as parliamentary candidates. Instead, the 129 delegates agreed with Hardie's argument that the party must have "flexibility for development." The former Scots coal miner

---

[9] Douglas, *The Making of a Socialist*, 18.

trilled, "It has come. Poor little child of danger, nursling of the storm. May it be blessed."[10]

In 1905, a royal commission was established to examine what was known as the New Poor Law — essentially, an early-nineteenth-century updating of the Elizabethan Poor Law of 1601 — which retained the original legislation's underlying principle that poverty was, at bottom, the fault of the poor. The commission found that the law was not working very well. There were more poor than ever, and despite the constant assurances that jobs were to be found, if only the slackers would look hard enough, such jobs remained elusive. Even the best endeavours of the workhouses to drive what we would now call social-welfare bums out to shift for themselves, by making life miserable within the institutions (a variation of the same basic approach of many modern governments), did not seem to produce employment. Moreover, the private charities on which most of the burden for caring for the underprivileged fell were, at best, indiscriminate, and at worst, bereft of reason. The commissioners described a woman who was so moved by a Sunday sermon on the perils of the poor that she took to the streets to distribute champagne and grapes to London's helpless hordes.[11]

The majority report of the commissioners abandoned the cosy notion that most of society's ills were caused by sinful sloth, and suggested that instead of deterring the poor from applying for assistance by making its availability as harsh and spare as possible, the government should recognize that at least some poverty was a direct result of the way the industrial system operated — an argument we appear to be revisiting today. There ought to be an old-age pension, the commissioners concluded, free hospital treatment for those in need, and more residential homes for orphans and foundlings. These would be provided in the main by the existing charities on a voluntary basis, but where it was required — and especially in the matter of old-age pensions — the necessary funding would come from government.[12]

All of this was directly contrary to the doctrines that most Scots had imbibed with their haggis, doctrines that left the poor pretty much to

[10] Clifton Daniel, ed., *Chronicle of the Twentieth Century* (London: Dorling Kindersley, 1995), 13.
[11] Anne Daltrop, *Charities* (London: B.T. Batsford, 1978), 62.
[12] Ibid., 58.

the care of Lady Bountiful, church charity, and the workhouses. But worse was to come. A minority report by two of the commissioners took the debate to another stage. This report was written by Beatrice and Sidney Webb, early members of the Fabian Society and supporters of the Labour Party (Beatrice Potter, daughter of a wealthy industrialist, had married Sidney James Webb, a senior civil servant and economist; together they helped to launch the London School of Economics in 1895, and the *New Statesman* in 1913). They proposed scrapping the Poor Law entirely, and bolstering private charity with state social services to protect everyone, not merely the poor, against illness and misfortune. They advocated that it should be the task of government — and not the vicar's daughter — to provide a framework of prevention, and that a state-supported pension should support not only the poor but the general populace in old age.

Charity Did More Harm than Good

Indeed, the Webbs argued in a series of books and tracts, private charity was doing more harm than good, since it relieved some of the symptoms of poverty without attacking the base cause, which was an industrial system founded on the exploitation of one class by another. Voluntary agencies would always be needed to supplement the state, but the main burden ought to be borne by government. The Webbs, reflecting European experiments, foreshadowed the welfare state, with its underlying principles of universality and government funding of the major elements of social care. Their minority report was a direct attack on the private charity system then in place, and its arguments provided the fundamental divide in the Douglas household: the split between the gradual and long-drawn-out reforms advocated by the Liberals and the rough surgery that the Labour Party (not the present one, of course) held to be the minimum possible change to combat unbridled capitalism.

The majority report of the commissioners, though seen as too timid by the Webbs, did represent real change, and became the rationale behind the budget of 1909, drawn up by David Lloyd George and adopted by Herbert Asquith's Liberal government.

"Four spectres haunt the poor," Lloyd George told Parliament. "Old age, accident, sickness and unemployment. We are going to exorcise them."[13] And his budget proposed just that, not by having the state take over the work of private charities, but by having it supplement them to a degree unheard of in England, though well known in continental Europe. It provided for a system of social insurance, including non-contributory old-age pensions, labour exchanges, and a fledgling program to provide at least some unemployment and sickness insurance. This would be financed to some measure by contributions from earnings, but also from land and income taxes; the general purse would be called on to take at least part of the place of Lady Bountiful. What is more, the dreadful deed would be accomplished by a tax of nine pence on the pound on incomes up to £2,000, and a shilling on the pound on incomes above that level. A "super tax" was also proposed: an additional tax of six pence on the pound on income above £3,000.

The House of Lords rose as one to veto the budget, and Asquith asked King Edward VII to create enough new Liberal peers to overwhelm the old Tories and get the budget through. Edward hated this idea, so he dithered and did nothing, and died instead. In the end, the Liberals fought and won a new election on the basis of the budget of 1909, which became the budget of 1910, with the support of Labour members. However, that spasm of reform seemed to sap the energies of Liberalism, which lapsed back into fiddling gingerly around the edges of the status quo.

By this time, Tom Douglas had decided, as had many of his fellow countrymen and -women, that there was no great future for individuals of his class and views in Scotland. The debates about poverty, its causes, and its cures echoed as stridently in the streets of Falkirk as in the thoroughfares of London, but the lives of ordinary people never seemed to change. There was an income tax, yes, and there were the timid beginnings of publicly supported social assistance, but these grudging gifts seemed

---

[13] John Grigg, *Lloyd George: 1902–1911, The People's Champion* (London: Methuen, 1978), 194.

to empty the Liberal locker. Not long after the Lloyd George budget staggered through an embattled House of Commons for the second time, Tom Douglas, fed up with the laggard pace of reform, was on board a ship for Canada and a new life entirely. It would not work out quite the way he expected — or, at least, not at first.

———————————————

Chapter TWO

The False Start

I felt that no boy should have to depend either for his leg or his life upon the ability of his parents to raise enough money to bring a first-class surgeon to his bedside . . . I came to believe that health services ought not to have a price-tag on them, and that people should be able to get whatever health services they required irrespective of their individual capacity to pay.

— Tommy Douglas, *The Making of a Socialist*

It was Tom's younger brother, Willie, who persuaded him that there were more opportunities in Canada than in Scotland. Willie had already spent some time in western Canada, and could sense that Winnipeg, launched into a period of growth and prosperity by the completion of the Canadian Pacific Railway in 1885, was the natural focus for western expansion. Despite the plethora of muddy streets and plank buildings, to say nothing of outhouses, it was no longer just a railhead and grain town, but the administrative centre of a booming territory, and a growing manufacturing town as well. In 1911, the year after Tom Douglas made his move, Winnipeg ranked fourth in Canada in manufacturing. Lots of jobs for iron moulders.

In the fall of 1910, Willie and Tom walked from the Winnipeg train station to a boarding house on Disraeli Street, where Mrs. Mariah Finn welcomed them in, and asked for a week's rent in advance: $4.55. They paid her with two gold sovereigns they had brought from Scotland.[1] Tom quickly got a job at the Vulcan Iron Works, whose belching furnaces must have made him feel at least a little at home in the strange new city. As soon as he had saved up the money, he sent Willie back to

[1] McLeod and McLeod, *Road to Jerusalem*, 5. Mariah Finn was the great-grandmother of Tom McLeod, the man who was to become Tommy's friend, co-worker, and biographer. She held on to the gold sovereigns, which passed down through the family. Tom's wife, Beryl, wore one attached to a bracelet, but had no idea where it had come from until 1986, when Tom's Aunt Kate, in a discussion about the early days in Winnipeg, mentioned it.

Scotland to bring over Anne and the two children, Tommy and Nan. The second daughter, Isobel, was born soon after their arrival.

Tommy later recalled that the sea voyage from Glasgow to Halifax took seventeen days because of fog, and the train trip in the old, crude colonist cars, another five days.

> We cooked our meals in a little kitchen at the end. [The cars] were pretty dilapidated. We slept on the hard boards. I can remember my father meeting us. I can remember coming out of the CPR station and seeing the old Countess of Dufferin, the old locomotive. I can remember a few days after arriving, the big Decoration Day parade . . . to decorate the graves of the men who fought in the Riel Rebellion. My father, as a South African veteran, was in the parade . . .
>
> . . . Winnipeg in those days was a fascinating place. People were pouring in between 1910 and 1912 from all over central Europe and the United Kingdom. Housing was hard to get, most of the houses that people like ourselves lived in were out in the suburbs, in Elmwood, houses that were not modern, where you had to carry the water.[2]

The Douglas family came to a city, and a country, that was mushrooming under the impetus of immigration. Three million immigrants poured into a nation of scarcely 5 million in the years from 1897 to 1914; about one million of these came tumbling up from the United States, another million, roughly, from Britain, and the final million from eastern and southern Europe — Germany, the Austro-Hungarian Empire, the Ukraine, the Balkans, and Italy, in the main. The populations of Montreal and Toronto were doubled, but the population of Winnipeg increased fivefold and by 1911 stood at 136,035; it was the third most populous city in Canada.[3]

---

[2] Douglas, *The Making of a Socialist*, 12.

[3] Robert Craig Brown and Ramsay Cook, *Canada 1896–1921: A Nation Transformed* (Toronto: McClelland & Stewart, 1974), 98–99, table III.

Chicago North

Winnipeg was, in a phrase popular at the time, "the Chicago of Canada," because of its hustle, its rapid growth and change, and its crudity. Two contemporary commentators described two entirely different cities within the single bounds of Winnipeg. The first, in a *Canada To-day* article that shied away from the back alleys, said:

> The present handsome and commodious railroad station is the third in twenty years, while the huge building going up on Main Street is the third post office. The "best hotel" last year is replaced by a better one this year, and the omnipotent CPR is erecting a palace of its own, which will absorb the wealthy travellers next year.
>
> All the modern conveniences of street railways, electric light, etc., are furnished in abundance; the brand-new Manitoba Club, where the city magnates meet for lunch, leaves nothing to be desired in comfort and "elegance," while the store set up by Eaton of Toronto occupies a solid block.[4]

Meanwhile, J. Woodsworth, the superintendent of the All People's Mission in Winnipeg, and a man who was to become so crucial to Tommy, saw things somewhat differently:

> The tendency is that the well-to-do gather together in more or less exclusive suburbs, while the poor are segregated in slum districts, and in between these there is comparatively little direct intercourse ... A woman may superintend laundry operations in her own house, but she knows little or nothing of the home life of her washerwoman ... They live in two worlds ... This condition is intensified and more complicated when large numbers of foreigners are brought into our civic life. Differences of language, of race and of religion, often

---

[4] J.A. Hobson, in *Canada To-day* (London, 1906).

running parallel, deepen and broaden the chasm. The people who most need help are separated from those who could best help them.[5]

If the Douglas family had to carry water, they were, compared to many of the other immigrants around them, well off. Tom was a skilled journeyman, with fairly regular work at modest, but adequate, wages. They lived in a comfortable rented house, first on Jarvis Street, later on Gladstone, in Winnipeg's north end, not far from the Vulcan Iron Works on Sutherland Avenue, and the All People's Mission.

The mission, run by the Methodists, was spread out over the neighbourhood, part school, part church, part social centre. It offered immigrant mothers classes in English, nutrition, and child care, and before long, the energetic Anne was a volunteer there. Anne took in boarders to augment the family income, while Tom, a gifted gardener, grew vegetables in the back yard for pleasure and the table. Tommy started school in Winnipeg, at Norquay Public School, and spent much of his spare time, when he was not running errands for his mother, at the mission, where he met J. Woodsworth, a slight man with a brown beard, a man he soon admired tremendously, but whose austere demeanour kept a seven-year-old boy, as Tommy was in 1911, at some distance. Tommy never spoke to J., that remote and godlike figure; he had much more to do with the Reverend Harry Atkins, who ran the boys' program at the mission.

Tommy carried two strong impressions from this time. One was, "I realized how much what I would call underprivileged boys need help, and how little the organized church and society was supplying at that time."[6] It was the renegade church, if you like, the church run by a radical like Woodsworth, that carried the load, while the wealthier institutions contented themselves with preaching sermons designed to instruct the downtrodden to accept their lot in life, and live in hope that if the rich got rich enough, some crumbs would slide off the banquet table in the right direction. Today, we call this the trickle-down theory, and it is much admired, still, in the right circles.

---

[5] J.S. Woodsworth, "Some Aspects of the Immigration Problem," *Young Women of Canada* (December 1909).
[6] Douglas, *The Making of a Socialist,* 14.

The second overwhelming recollection for Tommy was "the fact that I was tossed into the middle of what was a Tower of Babel."[7] The boys Tommy knew at school and from play spoke a dozen different languages.

> You lost all sense of national or racial pride, and began to realize the value and worth of other people of other races. They were wrestling the same problems we were. They were trying to get established. They were trying to get jobs. They were trying to get decent houses to live in. They were trying to speak the language properly and adapt themselves to the country. The fact that they had sheepskin coats and the women wore babushkas was secondary. You found that basically you were the same.[8]

Nothing in his later life ever changed these two strong impressions, and they explain something of what was developing in the skinny little lad from Scotland who went to school, played basketball, swam, and even began to box at the boys' club of the mission.

But it was not a time of much happiness for Tommy. First of all, there was the common, basic unfairness of the treatment of labour:

> Even the men who were working, like my father, were working short time, three days a week. A man would go down and stand around maybe half a day, to find out if he was going to get any work, and finally at noon be told there was nothing, and come back home not having earned a five-cent piece. Those were pretty grim times for us. We didn't suffer, but there was a feeling of uncertainty and we didn't have much other than just the basic necessities.[9]

Then there was the matter of Tommy's leg. His osteomyelitis flared up frequently, and Tommy spent quite a lot of time in the Sick Children's

---

[7] Ibid.
[8] Ibid.
[9] Ibid., 13.

Hospital. He had three operations, none of which seemed to improve matters much, and was often confined to crutches. In the wintertime, this made it very difficult to get to school, until two young boys came to the Douglas home one day in the winter of 1913, with a sleigh and an offer to pull Tommy back and forth to classes every day.

> These boys speaking broken English, the kind of people that some folks referred to as dagos and foreigners and bohunks, these were the people who came and took an interest in another immigrant boy. Otherwise I just wouldn't have got to school.[10]

The constant pain made the years between 1911 and 1914 "the most unhappy period of my life."[11] Not long after this, Tommy was back in hospital for more treatment, and learned that his right leg would probably have to be amputated. This was devastating news, not only to Tommy, but to the family. And then, by a fluke, an orthopaedic surgeon came through the ward, saw Tommy, and decided that his case would make an ideal teaching project for his students. Dr. R. Smith explained to Tommy's parents that he could save the leg, although the knee might be permanently stiffened, and received permission to operate. The operation was a complete success. When the doctor noted afterwards, "It is too bad he cannot bend his knee," Tommy promptly piped up, "Doctor, I *can* bend it." And so he could.

At the time, the youngster felt nothing but gratitude, but in later years, he reflected on the fundamental unfairness of a system under which any rich patient could have had the services of a surgeon with the skills of Dr. Smith, but he got them only by the coincidence that the physician wanted to make him into a teaching lesson. Doris Shackleton, another biographer, would later write:

> The Medicare program of Saskatchewan when Tommy was Premier came directly from the fear of a poor boy

---

[10] Ibid.
[11] Ibid., 14.

that he would lose his leg, and a sense of the unfair caprice that saved it for him.[12]

When the First World War broke out in the autumn of 1914, Tom Douglas found himself confronted with a dilemma. The political figures he admired most, which soon came to include J. Woodsworth as well as Keir Hardie, were pacifists by conviction and strongly suspicious that this conflict was just another sparring match between two empires. But most of their followers — and this was a phenomenon that was to occur again — once the blast of war rang in their ears, ran towards the sound of firing. Tom was a soldier; he would have to go back to Scotland and re-enlist. However, he decided that he would go only on the condition that he did not have to carry a gun. He enlisted in the 12th Field Ambulance, a Scottish unit.

Soon, Anne and the three children were back in Scotland, although not in Falkirk. They lived with Anne's parents in their Glasgow apartment. Tommy shared a room with his grandfather, while the two girls lived in an alcove off the kitchen, along with their mother. Grandmother Clement slept in the living room.

Before long, their brief adventure in Canada began to fade from the forefront of their memories; for all Tommy knew, he was destined to spend the rest of his life in Scotland.

---

[12] Doris Shackleton, *Tommy Douglas* (Toronto: McClelland & Stewart, 1975), 17.

Chapter THREE

Glasgow: A Radical Forcing Ground

Much may be made of a Scotchman, if he be caught young.
— Boswell's *Life of Samuel Johnson*

When the Douglas family arrived in Glasgow in 1914, it was a dirty, rough city, and proud of it. A "Glasgow kiss" meant smashing your head into another man's face, and the stink of industry, a pall of pollution that choked not only the Clydeside, where the ships were built, but the entire downtown area, was embraced as the stink of prosperity. Which, in a booming wartime economy, it was, in a way. But the prosperity was not shared around, to put it mildly. Most Glaswegians lived in tenements, filthy hovels with no indoor plumbing, cesspools of squalor and despair. These were the "ticketed class," so called because, outside the door of each of the tiny apartments that made up the beehive of a tenement, a ticket was attached to indicate how many people were allowed to live inside. A typical ticket might read, "2000 Cubic Feet 5 Adults." It was illegal to cram more than five adults, with however many children survived the diseases that decimated the population from time to time, into this tiny space.

Most of these little caves were "single end" apartments, with one door opening into a space split into a kitchen and one other room, with shelves for sleeping. There would be a bathroom a couple of floors away, shared by several dozen families, and, if you were lucky, it would be lined with "Wally tiles," which could be cleaned, as opposed to the wooden walls that could only be whitewashed. There would also be a "Steamie" somewhere in the neighbourhood, and once a week, the women would pile all the dirty things into a baby buggy and wheel them over to the hot water there, to boil their clothes and exchange views. Not much point in talking politics, of course; it was not until 1918 that all men over twenty-one and women over thirty were given the vote. Things got restive after the war.

The tickets that defined the tenements were made of tin at first, but the people, who can be very naughty, and inclined to disobey the rules made for their own protection, might tear these down or alter them, in order to reduce the amount of rent by stuffing seven adults in a space where the rent was set for five. So cast-iron tickets were stamped out and fastened over the door. To remove this marker or alter it was a criminal offence, just as it was a crime — punishable by a fine or eviction or both — to jam more souls into the allotted space than the city sanitary inspectors allowed. David Watson, one of the ticketed class, and a witness in 1915 before the Royal Commission on Housing in Scotland, knew what the ticket meant:

> It means your house is not your own, that you may be surprised at any moment of the night, roused up out of your sleep to let in a sanitary inspector, who comes hammering at the door and says, "The sanitary!" and the man must rise, and it may be two o'clock in the morning, and then he cannot fall asleep again, and he has perhaps to go out at five o'clock to work.[1]

The landlords did not collect the rent themselves, which would have meant visiting their own tenements, but instead hired factors — thugs, mostly — to do the job for them. The tenants were required to pay by the year. When the city fathers, in 1912, ruled that leases for shorter periods must be given, because it was so hard to raise a year's rent all at once, the landlords naturally all increased their rents to compensate.

When the tenants could no longer pay the rent, they went to the poorhouse, where they could be penned up "to save the property of hard-working men from destruction by putting an end to the monstrous

---

[1] This excerpt from Watson's evidence is printed on a placard in the People's Museum in downtown Glasgow, beside a mind-numbing display depicting life in the tenements.

system under which laggards who would not toil for their own support lived at the expense of their industrious neighbours."[2] Old men confined to a poorhouse could be, and were, deprived of tobacco if they refused to attend church to learn that all of this was according to heavenly decree.

It was thought necessary to treat the underclass in this rough way: in the first place, their poverty was either their own fault or God's will, so what was the point of treating them any better? And, in the second place, if you did anything to help them, they would only take advantage. Or, as a Scottish royal commission put it in 1910 (sounding like an editorial from today's *National Post*):

> If Parochial Boards desire to discourage indolence, to detect imposture, and to reform or control vice, they must make work, confinement and discipline the conditions on which paupers of this class are relieved.[3]

The Lap of Luxury

Tommy Douglas lived near the tenements, but not in one. He lived in the comparative lap of luxury in his grandfather's home, with half a bed to himself, decent meals, and clean clothes. Anne took in sewing to earn extra money, while Tommy ran errands, took part-time jobs, and went to school.

The house the family rented was on Clarence Street, on the south bank of the Clyde — not much more than a caber-toss from the river, its excitement, its industry, and its gritty grey water. Just around the corner, on Morrison, was the giant Co-operative Wholesale store, where his grandfather Andrew Clement worked at this time. (Today, Clarence Street has become Dalentober, the house is a pile of rubble on its way to becoming a block of condominiums, and the Co-op, still a massive and magnificent structure, is being turned into chi-chi lofts, which will sell for about half a million pounds apiece.)

---

[2] A.V. Dicey, *Law and Public Opinion During the Nineteenth Century* (London: Macmillan, 1962), 233. And no, historian Dicey was not being ironical when he wrote this.

[3] Royal Commission on the Poor Laws, *Minutes of Evidence* (Scotland), 1910.

The Lady's Not for Caning

Tommy attended Scotland Street School, about ten blocks away from his home. (The school is now a museum, closed most of the time, sitting forlorn on a broad thoroughfare; most of the working-class neighbourhood it used to serve has been flattened to make more room for roads.) Tommy was a good, but not outstanding, student; he had an excellent memory and, even then, a facility for expressing himself easily and well, but "I really never was the type of student who tried very hard for academic distinction."[4]

The principal at Scotland Street School, a man named David Strachan, was an Oxford graduate and a strict disciplinarian, although Tommy pointed out, "He would never cane a girl."

> But he did a great deal for us. He used to have the classes read selected portions of the Bible for half an hour in the morning, and sometimes sing Scottish psalms. He used to give us little talks, little homely things about honesty and dependability and loyalty, punctuality, the difference between being a gentleman and just being a boor, personal cleanliness, and the fact that when you went to look for a job how important it was that you look neat, that your shoes were shining, your fingernails clean. When you were given responsibility by your boss, every penny must be accounted for; this was a great trust and you must never betray it. These things sunk in.[5]

Tommy was also learning from a different sort of teacher. The radicalism that was beginning to reshape politics all over Britain was vividly expressed in Glasgow by public speakers like John MacLean, a revolutionary socialist and founder of the Scottish Workers' Republican Party; Willie Gallacher; and Jimmy Maxton, a fiery socialist and pacifist. Their public pulpit was in the greenswarded expanse of Glasgow Green, little

---

[4] Douglas, *The Making of a Socialist*, 22.
[5] Ibid.

farther than a mile from where Tommy lived. This was Glasgow's Hyde Park, a speaker's corner where anyone who thought he or she (seldom she) had something to say to the general public by way of instruction, enlightenment, or mere entertainment could hold forth.

Here, souls were saved, home remedies dispersed, myths dispelled, other myths propagated, and political and economic theories expounded, often all at the same time. In a world before television, movie theatres, even radios, Glasgow Green provided some of the finest entertainment available, and many a youngster who went to mock came away impressed, perhaps even converted.

Oratory was not just mouthing off; the speaker was expected to be a performer for a captious crowd whose jeers could drive the unskilled into sputtering silence. A carrying voice, leather lungs, an impermeable hide, and a quick wit were standard tools of the trade. This was quite different from the elocution lessons Anne provided for Tommy; it was speechifying as mud wrestling, and the devil take the hindmost. When someone like Jimmy Maxton stepped up to the podium to vent his righteous wrath on employers, landlords, armament makers, and King George V — a favourite target — the crowd expected thunderbolts. (Years later, when Tommy was on a conducted visit of Glasgow, which included a tour of the Kelvingrove Museum, the Lord Mayor pointed out proudly that the city fathers had seen fit to honour the old socialist Maxton with a bust of his likeness, set on a pedestal. Tommy remarked that "it confirmed my impression that there is nothing the upper classes are so fond of as a dead radical.")[6]

Tommy also went to hear David Lloyd George, a great orator, but a man subsiding into Liberalism with a capital L; his radical days were ebbing fast. Where Maxton, Gallacher, and MacLean poured forth denunciations of the king and urged workers to down their tools and cease making armaments, Lloyd George laid more emphasis, as Liberals tend to do, on the good things to come via reforms that shall be with us presently, providing always that we do the needful at the ballot box.

Tommy also frequented the public library on Paisley Street, just along

---

[6] Shackleton, *Tommy Douglas*, 21.

the Clyde from the Douglas home. He spent hours there, reading G.A. Henty, James Fenimore Cooper, and other authors of boys' adventure stories. Like most of his friends, he roamed the waterfront, and was determined to go to sea as soon as he was old enough, an ambition that was knocked on the head when the family later returned to Canada.

$1.10 a Day

Tommy's father was transferred from the Scottish ambulance corps to the Canadian army, where he earned $1.10 a day. Out of this, one dollar was consigned to Anne and the family, and Tom spent the other dime revelling.

With money so tight, Anne sold sewing machines to help make ends meet, and Tommy contributed whatever he could from his work as an errand boy. When the time came for high school — the Academy on Paisley Street (today also gone beneath the concrete) — he paid his own school fees with money earned from odd jobs. He worked for a time in a barber shop, for tips. He got his uncle to make him a little wooden box, with a note that said "For the Boy." It provided enough to cover his fees. His route to school took him along the waterfront, where a gang of youngsters hounded him with cries of "Canuck!" Tommy promptly picked a fight with the largest of his besiegers, got licked, went back for more, and got accepted. His pugnacity was natural, built in; he would learn more skill later.

In the fall of 1918, without saying anything to his mother, Tommy dropped out of high school — he had been in his second year — and went to work for a man named Hunter, who had a cork factory just across the river from Clarence Street. Tommy worked in the office, answering the telephone, taking orders, running errands. He also put in some time burning distillers' names onto corks for whisky bottles, an occupation that would have upset his teetotaller Grandfather Clement, had he known about it.

While on the job, he met a man who drove a team of Clydesdales. Tommy had helped to care for his grandfather's team when he was younger, and now on his days off he was delighted to help this man — polishing brass, cleaning harnesses, and performing other stable tasks that required a shovel rather than a cloth. Tommy spent a good deal of time talking about horses, the advantages and disadvantages of various breeds. (In later life, this knowledge would turn out to be an undreamed-of advantage.)

Because he was bright, energetic, and willing, Tommy was given more and more responsibility in the cork factory, and within a short time was making three pounds a week — more than his father had made in Falkirk as a moulder. Hunter wanted Tommy to go to night school to learn Spanish and Portuguese, with the eventual goal of becoming a cork buyer. The idea appealed to Tommy. But nothing came of it, because the family moved back to Canada. His father was dead opposed to this career choice in any event; when he came home on leave and learned that Tommy had dropped out of school, he was appalled. Education was important, even more important than money; as soon as it could be arranged, he told his son, Tommy was to go back to school.

The Sweet Here and Now

Tommy went to the Baptist chapel with his mother, and, just as often, on his own. He was as intrigued with the social message and the techniques of preaching as with the religiosity of these occasions. He studied the discourse of the preachers: how they developed and expanded a text; how they used gestures, changes of tone, variations of mood and colour to get their messages across. His own speeches would later carry a mixture of the elements of home elocution, fine preaching, and the rough-and-tumble oratory of Glasgow Green.

It was a time when political oratory was becoming joined to religious sermonizing. (This was always true, in a sense — John Knox, for instance, carried a political message into the pulpit — but it was always presented as divine advice rather than ballot-box dogma.) Ministers were beginning to feel that acceptance of the way things were done, and patient exhortations to the poor to bear their lot as meted out by a power higher than the factory owner, could no longer be defended. Morgan Phillips once famously said, "The Labour Party owes more to Methodism than to Marxism," which was another way of noting that it was not economic theory that was pushing preachers more and more into taking an active role in politics, but simple observation, and the need to comment on, even interfere in, the workings of an economic system that was so manifestly unfair.

Evangelism had cleared the way for the notion that it was not enough for ministers to expound the comforts that awaited the poor, the meek, and the humble in the sweet by-and-by. For Christians, according to the German scholar Albrecht Ritschl, who dominated European Protestant theology in the 1870s and '80s, the lesson was that there was no great gulf between mankind and Jesus. Christianity was a social religion, not just a highway to heaven. A new society was unfolding, thanks to Karl Marx and Charles Darwin, among others, and the doctrine of original sin, which instructed us all that we deserved the rotten lives we led, was being gradually elbowed aside, not only by a hint that humankind was fundamentally good, and capable of becoming better, but by the suggestion that the church was, or ought to be, an agent in the process of improvement.

Jesus among the money-changers is a powerful metaphor, even if it is not particularly reassuring to the classes in charge of money, and many a young preacher who entered the church full of platitudes and piety began to see things in another, harsher light.

When J. Woodsworth, then an orthodox young Methodist preacher-to-be, first went to live in Mansfield House, in the east end of London, he found it bewildering, even shocking, that the place seemed to be more concerned with the practical needs of the citizenry around than with what had until recently been its only concern — their souls:

> Here they give beds from 4d up and the men buy half-penny's worth of tea, sugar, etc., and cook their own meals. Most of them are the very lowest class of people.

We are near the great docks and they get the dockers and such casual labourers. You would scarcely care to sleep or eat here, but this is splendid compared to the low dives which most men now have to stop at . . . There was a meeting in the Hall called the P.A. — Pleasant Sunday Afternoon — a political or social rather than a religious meeting . . . The ordinary religious meetings fail to reach certain classes and these men are trying to help them. I cannot now discuss methods. I cannot yet understand them. I am trying to study the whole thing which is certainly a sincere effort to uplift humanity.[7]

Mansfield House became the model for the All People's Mission in Winnipeg, which got Woodsworth into trouble with the Methodist hierarchy, as it was bound to do. Essentially, the preachers were confronted with a dilemma as old as time in their line of work: whether to bring spiritual enlightenment to the pulpit in the hopes that the rich would react by sharing their wealth, or to mix directly into social issues. Tommy, while still in his teens, was being shaped in a particular and radical direction by his surroundings, his family beliefs, even his religious convictions. In Glasgow, he could see around him the appalling gap between rich and poor, and he was beginning to grasp that one didn't necessarily have to simply accept whatever came to pass as the will of God.

His father, too, was primed to kick over the traces. Originally, he had expected, and all the family had expected, that once they were back in Scotland, they would stay there. But, home on leave, he began to talk about moving back to Canada again. There were two reasons. One was that he was determined to find a better life for Tommy than the one he had had himself. Tommy would recall:

When I was a youngster, people said to my father, "Now, Tom, I suppose you're going to make the young

---

[7] Quoted in Grace MacInnis, *J.S. Woodsworth: A Man to Remember* (Toronto: Macmillan, 1953), 35.

> fellow a moulder," and my father would say, "Like hell
> I'll make him a moulder. I'll break his neck if he ever
> goes near a moulding shop." . . . All his life my father
> said, "You're going to get out of this and break this tie,
> this staying a slave to a foundry."[8]

The other reason for the return to Canada was a growing rage at the
continuing class distinctions that marked Scottish society. Political
change was coming, but it was not in a hurry, and Tom had had enough
of touching his cap to the gentry.

> This idea that you were in classes, and that the working
> class boy didn't get up in the professional class and the
> professional class into the ranks of the gentry, and that
> the gentry would never expect to get up in the ranks of
> the nobility, this irked my father. He said, "Oh, you
> people, as soon as you can, get a boat, go back to Canada
> and I'll come back when we are shipped back. I'll take
> my discharge in Winnipeg so we'll start again in
> Canada."[9]

And since that was exactly what Anne and the children wanted, too, that
was what was done.

---

[8] Douglas, *The Making of a Socialist*, 28.
[9] Ibid., 26.

Chapter FOUR

Winnipeg: A Saint and Sinners

Winnipeg had always been a city in ferment with the ideas of way-faring strangers dropped off, from the single tax to British Israelism. In so cosmopolitan a community, everybody belonged to some minority, and the differences in both thought-processes and conviction made Winnipeg's minorities volubly aggressive.
— James H. Gray, *The Winter Years*

On New Year's Day, 1919, Anne Douglas, her son, and her two daughters sailed out of Liverpool bound for Winnipeg, their way paid as part of Tom's demobilization. There were several hundred returning Canadian soldiers on board. Also on board was the influenza virus that ravaged the post-war world, and although the Douglas family escaped, they saw many funerals at sea.

In Winnipeg, Anne got a job in the Singer sewing factory and rented a house on McPhail Street, again in the city's north end. Tommy had been carrying considerable family responsibilities while his father was away at war. Now a mature fourteen, he got a job as a messenger at the Winnipeg Grain Exchange. Tom had told his son that he would have to go back to school as soon as possible. But Tom wouldn't arrive in Canada for months, and in the meantime, the family needed Tommy's wages.

Very soon that same year, Tommy learned lessons about working in Winnipeg that would last all his life: he witnessed the outbreak of the Winnipeg General Strike. At the time of this first general strike in Canada, all labour upstarts were seen, in the phrases used by the *Canadian Annual Review of Public Affairs* to report on these events, as "Communists, Anarchists, Bolshevists, IWWs [that is, members of the

Industrial Workers of the World, or Wobblies], One Big Unionists [One Big Union was launched in Canada two weeks after the strike began, but never mind], and all the variety of Red Socialists helping to keep the world in miserable unrest."

The times were certainly ripe for unrest: unemployment was high, wages were low, prices were soaring, and the apparent success of the Russian Revolution in 1917 roused the submerged classes everywhere. But the Winnipeg General Strike did not begin as a political strike; Canada's conservative labour movement paid scant attention to the radicals on hand. What the workers wanted was a decent wage and the right to organize to get it.

Men in the Winnipeg building trades, faced with a jump of 73 per cent in living costs since 1913, while wages had advanced only 13 per cent, called a strike for May 1, 1919 — May Day. Metal workers, who had lost three strikes for union recognition due to companies' use of strike-breakers, civil liability suits, and *ex parte* injunctions against picketing, called a fourth strike for the next day, May 2. City police officers, street railwaymen, and telephone operators were also involved in labour disputes at the time; and they had learned, in a series of strikes during the three previous years, that if they stuck together, they could win. So, the Winnipeg Trades and Labor Council passed a resolution to poll every union member in the city on whether to call a general strike to settle all these disputes at once. When on May 13 the results were announced, 11,000 Winnipeg workers had voted for a general strike, and only 500 had voted against. At 11 a.m. on Thursday, May 15, the city came to a standstill.

In all, 22,000 workers went out — firefighters, police officers, postal workers, telephone operators, electrical workers, tradespeople, mechanics, and labourers. Down at city hall, the village elders, convinced that the Bolshies had landed and Red Ruin was at hand, were rending the general air with horrid speech. An anti-strike paper, the *Winnipeg Citizen,* bloomed forth to record "a determined attempt to establish Bolshevism and the rule of the Soviet," and a Citizens' Committee of One Thousand sprang up to take over some of the abandoned jobs.

Essential services were maintained throughout the strike, but, as the milk wagons and bread carts trundled around the city bearing signs that read "With the Permission of the Strike Committee," the authorities were sure that what they called "the James Street Soviet" was fixing its steely grip on the city economy.

Although not a single law or ordinance had been broken, the federal government sent in its heavies. Arthur Meighen, minister of the interior and acting minister of justice, and Senator Gideon Robertson, minister of labour, arrived in town and began spraying ultimatums. Postal workers who exercised their legal right to strike were fired for doing so. Striking police officers were given a pledge to sign, repudiating the work stoppage, and when they wouldn't sign, 240 of them were fired. Their places were taken by "special constables," mostly university students, who were paid six dollars a day, more than the regulars had been making when they went on strike. They were utterly unable to keep the city under control, and brawls, beatings, and mob demonstrations became increasingly frequent as the strike wound through June.

The government rammed through an amendment to the Immigration Act, permitting the deportation of any "enemy alien" involved in the strike. The law passed both the House of Commons and the Senate, and was signed into law within an hour. An "enemy alien" was anybody whom the authorities singled out for this distinction; since we were not at war with anyone, the definition of an "enemy" left room for creative imagination. On the basis of this law, many of the strike leaders were picked up on June 17 and bunged into jail. In the same rush, an amendment to the Criminal Code, Section 98, permitted any person to be arrested on suspicion, and placed on the accused the burden of proving his or her innocence.

Meighen, Canada's defender of the rule of law, wanted those who had been arrested chucked out of the country forthwith, even those who had never set foot on a foreign shore. Cooler heads prevailed, however, especially when it became clear that by arresting the strike leaders, the government had removed most of the discipline from the crowds, with a consequent sharp increase in violence. On June 20, the leaders were released on bail, but by that time, their followers had decided to hold a protest parade on Saturday, June 21: Bloody Saturday.

That morning, the strikers began to mass on Main Street near city hall, ignoring an official warning that their assembly was illegal (although what was illegal, in fact, was the warning). Just after 2:30 p.m., a streetcar containing two men tried to pass through the picket line and was attacked. That brought the Royal North-West Mounted Police into the fray. They charged their horses into the crowd twice, and on the second charge a Mountie was thrown from his horse, grabbed by the mob, and badly beaten. The Mounties wheeled and made a third attack, this time firing their revolvers into the crowd. They killed one of the demonstrators and wounded several more. The mob split and began to panic, boiling off into the side streets, where they were met by cordons of the six-dollar-a-day Specials, armed with guns and clubs. For hours, a series of bloody brawls went on, until the militia arrived, and a mixed group of cavalry and machine-gunners took over the downtown area.

A Witness

On the way home from work, Tommy and Mark Talnicoff, the leader of the Scout troop to which Tommy belonged, wandered through public parks jammed with strikers and their sympathizers and speakers urging the workers to remain calm and steadfast. Seeing and hearing the excitement, they clambered up onto the roof of a building overlooking Market Square:

> The police opened fire and killed a man who stood on the corner of Main Street and William Avenue, not very far from where we were. We saw the mounted police and the men who had been taken in as sort of vigilantes riding from North Main straight down toward the corner of Portage and Main, then reforming on Portage Avenue and coming back down again, riding the strikers down and breaking up the meetings, breaking up their parade.[1]

---

[1] Douglas, *The Making of a Socialist*, 26.

Young as he was, Tommy had no difficulty in deciding the political import of the strike and of the crackdown against it. It was

> All part of a pattern. Whenever the powers that be can't get what they want, they're always prepared to resort to violence or any kind of hooliganism to break the back of organized opposition.[2]

J.S. Woodsworth

The Winnipeg General Strike changed Canadian politics forever, as it brought to prominence one of the most outstanding personalities ever to grace the Canadian scene: James Shaver Woodsworth. Since Tommy had met him at the All People's Mission, soon after the family first moved to Winnipeg, Woodsworth had become increasingly active on the social and political side of his church. In 1913, the *Winnipeg Free Press,* a strongly Liberal newspaper, charged that E.L. Taylor, a Conservative, had been elected as a member of the provincial legislature for Gimli by bribery and fraud. Taylor was a prominent member of the Methodist Church, Woodsworth's church, as well as a personal friend of both J.S. and his wife, Lucy.

J.S. introduced a motion at that year's Methodist Conference in Calgary, demanding that the charges be withdrawn, or, if proved, that Taylor should resign his seat. The result was a bitter confrontation at the conference, where the motion was eventually passed, and no action whatsoever being taken by any of the parties concerned.[3]

Woodsworth had been becoming increasingly convinced that the church was not prepared, or willing, to act on the great social problems facing the nation, and resigned his ministry at the All People's Mission to become secretary of the Canadian Welfare League in September 1913. The league's purpose was to promote a general interest in all forms of social welfare, right across Canada. J.S. worked for two and a half years to promote and organize the league's programs until, after the outbreak of war, funds dried up. The league shrank to a prairie-based Bureau of

---

[2] Ibid., 32.
[3] MacInnis, *J.S. Woodsworth*, 83–84.

Social Research, centred in Winnipeg and supported by the Manitoba government. That didn't last long; Woodsworth was fired when he wrote a letter to the *Free Press* opposing conscription.

He got a job as a supply pastor to a tiny congregation in Gibson's Landing, British Columbia, but felt conscience-bound to resign from the Methodist Church, and therefore his job, on June 18, 1918, because the denomination continued its belligerent support of Canada's war effort.[4] He became a longshoreman in Vancouver, pitting his 130 pounds of frail health against the massive bales and bundles on the waterfront.

He was working at this increasingly uncertain job in the spring of 1919, when he received an invitation from Rev. William Ivens of Winnipeg to make a speaking tour under the auspices of the Labor Church, an intra-church body founded that year on the lines of a similar group in Britain. Woodsworth arrived in Winnipeg on June 8 on this tour, and spoke that day to a crowd of 10,000 strikers in Victoria Park.

J.S. stayed in Winnipeg to contribute columns to the *Western Labour News' Strike Bulletin*, which was edited by William Ivens. When Ivens was arrested under Section 98, Woodsworth stepped in to take his place, and was arrested in turn — two days after the police charges had broken the strike — on the grounds of "seditious libel" for his writings. These had included accusing those who had ordered the police assault of acting in a way that showed signs of "Kaiserism in Canada," as well as cautioning the strikers to eschew all forms of violence, and urging the government to investigate the underlying causes of the strife. Sedition is where you find it, apparently.

The actual charge against the strike leaders was "Conspiring to bring into hatred and contempt the governments of Canada and the province of Manitoba and to introduce a Soviet system of government."[5] There were, in fact, no Russians and very few foreigners among the strike leaders, almost all of whom had British, mainly Scottish, labour back-grounds.

The leaders, on bail, travelled widely and made speeches to promote the union cause. In the end, six of them were convicted under the crazy

---

[4] His letter of resignation, by one of those wonderful ironies of history, was directed to A.E. Smith, then president of the Manitoba Conference of the Methodist Church, later one of the leaders of the Communist Party of Canada. In it, Woodsworth said, in part, "For me, the teachings and spirit of Jesus are absolutely irreconcilable with the advocacy of war."

[5] Quoted in Walter Stewart, *But Not in Canada* (Toronto: Macmillan, 1976), 226.

laws enacted so hastily, but Woodsworth, who was dying to have his day in court, was never brought to trial. The Crown was required to specify which actual words constituted the crime of sedition, and wound up producing one quotation from the Bible and another from the Right Honourable Arthur Henderson (a British MP and, later, cabinet minister). The embarrassed federal lawyers stayed the charges, which remained over Woodsworth's head until his death in 1942. Two of the strike leaders, A.A. Heaps and F.J. Dixon, won acquittals, and many of those who were given sentences of one or two years came out of jail and went straight into the provincial or federal legislature. Woodsworth himself was elected to the House of Commons on December 6, 1921, as a member of the Independent Labor Party of Canada.

Woodsworth was never to become the close friend of Tommy's that M.J. Coldwell, Woodsworth's successor, became, but for both Tommy and Coldwell, he was the beacon and example that brought them into politics, and into politics on the lonely left of Canada.

Tommy began to work for labour politicians in municipal and school board elections, going door to door in north Winnipeg on the endless task of dropping off political pamphlets anywhere they might do some good.

He went to hear J.S. speak on the steps of Norquay Public School (his old school, from his first sojourn in Winnipeg); he went to church (he was baptized into the Baptist Church, his mother's faith); he took elocution lessons and boxing lessons (but not at the same sessions); and he became active in the theatre.

Tommy's father returned from military service soon after the strike was broken, somewhat broken himself — partly by poison gas in the trenches, partly by despair at the appalling carnage he had witnessed — a despair that would send him out often, late at night, to wander the streets alone with bitter memories. His pension from two periods of military service came to a little over twelve dollars a month. He went to work back in the Vulcan Iron Works, just about the worst kind of job for a man with wounded lungs.

Learning a Trade

One day, Tommy saw an advertisement for a "boy to learn the printing trade," and went around to the *Grain Trade News,* where the print-shop foreman told him, "I'll teach you all I know and you still won't know anything."[6] This was the beginning of a five-year apprenticeship, which led to his becoming a journeyman printer and member of the Winnipeg branch of the International Typographical Union; he would carry his card all his life. He started as a printer's devil, breaking up forms, stripping and cleaning type, and putting away the lead slugs. He earned twelve dollars a week for working from 8 a.m. to 6 p.m. from Monday to Friday, and to noon on Saturday.

Most of his time was devoted to the job; he not only worked all day as a printing apprentice, but went to night school once or twice a week to perfect his craft. By the time he was sixteen, he was operating a Linotype machine — the youngest fully fledged Linotype operator in Canada — and was drawing a full journeyman's wages, forty-four dollars a week, which was more than Tom made at the iron works. Tom did not belong to a union, as there was none at Vulcan; many days when he went to work, he was sent straight home again, with nothing to show for his efforts.

By this time, the family had determined to buy a small house in their neighbourhood, and the prospect of the mortgage debt was an intimidating one. Everybody — Anne, Tom, and the three youngsters — contributed from their weekly wages. There were no luxuries; one year at Christmas, Tommy was sent out to buy the family gifts, with two dollars. He bought a board game.

Meanwhile, Tom worked all the hours he could get, tended his garden, marshalled his memories, and went to meetings of the Masons. It was this connection that led his son into the theatre. Tommy joined the DeMolay order of the Masons, a club for youngsters between the ages of thirteen and twenty-one, which encouraged public speaking and acting. Tommy began to give readings and recitations at concerts and formal dinners, for fixed but small fees. His set pieces included Alfred Noyes's

---

[6] Douglas, *The Making of a Socialist,* 29.

"The Highwayman," Rudyard Kipling's "If," and "The Legend of Qu'Appelle Valley" by Pauline Johnson. He also developed a wide repertoire of Robbie Burns poems and monologues, which he delivered at Masons meetings and Scout concerts. The Scouts charged twenty-five cents for their concerts, and Tommy noted ruefully, "Usually I'd get stuck doing a monologue and probably get stuck for a quarter, too."[7]

One of the adult sponsors of the DeMolay order, a Dr. Howden, was part-owner of the Walker Theatre, and he arranged for Tommy, who still had a strong Scottish accent, to play a couple of bit parts that required that accent. Howden thought Tommy showed great promise as an actor, and offered to pay for his dramatic training if he would quit his printing job and agree to join Howden's repertory theatre. This was much too iffy a proposition for a sixteen-year-old with an established trade and a steady income, but it did lead to a role as understudy for the part of Jacques de Molay himself (a fourteenth-century martyr who was the last Grand Master of the Knights Templar; his name was spelled with a space and a small *d*, but the order, for reasons best known to itself, went with "DeMolay") in one of the plays put on for the Masons. Just as in the movies, the lead had to drop out at the last minute, and Tommy got to shine at a Masonic convention of 5,000 members at the Winnipeg Board of Trade Building:

> My father, who was sparing of praise as he was of most things, was somewhat pleased when we got out of the Board of Trade Building. He said, "Let's walk." I knew from that that he'd been deeply moved by the performance. We never exchanged a word all the way home, but as we were going up the front step, he tapped me on the shoulder and said, "You did no bad." That was as close as he ever came to giving me a word of praise. He might tell my mother that he was pleased, but he found it very difficult to tell me.[8]

[7] Ibid., 34.
[8] Ibid., 35.

Tommy Becomes a Boxer

Tommy certainly received no praise from either parent when he took up boxing in a serious way at the OBU gym. One Big Union grew out of the Western Labor Conference of March 1919 in Calgary. It was western in orientation — its leaders felt they had been betrayed by the eastern-dominated Trades and Labor Congress of Canada, which came out for conscription in 1917 — it was industrial in design, and it was radical in disposition. Tommy never joined the OBU, although Woodsworth was a strong supporter, but he did use the gym. He began boxing during his second year back in Canada, at the age of fifteen, and with his wiry strength, quick hands, and natural pugnacity, was soon fighting preliminary bouts on cards that also included wrestling matches. He was proud to have appeared with Jack Taylor, the Canadian heavyweight wrestling champion, and Ed "Strangler" Lewis, the American titleholder.

Tommy, at 135 pounds, fought as a lightweight, and in 1922, when he was eighteen, he fought for and won the Manitoba Lightweight Championship in a six-round bout at the arena across from the Fort Garry Hotel. He repeated the victory the next year as well, but neither of his parents would ever attend a bout, and his father was "quite disgusted." Tommy recalled:

> The first time I fought in the championship, I already had a broken nose, a couple of teeth out, a strained right hand, and a sprained thumb by the time we came to the finals. My father looked me over before I went the last night and said, "It serves you right. If you're fool enough to get into this sort of thing, don't ask for any sympathy." I didn't get any.[9]

Tommy Douglas, boxer, printer, Baptist, and Boy Scout, was an odd sort of teenager. He had joined the Beulah Baptist Church, his mother's church, and spent Tuesday evenings there at Scouts, returned on

[9] Ibid., 38.

Wednesday for a prayer meeting, and was back again on Friday for a young people's club. While his fellow printers were playing poker over the lunch hour, Tommy was usually reading. On Saturday, after work, he often went to a youth group called Christian Endeavour, which organized frequent outings, and he attended three church services on Sunday.

At work, he was surrounded by men who were older than he was, and often more radical. One of these, Tom Campbell, a shop foreman, was an omnivorous reader, interested in Old Testament documents and in archaeology, passions he told Tommy he had acquired while setting the type for an archaeology book that dealt with the old scrolls that had produced the early scriptures. Soon Tommy was reading voraciously, at odd moments, about religion, history, and politics.

His introduction to the world of western agricultural politics came through a book called *The Farmers in Politics,* written by William Irvine of Calgary. Irvine was a fellow Scot, a preacher, and a guiding spirit of the United Farmers of Alberta. He was an ardent advocate of the co-operative movement, which he called "the gospel of the United Farmers." He wrote with great vigour; you can almost see him pounding the pulpit through his paragraphs:

> The drunk traffic, graft, profiteering, greed and poverty
> are being arraigned from every quarter as incompatible
> with Christian principles. The protest may come from a
> Labour Hall, a church conference, a United Farmers'
> convention — but whatever the place of origin, the spirit
> is the same. The line between the sacred and the secular
> is being rubbed out.[10]

Gradually, Tommy began to give brief speeches at young people's meetings, and even to deliver the sermon on a quiet Sunday evening. Tom Campbell convinced him that he was cut out for something better than the itinerant printer's life Campbell himself had led for most of his career. Tommy was combining part-time work in the church with

[10] William Irvine, *The Farmers in Politics* (Toronto: McClelland & Stewart, 1976), 147–48.

his full-time job, but he was becoming more and more convinced that "if I had any useful contribution to make at all it was probably in the Christian church."

The trouble was, he had only a very sketchy education, and no money whatsoever to finance the years of college that would be required to turn him into a Baptist minister. With the enthusiastic support of Anne, and the less vocal but no less sincere support of his father, he began saving money for this ambition. Dr. W.C. Smalley, the Manitoba superintendent of missions, got him as many jobs as he could as a weekend supply preacher in the little country towns around Winnipeg.

At Stonewall, one of these towns, Tommy — who looked about fourteen at the time, although he was in fact eighteen — went up to a boy who was leaning against his bicycle on the railway station platform, and asked for directions to the Baptist church. The boy asked, "What do you want at the Baptist church?"

"I'm supposed to be taking the service there this morning," Tommy replied. And the kid shouted down the platform, "Mom, this kid says he's the new preacher!"[11]

Despite this inauspicious beginning, Tommy did so well in the pulpit that morning that he was asked back to that church, and by the end of a year, he had saved up enough money to apply for a post at the nearest, and only western, Baptist theological academy, Brandon College. He and Mark Talnicoff (who later changed his name to Mark Talney, and still later married Tommy's sister Nan) resolved that they would study theology together, become preachers, and do what they could to bring Christianity into the social arena in western Canada.

---

[11] Douglas, *The Making of a Socialist,* 41.

Chapter FIVE

Brandon: A School for Thought

Tommy Douglas, our Senior Stick, is too well known to need any introduction to College Students. He has taken a leadership part in dramatic, administrative, scholastic and debating activities.
— entry in *The Sickle,* Brandon College yearbook, 1929–30

One bright afternoon in the autumn of 1924, the train from Winnipeg disgorged at the Brandon, Manitoba, railway station a wiry five-foot, five-inch young man with ninety dollars in his pocket and a burning ambition in his heart. Tommy Douglas was nineteen, and about to begin a six-year course that would take him, in effect, through high school and college on the way to a preaching career that had the potential to rival the fame of Charles Hadden Spurgeon, the best-known Baptist cleric of his time, whose works were almost as familiar to Tommy as those of Robert Burns.

His original idea was simply to take a course in theology, which he could have done in three years, but Dr. F.W. Sweet, the college president, persuaded him that it was better to take a full high school curriculum, and then go into theology. Tommy later called it "the best advice I ever got."[1]

The ninety dollars was all he had been able to hang on to once his fees were paid, but Dr. Smalley, the Manitoba superintendent of missions for the Baptist Church, had promised to get Tommy as many stand-in preaching appointments as he could. At an average of eight dollars a week for sermons, and fifteen dollars a week to serve as a standing pastor during the summer, this should see him through. He had already picked up his first assignment on the way to Brandon, at Austin, a small town west of Portage la Prairie. The Baptist congregation there had suffered a

---

[1] Douglas, *The Making of a Socialist,* 43.

doctrinal split, the preacher had gone, and Tommy was brought in, ostensibly to close the place down.

The young pipsqueak, as he no doubt appeared to most of the congregation, went into the pulpit and gave the members hell. The young people in the community needed religious education, he said, and it was nothing short of disgraceful that they should be deprived of this because their elders couldn't agree on how to interpret passages of the Bible. As a result of this diatribe the chastened body agreed to keep the church going — if Tommy would agree to come and give them hell every Sunday. Tommy was delighted. But Brandon College was not: with the heavy workload Tommy would be carrying to catch up on his formal education, he could not afford to be away one day every week. A compromise was worked out: Tommy arranged to travel to the pulpit at Austin every second Sunday, and his friend and co-student Mark Talney would take the other weeks.

Mark and Tom also made money waiting tables and answering night bells at the college residence. Students who came in late were fined twenty-five cents, and the bell-tenders got to keep the fines in return for getting up to let them in. Served them right for waking him up, was the way Tommy looked at it. To keep up his elocution training, and to make money, he performed monologues at church suppers and service-club affairs for five dollars a performance. These talks included such then-favourites as "Shopping at Eaton's" and "Is He at the Wedding?" One night, he was featured for the entire program, and came away with twenty dollars (more than $200 in today's funds).

The college he had come to was just about the ideal place for him to be, in retrospect, precisely because it was in the midst of the controversy surrounding the new — well, fairly new — doctrine of the social gospel. To make matters worse, or better, depending on your point of view, it was also in the midst of a prairie population busy fanning the flames of political discontent.

Brandon College was founded in 1899, and together with what emerged as the Baptist Union of Western Canada, it sought to turn out

Baptist ministers with a liberal arts education — and a capacity for critical analysis — as well as non-clerics with a firm grounding in their religious (i.e., mainly Baptist) roots. It was established on the edge of the Assiniboine River in Brandon, the only sizeable town (population then of 18,000) in western Manitoba. (It is still there, a full-fledged university now; the original two buildings joined by a chapel, which were all that existed in Tommy's day, look much as they did three-quarters of a century ago.)

The Baptists, like the Methodists and the Presbyterians, were going through a trying time. Recent discoveries in geology and biology appeared to undermine — to put it at its mildest — the story of human creation as recorded in the Bible. The fundamentalist wing of the churches decreed, as they still do, that the Bible was the literal word of God — argument over. However, many parishioners, and many preachers, saw the new knowledge as liberating rather than threatening, and it opened up whole fields of speculation, argument, and hope.

Inevitably, the social milieu in which these arguments took place became part of the debate. If theology was open to question, what about the social order that rested on it? Were we indeed to accept whatever arrangements had been arrived at for the division of the world's wealth because, after all, that was the way things were, and no doubt the way they were meant to be? Or was it possible, indeed dutiful, to question the fact that while some of our fellows wallowed in wealth, others lived in appalling poverty?

Suddenly, these were not abstract arguments, like the famous metaphor of attempting to figure out how many angels could dance on the head of a pin; they came down, in a vivid western example, to where you stood on the Winnipeg Strike. Was that event, as the *Presbyterian Witness* claimed, the product of Bolshevism, alien thinking with "more than a hint of the smouldering fires of revolution?"[2] Was the whole idea of a general strike fomented by "Ukrainian priests and demagogues" who dared to attack "British government and institutions"? Or was it, as William Ivens, pastor of the MacDougall Methodist Church in Winnipeg, told his parishioners, the inevitable result of the exploitation

---

[2] Quoted in Richard Allen, *The Social Passion: Religion and Social Reform in Canada, 1914–28* (Toronto: University of Toronto Press, 1971), 1.

of labour and, more ominously, the capture of the church itself by a secular, capitalist, and anti-labour spirit?

Social Gospel

"The great need of the hour," William Ivens said, was "that the Church herself should be Christian," and this would not happen unless and until the common people, the world of labour, re-Christianized the institution.[3]

This was heady stuff, heady enough to get Ivens arrested during the strike, then jailed, and then elected as a provincial member of the Dominion Labor Party in 1920. Ivens was one of the heroes of restive young men like Tommy Douglas; he was a socialist, a religious radical, a key member of what came to be called the Labor Church, and a man of rolling rhetoric: "Turn on the light. Turn on the light. Let every worker do his part and the promise of the dawn will not be in vain."[4]

It had been a while since people on the left had a Red Dawn to look forward to. For churchmen like Ivens, J.S. Woodsworth, and Dr. Salem Bland — a Methodist minister at Winnipeg's Wesley College who was hounded out of that post for his radical views — the social gospel was clear in its message. It was the duty of the church to be involved in issues of political and social reform, and if that led to criticism, even banishment from the pulpit, so be it.

Woodsworth embodied this approach in his "Grace Before Meat," which went:

> We are thankful for these and all the good things of life. We recognize that they are part of our common heritage and come to us through the efforts of our brothers and sisters the world over. What we desire for ourselves, we wish for all. To this end may we take our share in the world's work and the world's struggles.[5]

Not what most church deacons wanted to hear when they carved into the Sunday roast; and what made it doubly dangerous was that it was not just pious platitudes — Woodsworth meant every word of it.

---

[3] Ibid., 84.

[4] From an article in *The Searchlight,* the newspaper of the OBU, in 1919.

[5] Quoted in Walter Stewart, *M.J.: The Life and Times of M.J. Coldwell* (Toronto: Stoddart, 2000), 82.

Brandon College was in the middle of this controversy. In 1922, several teachers at the college were charged with heresy on the complaint of a group of Baptist ministers in British Columbia. The charges included "perpetrating the reprehensible crime of sowing the seeds of rank infidelity in the minds of the Young" (in those days, the coming generation rated a capital Y) and "polluting the springs of learning" with "rationalism."

The main target of the complaints was Professor Harris Lachlan MacNeill, who taught Greek and Latin at Brandon, and was not entirely sure whether he believed in the details of either the virgin birth or the physical resurrection of Christ.[6] The school's principal, H.P. Whidden, was also charged with heresy as one of those "men who love darkness rather than light," a somewhat difficult charge to defend against. The executive board of the Baptist Union of Western Canada established a commission to inquire into the charges, and after long hearings and abstruse arguments, this learned body brought in acquittals in 1923. MacNeill, the commission reported, did believe in the place of the supernatural in Christian revelation, but also stood for "the liberty to investigate certain facts and events."[7]

The fundamentalists did not — would not — accept the findings of the commission, and continued to agitate for a literal interpretation of the Bible, at Brandon and everywhere else. Their view, as Tommy put it, was: "I want complete freedom of thought unless your point of view is different from mine, in which case you'll believe what I believe."[8] The heresy trials did not end the controversy by a long shot, but for the moment the right to inquire into all questions was a fundamental part of the college creed. For the time being, anyway. (In the end, the eastern Church dried up the funding for Brandon, gradually, and the college survived only by turning itself into a secular affiliate of McMaster University in Hamilton, Ontario, with no ties to the Baptist Church.)

Harris MacNeill became Tommy's favourite teacher, a man he described as "a giant among pygmies." MacNeill's form of rationalism, which embraced both faith and open inquiry, suited the young preacher down to the ground:

---

[6] He was cross-examined on these points during the heresy hearings and said that he could just not get his "head around" exactly how these things happened.
[7] McLeod and McLeod, *Road to Jerusalem*, 21.
[8] Ibid.

> I would say that any intellectual curiosity I have came
> from him. He recognized that you have to have answers
> to the questions about what we are here for, what we
> are supposed to be doing . . . How do you work with
> your fellow man to build the Kingdom of God?[9]

MacNeill had been acting dean of the college, but was considered to be too controversial for a permanent appointment to that post. Still, by teaching his students Greek, he was able to explore with them all the major issues of philosophy. The rigid elders were no doubt right to suspect that he was upsetting the ordered thinking of his students, most of whom were conservative to the bone when they entered the college. Upsetting their thinking was, after all, part of what he was paid to do.

Brandon was a small college; it never had more than 200 students in Tommy's time there, so he got to know his teachers well. And the best of those teachers, men like MacNeill and J.R.C. Evans, who taught science and coached the debating team, were well worth knowing. For the rest of his life, Tommy would structure his debates the way Evans had taught him: introduce the main line of argument, elaborate the key points, and conclude with a summary of the argument. Evans, like MacNeill, had a wide-open, inquisitive mind, and he instructed Tommy in the importance of framing questions in a scientific way.

The world around Brandon was also in the grip of unrest, and ordinary citizens increasingly sensed that the standard political parties then on offer — the Liberals and the Conservatives — did not, and could not, represent the views of most westerners, nor act to correct their problems. (The income tax was supposed to be temporary when it was enacted in 1917; so was western discontent. They have enjoyed parallel longevity.) The East, with a capital E, was generally for high tariffs, high freight rates, and low wheat prices, which meant adopting policies that made it expensive for westerners to buy machinery and left them at the mercy of the banks, which conveniently arranged crop loans so that they came due at harvest time, ensuring that the markets would be flooded

---

[9] Ibid.

with low-cost wheat every autumn. Western objections to this arrangement went unheeded. Cornelius Van Horne, the railroad mogul, told a delegation of Manitoba farmers demanding lower freight rates to "Raise less hell and more wheat," and eastern MPs all nodded their heads in unison.

The agrarian revolt joined the Christian socialism of men like Bland and Woodsworth to the American prairie populism of men like Henry Wise Wood — the American farmer who moved to Carstairs in southern Alberta and became head of the United Farmers of Alberta — and William Irvine, a strong supporter of "Co-operative Government" as opposed to party politics. The old parties would never act in the interests of the western population; indeed, it was strongly argued that no parties could ever do so. The solution was to form groups in the legislatures that would co-operate with any other groups to bring about the necessary changes. Not parties, but temporary coalitions.

The Progressives Fail to Progress
When Thomas Crerar, a Liberal, resigned from the federal cabinet in 1919 to oppose high tariffs, the Canadian Council of Agriculture propelled him to the head of a new movement, the Progressives, which would embrace free trade, nationalization (starting with the railways), and direct democracy. In 1921, the Progressives won 65 seats in the House of Commons, and formed the second-largest bloc in Parliament. However, because they wouldn't cling together like a regular political party, but allotted their votes to any policy that attracted them, the movement soon lost any cohesion. It was soon absorbed by the wily Mackenzie King, and Crerar wound up with a Liberal cabinet portfolio and a faintly puzzled look on his face.

But the problems of western farmers had scarcely been touched, and the same issues that agitated Crerar's followers led to the founding of the United Farmers of Alberta, which won the provincial election of 1921. (Henry Wise Wood, true to form, refused to accept the post of premier, and the party became a moderate, then conservative, government that held office until 1935.) In Manitoba, the Manitoba Grain Growers' Association, the main farm group, was replaced by the United Farmers of Manitoba in 1920, and this group propelled John Bracken into government in 1922, with pledges to encourage co-operative marketing, government intervention in transportation policies, lower manufacturing tariffs, and the creation of a central bank.

This government, too, would gradually become one more conservative regime. But at the time Tommy entered Brandon, anything seemed possible — in politics, social policy, and religion — except the status quo.

Senior Stick

Tommy was an able student; he won the general proficiency scholarship in each of his three years at the Brandon academy — the high school section of Brandon College — and two gold medals in the senior school, one for debating and the other for oratory. He also, to his delight, walked off with the senior prize in Hebrew in a class that contained only himself and two Jewish scholars preparing for the rabbinate. He was active in school sports (although he had to give up boxing: there wasn't enough time for training), drama, debating, oratory, and school politics.

In the senior school, he ran up against stiff academic competition in the form of a lanky young Canadian who had been living in Los Angeles — Stanley Knowles. Knowles, like Tommy, had been a printer and held his card in the International Typographical Union. Like Tommy, he had decided to become a preacher and was paying his way through school as a supply preacher, although he was a Methodist, not a Baptist. On the day they met — Knowles remembered the date to tell his biographer — September 27, 1927,[10] he was entering the B.A. program, as was Tommy. Knowles would later joke that he spent three years at Brandon and came away with the same degree it took Tommy six years to collect.

They were instant friends, and instant allies. The school curriculum had promised a course in socialism, but when it was not forthcoming,

---

[10] Susan Mann Trofimenkoff, *Stanley Knowles: The Man from Winnipeg North Centre* (Saskatoon: Western Producer Prairie Books, 1982), 185.

the two led a group of students in a protest that resulted in the course being taught after all (albeit by a conservative economist who probably knew a good deal less about his subject than some of his students).

Knowles backed Tommy in the election for Senior Stick — president of the school student population — and even adapted some football yells in pursuit of this end (alas, those yells are lost to history, although Knowles did a splendid rendition of something called "Hippy Skippy"). Knowles was the more brilliant, and more applied, student, and won the overall gold medal in their graduating year. Tommy was the wider-ranging, with a strong reputation as an orator and debater. In his first year of the B.A. program, he and a partner emerged victors in a debate against the University of Manitoba, arguing the negative of a high-minded argument, "Resolved: Western Civilization is Degenerating." Tommy also debated against the Imperial Team, a university debating team from Great Britain that toured Canada and lost only one debate — against Brandon.

Tommy acted in several dramatic productions and directed others, and was active in the Student Christian Movement, representing his school at a student convention in Detroit, Michigan. Amidst all this, he found time to serve on the student administrative council, in successive years running the programs in drama, debating, and the literary group that put out the student newspaper, and then finally running the whole council as Senior Stick. He learned a good deal about working with others and about administration, and later concluded that his extracurricular activities were probably at least as important to him as anything he learned in a classroom.[11]

A Terrible Predicament
Tommy also spent much of his time preaching. Because he took these supply posts seriously, not only would he give his sermons on Sunday, but he would go out to visit his parishioners throughout the week, first on a bicycle that he hauled along on the train, and later in a second-hand Ford car that sometimes ran and sometimes had to be pushed.

---

[11] Douglas, *The Making of a Socialist,* 49.

Doris Shackleton asked him what he preached about in these small churches, and his reply was illuminating:

> Oh, you always start with a text. But the Bible is like a bull fiddle, you can play almost any tune you want on it. My background, being interested in social and economic questions, naturally inclined me to preaching the idea that religion in essence was entering into a new relationship with God and into a new relationship with the universe. And into a new relationship with your fellow man. And that if Christianity meant anything at all, it meant building the brotherhood of man. If you really believed in the fatherhood of God, if you believed what Jesus said, that we live in a friendly universe, then the brotherhood of man was a corollary to it. And that meant a helpful relationship between man and man, building a society and building institutions that would uplift mankind, and particularly those who were the least fortunate, and this was pretty well the message I was trying to get across.[12]

One day in his final year of the academy, when Tommy was on his way to Austin, a man came up to him, having seen the youngster reading the *Sunday School Times,* and they got chatting. The man turned out to be the superintendent of the Presbyterian church at Carberry, a tiny farming community about sixty kilometres straight east of Brandon. The church was, he told Tommy, "in a terrible predicament." The 1925 union of the Presbyterian and Methodist churches to form the United Church was not universally accepted. Every congregation was entitled to vote whether to join or to abstain from the union; some went one way, some the other, so that Canada had Presbyterian, United, and Methodist denominations in close proximity. The Carberry congregation remained Presbyterian, but was unable to get a minister for the summer. Would

---

[12] Shackleton, *Tommy Douglas,* 32.

Tommy be interested? Tommy pointed out that he was a Baptist, not Presbyterian or Methodist, nor even United, but the superintendent said not to worry about that; he would clear it with the Baptist supervisors himself. He did, and Tommy became a regular preacher at the Knox Presbyterian Church for two years. Before he had even begun his formal study of theology, he was in full charge of a church.

One of his parishioners was a slim, dark-haired, vivacious girl named Irma Dempsey, daughter of a local horse dealer, Hull Dempsey. She was a Methodist, but attended Knox after Tommy became known in the community for his lively sermons, as well as his active programs for youth, which included plays, variety nights, and music programs. Irma was a music student, so it was natural for her to attend many of these evenings. She was also a skilled debater; indeed, the only debate Tommy remembered losing during his days at Brandon College was in his fourth year, against a visiting team that she headed.

Tommy was the only young preacher in town; the Methodist church had been joined to the United Church, and the minister there was seventy-five years old. Tommy therefore became the mentor for nearly all youth activities, including Guides, Scouts, Cubs, Brownies, and two basketball teams.

Tommy's sermons included dramatizations of some of the Bible stories, and the rock-ribbed conservatives of the community were gradually won over by sermons entitled "God Provides Food for Every Bird, but He Doesn't Throw it in to the Nest," "The Gospel in a Nutshell," or "The Woman Who was a Hustler in the Church." Overflow congregations became the rule, rather than the exception.

In 1928, the second year Tommy ran Knox Church from his base in Brandon, Irma moved to Brandon, with her mother along as chaperone, to further her music studies at the college. She and Tommy were soon engaged. Tommy believed his knowledge of horses, from his days in the cork factory back in Scotland, played a part in his winning of Irma: "If I hadn't been able to talk to Irma's dad about horses, I doubt that he would ever have let me marry his daughter."[13]

---

[13] Quoted in McLeod and McLeod, *Road to Jerusalem,* 28.

In 1929, Tommy's leave to preach in Carberry was cancelled by the officials of the Baptist Union of Western Canada, which was itself running short of preachers, and he took over two small churches at Shoal Lake and Strathclair, close to Dauphin.

A cheerful little book called *Touched by Tommy,* compiled by his long-time friends and political allies Ed and Pemrose Whelan, consists entirely of quotations from people who knew him, and contains a number of stories of his preaching style. This excerpt is from my favourite of these, contributed by Mrs. H. Lindsay:

> I was thirteen or fourteen when Tommy Douglas took the Sunday services at our church in Shoal Lake. He was someone you didn't forget.
>
> One sermon I remember was in the Christmas season, about the Fourth Wise Man. He told it in the first person. He had started out with the other three wise men to follow the star in the east, but he turned back . . .
>
> . . . When [Tommy] got up to give his sermon, he took out his watch and placed it on the altar and said it reminded him of a story. Two neighbour women, one Catholic and one Baptist, agreed to go to each other's church for a Sunday service.
>
> They went to the Catholic church first and the Catholic woman explained everything about the service to her friend.
>
> The next Sunday they went to the Baptist church and when the minister got up to speak he put his watch on the altar, and the Catholic woman said to her friend, "What does that mean?"
>
> Her friend replied, "It doesn't mean a thing."[14]

In his final year at Brandon, when he was, in the phrase of the time, "preaching for a call" — that is, looking for a permanent job after graduation —

---

[14] Ed Whelan and Pemrose Whelan, *Touched by Tommy* (Regina: Whelan Publications, 1990), 5.

Tommy was invited to preach at a dusty little town called Weyburn, south of Regina in neighbouring Saskatchewan. His friend and political ally, Stanley Knowles, was also invited to try for the post at Weyburn, and the two young men preached alternate Sundays there through the winter of 1929–30. On February 23, a special general meeting of Calvary Baptist Church made its decision: the new pastor, to take up his duties full-time that fall, was to be Tommy Douglas. He was ordained in the Weyburn church on June 30, after he was examined as to his training, faith, and beliefs. Like the Anglicans, the Baptists had no formal dogma or set of articles of faith; the New Testament was the basis of this formal examination. His ordination complete, he was set to start at a salary of $1,800 per annum, or about $20,000 in today's terms.

It was good money at a time when the entire nation, and especially the Prairies, was in the iron grip of the Great Depression.

Chapter SIX

Weyburn: The Call

What do you say to a woman whose family is on relief, whose husband has died because they couldn't get the kind of medical and hospital care he needed, a woman who has no prospects for the future and very little in the way of social assistance? It is awfully hard to know what to say to people like that.

— Tommy Douglas, *The Making of a Socialist*

Irma Dempsey and Tommy Douglas were married on August 30, 1930, two months to the day after Tommy's graduation, at Brandon. The ceremony was performed by Mark Talney, and Stanley Knowles was the best man. After a short honeymoon in Winnipeg — they stayed with Tommy's parents; they could not afford anything grander — the newlyweds took the train out to Weyburn, where the bride might well have asked her new lord and master what the heck the big idea was. Weyburn was, in the redolent phrase of authors Tom and Ian McLeod, "a place of constant hope and crushed dreams."[1] With an official population of 5,002, it was officially entitled to call itself a city, but it was, in fact, a windblown, sundried, dust-devilled straggle of a place. The only water came from wells, and the toilet arrangements were mostly outdoors. The houses, like the people, were plain; the streets wide; the wind constant. W.O. Mitchell based his fictional town of Crocus on Weyburn, for the very good reason that he had been raised there. Intriguingly enough, his descriptions of the stores, and the people, are detailed and evocative, but the town itself remains a blurry background, formless and forlorn.

Tommy, as a gold medallist and a seasoned and popular preacher, no doubt could have won the call from an urban church (after Weyburn

---

[1] McLeod and McLeod, *Road to Jerusalem*, 1.

chose Tommy, Knowles went to the First Baptist Church in Winnipeg as assistant minister). But he never regretted his choice:

> It was a young people's church. This fitted in with my whole background. From the time I'd been sixteen or seventeen years of age, I'd done Scout work and athletics and drama among young people . . . So this was a very natural habitat for me and I suited their specific demands as a pastor.[2]

Irma accepted the town, the job, and the challenge with an equanimity that seldom left her. She played piano in the church, helped with a sewing circle that her husband quickly established to provide clothes for those who had none, visited in the community, and put up with some of the surprises Tommy handed her, such as arriving home with unexpected guests at any time. She was a very private person, not outgoing like Tommy, and was never very popular with his political cronies.

I once spent most of an afternoon with the Douglases at their apartment in Burnaby, British Columbia, when I was researching a profile on Tommy for *Star Weekly Magazine*. I had been told that Irma was somewhat prissy and completely under Tommy's thumb. Instead, I found her to be lively, humorous, and attractive. She was very much up on politics, and when I was pressing her husband on a couple of subjects, and he answered me sharply, she nodded her head vigorously, as if to say, "That'll hold *you*, buster." Which it did.

In their generation, the wife of a preacher or a politician, to say nothing of the wife of both, was expected to be a helpmate, to subsume her own talents and career — Irma was a gifted musician — to her husband's. The Douglases certainly played by those rules, but Irma was clearly her own person. The church, as is so often the case, got two workers for one salary.

In 1930, the Calvary Baptist Church had a congregation numbering about 140; with non-members and droppers-in, the figure rose to about 250.

---

[2] Douglas, *The Making of a Socialist*, 53.

As part of his arrangement with the Board of Deacons, Tommy volunteered to minister on a regular basis in other nearby towns where there were no permanent pastors. In these congregations, most of the members were farmers. In Weyburn, the parishioners were mostly working people, with one or two professionals and a few business people. Many of them were pledged to contribute four or five dollars a week — a lot of money in the 1930s. Tommy was later "staggered" to find congregations in Ontario in which wealthy industrialists gave the church two dollars a week and thought themselves generous.[3] Finances were not so much a problem within the church, then, as they were in the community, as the drought, and the Depression, took firm hold.

A kind of nostalgia now washes over those days of the Great Depression, leaving us with images of neighbour aiding neighbour and everyone getting by on less, but there was nothing romantic about huddling in a shack, lining up for scant sustenance at a soup kitchen, or freezing to death in the street. The federal government maintained throughout the Depression that social assistance was primarily a matter for the provinces, while the provinces held that it was primarily a matter for the municipalities, which passed the buck to the churches and charities, until it became evident that hundreds of thousands of people were living in privation and despair through no fault of their own. Even then, not much happened, because the wisest of Canada's political elders kept assuring voters that the economy was about to correct itself and that to interfere with the right of the poor to suffer was wanton disobedience to the will of God, or even worse, to the will of the Market.

Almost the only government assistance available was a twenty-dollars-a-month pension payable to those over seventy years of age, as long as they could pass a means test to prove that they were destitute. This pension was forced on the minority Mackenzie King government by J.S. Woodsworth and his Laborite group (which consisted of A.A. Heaps and Woodsworth).[4] It was the sole program of social legislation put into place during the crisis. Under the Old Age Pension Act of 1927 (the legislation forced on King), Ottawa agreed to share the cost of providing

---

[3] Ibid., 52.

[4] Prime Minister King needed their support to survive a vote of confidence, so Woodsworth offered to back him in return for a written promise to introduce a modest pension scheme within a year, even though it was not included in the Speech from the Throne. King's letter is now on the wall of the offices of the NDP in Ottawa.

this pittance with the provinces, although, in fact, only the four western provinces and Ontario took it up at the time.

As unemployment soared, people began to lose their homes, farms, livelihoods, and health. Thousands of families were broken up because the men took off, either to rid themselves of the burden or because it was the only way their families would be eligible for provincial or municipal relief. When a "standard of relief" was finally established, it set the maximum — not the minimum — that the local authority could provide at $5.00 per week for a family of five, $8.25 for a family of ten. There was no rationale for these numbers; they came from the brain of H.L. McNally, sales manager of National Grocers, and sounded about right to him.[5]

In Return for Help, Humiliation

In response to the crisis, the Canadian Red Cross and the churches gathered and distributed food and clothing. The Saskatchewan Voluntary Relief Committee distributed gifts and donations, and developed a voucher system to help the poor buy needed articles. The humiliation, for most of those who needed this help, was unbearable; they knew, because they were constantly told, that their presence on the dole was a mark of personal failure, and that, as W.K. Baldwin, the Liberal MP for Stanstead, Quebec, insisted, "There is work in Canada for anyone who wants it."[6] Baldwin wanted anyone who wouldn't work deported, and then, contrarily, wanted to pass laws so that the agrarian poor could be blocked from flocking to the cities to look for work. To bolster his argument, he cited the example set by that fine fellow Benito Mussolini: "In Italy," Baldwin declaimed, "the chief ruler makes the people stay on the land."[7] So the people lined up, or they begged, or they stole, because the ramshackle system of voluntary aid was swamped.

In Saskatchewan, the pitiful medical services then being provided to the impoverished were curtailed when many of the doctors themselves went on relief. A Red Cross worker travelling the province found a family of nine children near Shaunavon dressed in gunnysacks. One of

---

[5] James Struthers, *How Much Is Enough?* (Toronto: University of Toronto Press, 1994), 84.

[6] Pierre Berton, *The Great Depression* (Toronto: McClelland & Stewart, 1990), 51.

[7] Ibid.

the children had died, and another wanted to commit suicide. At Bone Creek, a family of eleven lived in a one-room shack whose walls were so flimsy that drinking water froze in the pail.[8] And there was absolutely nothing the Red Cross worker could do to help.

Well, there were things Tommy could do, and he did them. He began to organize drives for food and clothing, and worked with members of the local Ministerial Association and the local union leaders to badger the authorities to provide jobs and help for the unemployed. They were told to mind their own business, to which Tommy replied, "Anything is my business that affects the people I am in contact with."[9]

The combination of depression and drought produced conditions under which once-prosperous farmers became destitute, unable to feed even their own families. There was no water in the wells: no water to feed livestock, to tend gardens, even to keep chickens alive for the pot. Ninety-five per cent of the farmers in the Weyburn area were on relief, such as it was. As they ceased buying in town, local businesses went under, as well. Even more devastatingly, there was no money for children to stay in school, and certainly not to go on to university. Youngsters with bright minds who would have had brilliant careers ahead of them in normal times were suddenly cut off from learning. Tommy set up classes in the church to engage the energies of young people who had finished high school but who could not go on to university and couldn't find work. They took classes by correspondence.

But the worst impact of all, he found, was the absolute lack of any kind of medical care:

> Out in the country I performed funeral services. I remember burying a girl fourteen years of age who had died with a ruptured appendix and peritonitis. There isn't any doubt in my mind that it was just an inability to get her to a hospital. I buried a young man at Griffin, and another one at Pangman, both young men in their thirties, who died because there was no doctor readily

---

[8] Ibid., 358.
[9] Quoted in McLeod and McLeod, *Road to Jerusalem*, 32.

available, and they hadn't the money to get proper care. They were buried in coffins made by the local people out of ordinary board. This boy at Griffin was buried on a hot day in August. The smell permeated the church. This was a difficult thing.[10]

A Gaggle of Delinquents

While serving as a local social service co-ordinator, Tommy also performed all the duties required of him as a preacher and minister, and the Calvary congregation grew by leaps and bounds. He put on dramas to replace sermons, ran the youth clubs, joined the Young Fellows' Club, helped raise money for a civic swimming pool, and won the enthusiastic support of the Board of Deacons. And he took it upon himself, one day, to save a group of youngsters from incarceration.

This situation came about when he got a telephone call from the police magistrate saying that he had a gang of eleven juvenile delinquents before him, repeat offenders, and he would have to send them to the Industrial School in Regina, unless . . . So Tommy went down to the court, where he found a gaggle of dirty, scruffy teenagers in need of haircuts, manners, and moral regeneration, and who had been into almost every sort of crime, including breaking and entering. He found himself offering to take them into his care, and marched them home. Irma "just about went home to mother."[11] But although she rolled her eyes, she rallied around, provided lunch, and never made a complaint. Tommy badgered members of his congregation to provide the boys with decent clothing, got them cleaned up, gave them haircuts, and lined up after-school jobs to keep them busy and out of trouble. And he discovered to his astonishment that they didn't know how to play:

> They could fight at the drop of a hat, and knew everything except the Marquis of Queensbury rules. They could pick a lock. They could get into a building and out again, and you'd never know how they got there.

---

[10] Douglas, *The Making of a Socialist,* 59.
[11] Ibid., 56.

> But they couldn't play games. And so these other boys
> [i.e., in the Calvary's youth groups] who could play bas-
> ketball and who could box, whom I had been training
> in athletics so far as we had equipment, joined in and
> taught these boys how to play.[12]

Then came the Sunday when Tommy had to go over to Stoughton to take the service there. He came home to find a Weyburn storekeeper at his house, radiating fury. The delinquents had broken into his store and stolen a good many things, including cigarettes and chocolates. He wanted them charged. Tommy tracked down the boys and found them smoking cigarettes and gorging themselves on chocolates. He put on his sternest voice and told them he was going to have them all back before the magistrate the next day. But that day, they should come to church, after which he wanted to see them all in his study. They turned up look-ing like angels, brushed and polished, and after the service they all trooped into the study, where Tommy told them how disappointed he was in them, and how they had let him down. He had no choice but to take them back to the magistrate, who would commit them to an institution.

The guilt-stricken boys began to sniff and cry, promised that they would behave in the future if they were given just one more chance, and vowed to return to the store all of the goods they had not yet con-sumed. As they filed out, the toughest boy of the bunch stopped and said, "Mr. Douglas, I'm terribly sorry for what we've done. I'm so sorry, I want to give you back your things." And he proceeded to unload on Tommy's desk Tommy's watch, fountain pen, penknife, and half a dozen other items he had whipped off the preacher's desk while he had been holding forth.[13] Years later, Tommy met the young man again in Holland, during the war. He was a master sergeant, and doing well.

A Wind Tunnel for Politics
It was inevitable that the young pastor would see his role as more than youth counsellor, comforter, and, to the extent that he was able to be,

---

[12] Ibid.
[13] Ibid.

provider of emergency assistance. There was clearly something drastically wrong with an economy that ran the way Canada's did, and Tommy soon found himself working with a network of clergymen, teachers, co-op organizers, and labour leaders, who met in the print shop run by Tom McLeod's father, a place McLeod remembers as "a sort of wind tunnel for local politics."[14] They talked about other ways of doing things, and how to go about creating a new and more responsive kind of politics. As word of these rumblings spread, some of Tommy's wealthier parishioners became concerned. One day after church, a prosperous local lawyer came up to Tommy to ask him, "Why do you get mixed up with this crowd?"

The pastor replied with a question of his own: Had the lawyer ever seen the conditions in the poorer part of Weyburn? Well, no; he had lived in the city for twenty-five years, but had only been, you understand, in certain kinds of homes. Then, would he be willing to spend just one day visiting the houses of some of his fellow citizens? After some hesitation, the man agreed to do so, and the very next day the two men went for a walkabout in Weyburn. Tommy took him to homes where children couldn't go to school because they had no shoes or clothing; homes where there was little coal and less milk; homes where real hunger was not a distant nightmare, but a daily fact. Near tears, the lawyer said to Tommy: "I wouldn't have believed it. I know this might happen in the east side of London, but for it to be happening in the town where I live, I'm ashamed that I don't know this."[15]

American Pie in the Sky

One could not cure the country's ills one lawyer at a time — that much was obvious. A new political alignment would soon take on the job, and it would reach out to bring Tommy in; in the meantime, he wanted, amidst all his other tasks and duties, to continue his education. He went to the University of Chicago in the summer of 1931 to begin work on a Ph.D. in sociology. At the time, this was one of the few universities where sociology was studied seriously, and Tommy felt that it was the

---

[14] Thomas McLeod, interview by author, Victoria, 2 May 2001.
[15] Douglas, *The Making of a Socialist*, 69.

place to be. Tuition fees and living arrangements were minuscule, and he was able to pay his own way out of savings. For field work on his thesis (which he never did complete), he was put to work collecting case histories in the hobo jungle on the Chicago waterfront. About 75,000 men lived there, panhandling, stealing, doing whatever they could to keep alive. He interviewed men who had been bankers, clerks, medical students, budding lawyers, and came away convinced that a system that wasted its potential in this way could not last.

Tommy also studied the writings and teachings of the American Socialists, who, he soon discovered, were more interested in abstract theory than present remedies. They were waiting for a revolution, not passing out clothing, and he was not impressed. Nor was he impressed by the action, or rather inaction, of the established churches, including his own, in the face of disaster:

> It wasn't enough to talk about pie in the sky; it wasn't enough to talk to people about some sort of afterlife with no misery and sorrow and tears. We had to concern ourselves with the problems people had here and now. What I was trying to do, both in the church itself, and in meeting local organizations of various sorts, was to constantly remind people that Jesus said it was better for man that a millstone be hung about his neck and that he be cast into the depths of the sea, than that one of these little ones should perish. [16]

When he made this argument at a Baptist convention, he was attacked by a prominent minister, who told him that God had made two classes of people, the rich and the poor — the rich so that they would learn the lesson of benevolence, and the poor so that they would learn the lesson of gratitude — and that it was "interfering with the will of God to attempt to abolish poverty." [17] To Tommy, this was "sheer blasphemy." Although the religious community was beginning to believe that it had

---

[16] Ibid., 65.
[17] Ibid., 66.

some role to play in ministering to the victims of an economy run amok, it still insisted that it had no interest whatsoever in what caused the problem in the first place. This attitude concerned Tommy greatly.

Instead of finishing his Ph.D. in Chicago, he returned to Weyburn in late 1931 and began work in 1932 on a master's thesis, again in sociology, through McMaster University, Brandon's affiliate. (Brandon could not grant a post-graduate degree, so Tommy ended up earning his western degree through an eastern institution.)

Rearing an "Imperial Race"

He was getting ready to accept a call that came not from the church, but from politics. However, in his pursuit of a post-graduate degree, he was led into a rather nasty little side issue. Bear in mind that the socialism Tommy now embraced had its theoretical basis in Britain, in the Fabian Society led by Sidney and Beatrice Webb, Harold Laski, and George Bernard Shaw. It was nothing if not expansive. At one Labour Party conference (the Fabians helped to found the Labour Party, and have continued to be affiliated with it), a delegate got up to argue that a resolution outlining the areas to be covered by proposed reforms should be amended to include the words "and the Milky Way." Hugh Dalton later wrote of a dream he had in which he found himself at a party conference "moving a resolution to nationalize the solar system."[18]

These broad thinkers included in their proposals for reform an expurgated and misguided approach to genetics. Mankind was perfectible. Right. Science was king. Right. Therefore, we ought to be able to breed a better race of mankind — more intelligent, more humane, less criminal — by selection. It works with crops, why not with people? Let the most intelligent people have lots of children, and block the least intelligent from having any at all, and you will quickly have an entirely better class of human being. This line of thinking, based on a complete misunderstanding of genetics, was seriously argued, and widely accepted, both in the Labour Party and by some prominent Liberals.

Harold Laski, who was to become one of the most influential thinkers

---

[18] Isaac Kramnick and Barry Sheerman, *Harold Laski: A Life on the Left* (New York: Allen Lane, Penguin Press, 1993), 314–15.

of the Labour Party, proclaimed that the time had arrived "when man can consciously undertake the duties that have heretofore been performed by nature." He believed that, just as people inherit physical characteristics, so they inherit psychical and social qualities; thus social behaviour should be controlled by the regulation of marriage and mating. "Natural selection," Laski wrote, "must be implemented by reproductive selection." The way it was, the fitter classes produced smaller families, while the mentally defective proliferated. If the nation was not to decline, "the propagation of the unfit must be prevented." And to those feeble souls who insisted that the state had no right to interfere in the private matter of marriage, he replied, "Whatever action is fraught with national consequences rightly comes within the cognizance of the state."[19]

George Bernard Shaw weighed in with *Man and Superman,* which depicts John Tanner as the servant of a Life Force, relentlessly pursuing the selective breeding of national leaders as a way to cultivate rational brain power. Sidney Webb, in the 1909 minority report to the Royal Commission on the Poor Laws and Relief of Distress, wrote a chapter on "Eugenics and the Poor Law," which called on the state to "interfere, interfere, interfere" in the mating habits of the populace, because the alternative would be the eventual triumph of "the lowest parasite." Webb wanted the state to provide what later came to be called cradle-to-grave support for citizens to "ensure the rearing of an imperial race."

This bunkum, which reads today like something from the pen of Friedrich Nietzsche, was highly regarded by men the left took seriously. H.G. Wells, in *The New Machiavelli,* set out a society in which "desirable" parents were encouraged by state subsidies, and motherhood was "a service to the state . . . provided for like any public service" — it had to be "sustained, rewarded and controlled."[20]

There was no scientific basis for this argument, although some scientists did support it. It was a scientist, Francis Galton, who invented the term "eugenics" to describe improving the human race by selective breeding.[21] The theory of eugenics seemed so sure, so logical, so much a part of the

---

[19] This is the essence of an article entitled "The Scope of Eugenics," published in the *Manchester Review* in July 1910. This was the article that first brought Laski to public attention; won the praise of Francis Galton, inventor of eugenics; and converted many on the left of the Labour Party. The fact that it was piffle did not become clear until much later.

[20] Kramnick and Sheerman, *Harold Laski,* 41.

[21] Matt Ridley, *Genome: The Autobiography of a Species in 23 Chapters* (New York:

planned world that socialism promised, that it was bound to appeal to many, both on the left and on the right of politics. Arthur Balfour, the Conservative ex–prime minister, took the chair at the first International Eugenics Conference in London, in 1912. An enthusiastic delegate was Winston Churchill, who rumbled that "the multiplication of the feeble-minded" was "a very terrible danger to the race."[22]

When the new science of eugenics migrated to North America, the emphasis, fuelled in part by anti-immigrant feeling, came to be laid not so much on breeding the best as preventing the breeding of the worst. There was even a name for this wicked breeding: "dysgenic." Charles Davenport, an admirer of Galton, persuaded Andrew Carnegie to fund a laboratory to study eugenics, where Davenport was able to "prove" that families that produced successive generations of sailors inherited a gene for "thalassophilia," or love of the sea ("All the Nice Girls Love a Thalassophilian?"). Davenport was an arch-conservative, no left-leaning socialist, and his views appealed to Theodore Roosevelt, who pronounced, "Some day we will realize that the prime duty, the inescapable duty, of the good citizen of the right type is to leave his or her blood behind him in the world."[23]

With such prestigious backing, it was not long before American states began passing laws to permit the sterilization of the "mentally unfit." In 1927, the Supreme Court of the United States gave this approach official sanction in *Buck v. Bell*, where it ruled that the Commonwealth of Virginia had the right to sterilize Carrie Buck, a seventeen-year-old girl who had been committed to a colony for epileptics and the feeble-minded in Lynchburg, where she lived with her mother and her daughter, Vivian. Carrie was shown to have normal intelligence, but Vivian, at the age of seven months, was judged to be an imbecile. On this basis, Carrie was sterilized.[24]

Between 1910 and 1935, thousands of Americans were sterilized under various federal and state laws, and Virginia continued the practice into the 1970s. The United Farmers government of Alberta passed a

---

HarperCollins, 1999), 287. Galton was a first cousin of Charles Darwin, but unlike that quiet man, he was an extrovert, a showman, and a relentless self-promoter. He also, apparently, had mental problems.

[22] Quoted in Ridley, *Genome*, 293.

[23] Quoted in Daniel J. Kevles, *In the Name of Eugenics: Genetics and the Uses of Human Heredity* (New York: Knopf, 1985; reprint, Cambridge: Harvard University Press, 1995), 102 (page citation is to the reprint edition).

[24] Ibid., 291.

Sexual Sterilization Act in 1928, which remained on the books for decades. Under this law, an Alberta board of review ordered a twelve-year-old girl in a provincial institution sterilized in the 1950s on the grounds that she had deformed feet.

In fact, genetics showed that it was perfectly possible for two people of high intelligence to produce retarded children, and the notion that social characteristics could be developed and then passed on by inheritance had been disproved decades before its popularity in the 1930s, although it survived in the teeth of all evidence to the contrary within the Soviet Union in Stalin's day. Of course, this kind of approach reached its zenith in Germany. In 1927, the Kaiser Wilhelm Institute for Anthropology, Human Heredity, and Eugenics was founded in Berlin. On May 5, 1931, this institute sent out questionnaires to leaders of the professions in Germany, asking their assistance to help solve the serious problem faced by the nation — "making reproduction discriminate."[25]

Tommy Embraces Eugenics

If the academic world accepted eugenics, it is not perhaps so surprising that when Tommy studied sociology, he swallowed this tosh whole. At McMaster, he produced a forty-three-page M.A. thesis entitled "The Mentally and Morally Subnormal Family," based on a study of the Weyburn district.[26] It not only embraced the notion of sterilizing mentally handicapped people, it wanted to extend the same courtesy to the morally deficient.

He identified 12 "immoral or nonmoral" women from the area who had, among them, 95 children and 105 grandchildren. Of these offspring, he pronounced 34 to be "moral delinquents," either because they had police records or because they had produced children out of wedlock. To put it another way, 12 immoral women had produced 34 immoral descendants, by Tommy's reckoning. Where would it ever end?

From this highly dubious ground, he leapt to the breathtaking conclusion of his thesis, which declared, "The subnormal family presents the most appalling of all family problems," and went on to suggest definitions:

---

[25] Martin Gilbert, *A History of the Twentieth Century, Volume One: 1900–1933* (Toronto: Stoddart, 1997), 732.
[26] The thesis, on microfilm, is available in the Douglas Collection, Saskatchewan Archives, Regina.

By subnormal we mean 1) a family whose mental rating is low, i.e., anywhere from high-grade moron to mentally defective; 2) a family whose moral standards are below normal, and who are delinquent; 3) as a usual, but not necessary corollary, a family subject to social disease; and 4) so improvident as to be a public charge.

In short, mental and moral deficiencies are not only measurable by the truly wise, but they are inheritable. Wicked women beget wicked children, and that's all there is to it. And in this event,

Surely, the continued policy of allowing the subnormal family to bring into the world large numbers of individuals to fill our jails and our mental institutions, and to live upon public charity, is one of consummate folly.

As a solution, Tommy proposed a system under which couples who wanted to be married would first have to be certified as to their mental and moral fitness. Moreover, those people who were certified as "subnormal," under the definitions above, would be sent to state farms or colonies. And finally, the mentally defective and incurably diseased would be sterilized.

It is to be hoped that today a thesis arguing that a woman might find herself in a concentration camp because she had a criminal record, a venereal disease, or a child out of wedlock would be rejected. In 1932, it was accepted by McMaster, and Tommy got his M.A.

How could a man of Tommy's sense and humanity advocate what — for want of kinder language — may be called pernicious drivel? In practice, as opposed to theory, he could not. When he became premier of Saskatchewan, and minister of health, he was presented with two official reviews of the provincial mental health care system, both of which recommended a program of eugenics, including some sterilization of the mentally handicapped. Douglas rejected them out of hand and opted for an approach that emphasized vocational training for the mentally hand-icapped and therapy for the mentally ill.

Of course, by the time Tommy was premier, in 1944, the whole sub-ject of eugenics, and breeding for a master race, had been given a tainted reputation by the Nazis, although that did not immediately halt the practice of sterilizing women deemed mentally defective in the United States or, for that matter, in Alberta. (In Britain, by the way, where the whole fuss began, no law was ever enacted permitting the forced steril-ization of women on these grounds.)

As part of his research for his thesis, Tommy had done case work at the mental hospital in Weyburn, where he conducted services every three or four weeks. One day, having worked past the normal close of hospital visiting hours, he found that a new ward attendant, who didn't know him, was guarding the door.

When Tommy said, "Well, I'm ready to go home," the attendant told him to go and sit down: "Supper will be in a little while."

"But I'm writing a master's thesis for the university and I'm just here doing some cases," Tommy replied.

"That's fine, I'm sure the superintendent will be happy to know."

It took Tommy forty-five minutes to get off the ward. He later remembered that the hospital superintendent, Dr. A.D. Campbell, "Never let me forget that they had tried to keep me in there, and he said it was proof that the attendant was a better psychiatrist than he was."[27]

The visits to the mental hospital, when he thought back on them, gave Tommy a far better insight into some of the problems of mental health and hospital oversight than did his academic work. The latter became less and less important as he became increasingly drawn to what he would later call "a cumulative conclusion to go into politics."

---

[27] This story is told fully in Douglas, *The Making of a Socialist,* 73.

Chapter SEVEN

The Awakening

I felt that the church could not divorce itself from social and economic and consequently, political, movement and that I just ought to be active in relief, in helping the unemployed, helping distribute milk, or active in any mental health association, so I ought to belong to a political party and try to do something about these economic conditions. I hadn't the remotest idea at this time and a long time after, that I would become a candidate or pursue a political career.
— Tommy Douglas, *The Making of a Socialist*

The young man behind the counter at the Shell station in Weyburn, Saskatchewan, was regretful but adamant. He told me he had no idea where the Calvary Baptist Church might be. He had no idea who Tommy Douglas might be, either, and when told that he had been the premier of Saskatchewan for seventeen years, was mildly impressed. Not as impressed as if Tommy were to have once played third base for the Yankees, but a little impressed in spite of himself. He had heard that some old buildings had been hauled up Signal Hill on Tenth Avenue, and made into some sort of display. Now that he came to think of it, that was probably where the church wound up. Just follow this street, take the second left, drive for about a kilometre; you can't miss it.

Sure enough, the church is right where he said, and on this Sunday morning is still operating as a church. Well, a kind of church-museum; it is full of the hum of people readying their souls for a sermon. It was brought here when some of the locals learned in 1983 that it was to be demolished to make way for an apartment building. It was hoisted up onto a big flatbed truck and yanked halfway across town, put on a new foundation, complete with basement, and paired with an old grain elevator, another part of the prairie's fading past. A funding drive raised $300,000 to turn it into the T.C. Douglas Calvary Centre for the Performing Arts. It was opened on October 19, 1991, and Irma, along with her granddaughter, Rachel Sutherland, came to cut the ribbon.

Today, it looks much as it must have in 1930 or, for that matter, in 1906, when it was built by volunteers, except that there is a ramp for wheelchairs on one side and, at the back, a Memorabilia Room, containing photographs, letters, awards, and oddments. Oh, the lighting is much better, and there is a sound system to help out in the plays that are frequently put on here; but there are the same polished pews, the same combination of hush and bustle, the same sense of purpose, order, and worship. Tommy would walk in, go right up to the front, and begin to preach without a moment's pause. The sound system wasn't necessary then; he could pitch his light baritone voice to the back corner with no trouble at all.

Whether he would be disturbed by the fact that the young gent at the gas station had never heard of him is a matter for speculation. Probably not. He had a very strong ego, but it was tempered by a pretty good dose of humility — from time to time — and he had an unfailing sense of humour. His political career, after all, was nothing he'd intended; if those sons of guns in the upper echelons of the Baptist Church in 1935 hadn't been so stiff-necked, it might never have come about at all.

The Unemployment Association

When he returned from his brief sojourn in Chicago in late 1931, Tommy began to read more seriously on the subject of socialism, which had been, to that point, mainly a matter of listening to speeches and slogans rather than study. He read Fred Henderson's *The Case for Socialism*, which had become a standard text in the British Labour Party; *Christianity and the Social Crisis* by Walter Rauschenbusch, an American theologian who was one of the first proponents of the social gospel in the United States; and the increasingly popular writings of J.S. Woodsworth.

On a more practical level, he got the Weyburn city council to donate a house that had come into its possession for non-payment of taxes, and in the fall of 1931 he set up an unemployment association:

> We sawed wood and got a little bit of coal together, and turned it into a club room for the men. We also managed to get enough money to buy a telephone, and we set up an agency so that anybody who wanted a chair repaired, snow shovelled off their sidewalks, their lawns raked, their gardens dug, or their basement cleaned could phone and we'd send a man and they might give him twenty-five cents an hour, or fifty cents for the whole day. We also put on some entertainment for these people. This was the hardest of all because there was nothing to do. We got special rates at the picture show, and special tickets so that the men could take their wives to a show once a month. We put on the odd concert, and the odd dance, at which you would get lunch for ten cents. People would contribute the food. The unemployment association went on for some time.[1]

Note that Tommy did not then, or ever, believe in something for nothing, although that was a charge that would be constantly laid at his feet. He believed in hard work; he believed in earning your way; he believed that outside intervention should help you to find work, not make work unnecessary. The unemployment association led, almost imperceptibly, to the formation of a Weyburn Independent Labour Association, with the rather ambitious goal "to wipe out unemployment."[2]

Other ministers in Weyburn were sympathetic, but dared not actually mix in at the unemployment association or the labour association, for fear of alienating their congregations. Tommy was fortunate in his own congregation, which became more and more open to radical views as the Depression marched on, and more and more willing to back their

---

[1] Douglas, *The Making of a Socialist*, 68.
[2] Ibid., 70.

spunky young pastor in his non-clerical role. Things were vastly different in other churches. Relief was, in part, a charge on the local tax base, and the prevailing attitude was that when Tommy went to the relief officers, as he did more and more, to demand money for shoes and coal and milk, he was not only butting in where he wasn't wanted, but was helping to raise taxes on businesses that were already in trouble. He was a disturbing element, a nuisance; why couldn't he stick to preaching the gospel, and leave these larger economic issues to the men who knew what to do? Because, in brief, they clearly did not know what to do — not in Ottawa, not in Regina, not in Weyburn, and most emphatically not in the surrounding countryside, where once-proud people were reduced to beggary, or to fleeing the land their ancestors had settled and trying again elsewhere. Almost every day in the summer and fall of the early 1930s, you could see people who had piled all their pitiful possessions into a wagon, left their once-prosperous farms to the banker or the tax collector, pulled up stakes, and headed out, with an axe and a cow, to try to wrest a living in the northern part of the province, where there were even fewer amenities, but more rain.

Tommy was drawn into the complex machinations of a new political movement that had been growing up around him. The neutering of the Progressives had left the only reform element in Ottawa in the hands of a "Ginger Group" — made up of the remnant of continuing Progressives, mostly from Alberta; plus the Labour Group, consisting of J.S. Woodsworth and William Irvine ("Mr. Woodsworth is the leader of our group," Irvine explained, "and I am the group"); A.A. Heaps of Winnipeg; and Agnes Macphail, the first woman elected to the House of Commons, representing the United Farmers of Ontario.

The (Somewhat) United Farmers

As we have seen, there were successful farm groups already in operation in provincial politics. In Saskatchewan, this role was taken by the awkwardly named United Farmers of Canada (Saskatchewan Section), an affiliate of the United Farmers of Canada. However, the Saskatchewan group had, at its convention in the spring of 1929, specifically resolved not to play any direct part in politics.

That began to change. In Regina, a bespectacled school principal named Major James Coldwell (the "Major," which came from a family name, irritated him, and he was always known as "M.J.") had been lured and pushed into civic politics, in part by his own vice-principal, Clarence Fines, who was to become crucial to the Douglas administrations. M.J. ran for city council, and became its most popular member by far. Like Tommy, he made life hard for the relief administration, even though he was a member of the city's Relief Committee.[3] Once, after receiving complaints that local restaurants were skimping on the meals provided to relief clients, he passed himself off as one of the needy and obtained a fifteen-cent meal ticket from the relief officer. When he took it to the Blue Moon restaurant in downtown Regina, he got "some potato, some turnip, and a piece of meat that would have fitted neatly into the bowl of a tablespoon. I have no idea what it was." When he complained that he was entitled to soup and dessert, he was told, "Well, the city won't pay more than fifteen cents, so what you got is all it's worth."

He went home, changed, and laid an official complaint against the restaurant before his own Relief Committee, whose members wanted to have him charged for "obtaining a meal under false pretences." However, no charge was laid when the story came out in the Regina newspaper, although the incident caused one of the city's richest men to bemoan the fact that "this man Coldwell wants to hoist the Red Flag on the City Hall."[4]

M.J., like Tommy, was an immigrant — in his case, from Seaton, in Devon, England. He had come to Canada in 1910 at the age of twenty-one. As a student, he was a staunch Conservative, but he became convinced that the old ways would no longer work, and he was attracted more and more to a socialist solution. He ran for the Progressives in 1925, and lost his deposit. However, after this expected loss, J.S. Woodsworth, on a speaking tour, came to see him, and the two men got

---

[3] Stewart, *M.J.*, 78.
[4] Ibid., 78–79.

on famously. They resolved to stay in touch. Not long after this, Clarence Fines and Coldwell cobbled together the grandly named Independent Labor Party of Saskatchewan, whose main purpose was to keep the two men in their aldermanic posts in Regina. It began with donations of thirteen dollars, "to buy suitable stationary."[5] Before long, branches had been formed in Moose Jaw, Saskatoon, and Melville, spurred on by radio talks that M.J. gave in his deep, resonant voice, usually on the subject of economic planning. Donations from listeners paid for the talks, with a little left over to keep the fledgling party alive.

The problem with the provincial ILP, it quickly became clear, was that it was the farm vote, not the union vote, that mattered in Saskatchewan. Although the farmers were interested in politics, they were not interested in parties. They often embarrassed visiting MPs by quoting to them from Hansard to show that the statements these politicians were making in Regina and Saskatoon were directly contradictory to the positions they had taken back in Ottawa; the farmers opposed party connections of every sort. Some thought the solution was to plunge into politics with a new, honest party, but others felt their only hope was to stay aloof from the melee, and try to gain concessions that way. This was the Progressive solution; it had already been shown not to work, but hope springs eternal.

In an attempt to break this logjam, Fines, Coldwell, and Woodsworth brought together a meeting they called the Western Conference of Labour Political Parties in the fall of 1929, just as the stock market crash that instigated the Great Depression was beginning to collapse the general economy. In 1930, they met again, in Medicine Hat, Alberta; and in 1931, in Winnipeg. Fines, as president, worked busily to promote an alliance with the farmers' groups that would bind labour and agriculture together for reform. Invitations were sent out to anyone who might be interested in creating a "new social order."[6]

When the 1931 convention of the United Farmers of Canada (Saskatchewan Section) assembled, a somewhat different feeling was in the air. While all the purveyors of Received Wisdom in Ottawa and in

[5] C.M. Fines, "The Impossible Dream, An Account of People and Events Leading to the First CCF Government, Saskatchewan, 1944" (1982), 54.
[6] Ibid., 69.

Regina kept explaining that the best way to cure the evil of the Depression was to do nothing, to hope for the best, and to wait for the miracle of capitalism to refloat the economy, these people were losing their farms, their livelihoods, their accumulated savings — everything. A diet of gopher, which is what some of them had to feed their children, induced them to swallow their misgivings about mixing into politics. At Medicine Hat, 600 rural delegates adopted, with only six contrary votes, a resolution to form their own political party. They also passed a Charter of Liberty to guide the process. It called for nationalization of the Canadian Pacific Railway, social ownership of currency and credit, and "nationalization of all land and resources as rapidly as possible."[7]

These bold initiatives were all included in the platform of the Independent Labor Party, and indeed of all the groups that had been meeting annually under the umbrella of the Western Conference of Labour Political Parties. The farm component of this group in Saskatchewan, the UFC(SS), was increasingly dominated by George Hara Williams, a militant farm leader and committed socialist, who drew up a resolution, which the convention duly passed, calling in a straight-forward manner for "the abolition of capitalist robbery."[8]

It was the UFC(SS) — bear with the ugly acronym, it won't last long — that first approached Tommy in 1931 and asked him to address some of their meetings, which he did. The next step was for him to agree to form part of their delegation to call on Saskatchewan's Conservative premier, J.T.M. Anderson, who, like many politicians, was sympathetic but unhelpful.[9]

Murder in Estevan

Tommy was compelled to take a more radical stance by the Estevan coal strike of 1931. That year, the coal miners in this region had reached their nadir, and went on strike. Their wages had been driven down by the Depression to $1.60 a day, their working conditions were unsafe, and their living conditions were appalling. The sixteen-year-old daughter of a miner from Bienfait, near Estevan, later described her home to the Wylie Commission,[10] which investigated this little patch of history:

[7] Stewart, *M.J.*, 63.
[8] Quoted in McLeod and McLeod, *Road to Jerusalem*, 34.
[9] Douglas, *The Making of a Socialist*, 70.
[10] The commission's official name was the Royal Commission on the Industrial Dispute in the Coal Mines in the Estevan District, Saskatchewan.

> One bedroom, two beds in there, dining room, no beds in there, kitchen, one bed, and eleven in the family. I think we need a bigger place than that. When it is raining the rain comes in the kitchen. There is only one ply of paper, cardboard paper nailed to about two-inch wood board [on the walls] . . . When the weather is frosty, when you wake up in the morning, you cannot walk on the floor because it is all full of snow.[11]

These were not the idle unemployed; they were the working poor. Apparently, you needed more than a job to prosper. A union helped. This house belonged to the mining company; some of the privately owned shacks were worse. An inspection after the strike showed that of 113 miners' houses and shacks, 53 had inadequate heat, 43 were leaky, 52 were dirty, and 25 were overcrowded. Almost all needed repairs.

The miners had to trade at coal company stores that charged exorbitant prices, so the miners were going further and further into debt, while working harder and harder. When they tried to organize, they were decried as "foreign agitators" — a richly humorous cry in that almost all the miners were, in fact, foreigners. A union organizer did come to town, and was kidnapped and threatened with violence if he did not clear out.

The seven men responsible for the kidnapping were eventually tried and acquitted by a jury made up mostly of merchants. The accused included a corporal in the Saskatchewan Provincial Police. In those days, there was no attempt on the part of the police to pretend that they were either impartial or non-political. (In 1932, Major General James O'Brien, the commissioner of what had become the Royal Canadian Mounted Police, would make a speech in Toronto in which he made it clear who was to blame for the Depression — once again, it was "foreign agitators.")

Finally, the miners organized themselves without any outside help, and applied for membership in the radical Mine Workers' Union of Canada. An organizer from that body arrived and signed up members,

---

[11] Quoted in Walter Stewart, *My Cross-Country Checkup* (Toronto: Stoddart, 2000), 197. The description of the strike is drawn from this same source.

but the companies refused to recognize the union, which they said was connected with the "Red Internationale of Soviet Russia," although they did not explain how this could have come about. In response, a strike was set for September 7, 1931.

This move brought in a dozen members of the RCMP, who joined a force of thirteen "special constables" in the direct pay of the Saskatchewan Coal Operators' Association. Farm workers were brought in to dig the coal, but a mass meeting of strikers descended on the mines, and the farmers cleared off.

As the strike continued, the workers announced a protest meeting in Estevan for September 29, which would be addressed by Anne Buller of the Workers' Unity League, a Communist. The affair was to start with a parade, but the Estevan town council, meeting hastily the same day, passed a bylaw banning any sort of demonstration. A letter was dispatched to the strikers to inform them that, if they went ahead, they would be met by police force, but the letter did not arrive until several days too late. The postmark shows that it had been mailed at 10 p.m. on September 29, seven hours after the protest meeting began. The workers had heard by word of mouth about the council meeting, but they thought what had been banned at the meeting — which was closed, of course — was a parade. They changed their protest to a motorcade, and thought themselves very clever. (This series of events remained a secret in most of Canada until Stuart Jamieson's *Times of Trouble*, commissioned by the federal government to probe national labour unrest, was published in 1968.)

Accordingly, when a caravan of 400 miners and their families arrived on the outskirts of Estevan in the early afternoon of September 29 and were greeted by a cordon of police, they were outraged, and decided to push on regardless. A bloody battle broke out at Fourth Street and Eleventh Avenue, with the strikers using clubs and stones, and the police wielding guns and riot sticks. The RCMP were equipped with thirty rifles, forty-eight revolvers, forty-eight riding crops, and four machine guns. Police reinforcements soon arrived and the battle turned into a rout.

After about three hours of fighting, the streets were cleared, leaving two miners dead and one fatally injured. The injured miner died after the local hospital refused to treat him. The hospital director, knowing there was likely to be trouble, had issued orders that no wounded strikers were to be admitted unless they could pay, in advance, all the expenses for a week's stay; however, anyone in uniform was to be admitted because "the government pays." The detail that the miners had been making weekly payments to the hospital for years, as a form of insurance, was ignored.

In addition, eight miners, four bystanders, and one Mountie had non-fatal bullet wounds, and eight policemen had other injuries. Since the strikers had no firearms, the Mountie must have been hit by one of his own (nearly all the Mounties involved were raw recruits, with little training and no experience). No Mounties were ever charged or even reprimanded for killing and wounding miners and bystanders. The strike was broken and the union smashed, and twenty-two workers were convicted of various offences in connection with the fray. One of those jailed was Anne Buller, although no evidence was ever produced to show that she had participated in the riot.

About all that remains to record what happened that day is a monument in the cemetery at Bienfait, which names the three dead miners and adds: "Murdered In Estevan September 29, 1931." The original inscription added the words "By RCMP," but that phrase was removed by order of the Bienfait authorities.

Weyburn was the closest large community to Estevan — it is eighty-six kilometres northwest of Estevan, along Highway 39 — and some of the strikers who were refused treatment in Estevan were treated in the Weyburn hospital. Tommy visited the strikers and helped collect food for them. He also preached to his congregation on the topic of "Jesus the Revolutionary,"[12] asking how Jesus would view the strike. If Jesus came back to earth, would he be crowned, or deported? The mine owners complained to the Board of Deacons at Calvary, but the board made no attempt to curb its feisty pastor.

---

[12] McLeod and McLeod, *Road to Jerusalem*, 35.

The Winnipeg General Strike had taken place when Tommy was a fourteen-year-old, but he had never forgotten it; here was another clear case in which, as soon as working people tried to stand up for even the most minimal rights, they were faced with the full panoply of powers of the state and crushed to earth. He asked, "Would Jesus revolt against our present system of graft and exploitation?" To him, the answer seemed evident.

Tommy was not preaching socialism outright, but by this time he had certainly become convinced that socialism was the only way to get to the end desired, the brotherhood of man. Socialism at this time was a good deal more direct and demanding than its modern descendant (in large part, it may be argued, because its more vigorous approach, while easier to explain, later turned out not to work very well in a mixed economy). The state was to be the principal producer of goods, and the activator of the economy; it would not only see to the fair distribution of the wealth produced by the workers, farmers, manufacturers, and other segments of society, it would own the major means of production. Capitalism had failed, it seemed; driven solely by greed, it could produce goods in God's own plenty, but it blundered utterly at the task of distribution, and left the majority of the citizens at the mercy of their overlords, while doing nothing at all for the poor and downtrodden, whose misery was a built-in part of the capitalist system. (The strength of this argument was shown in the later decades of the twentieth century in the way that pure capitalism adapted itself to these charges and, step by step, enacted changes that would have astounded and enraged the system's champions in the days of the Great Depression. Capitalists got pliable and wily, in large part because of the insistent pressure from the left; their success left the socialists with only a watered-down villain to assail. Nobody said life was fair.)

A Fateful Meeting

Tommy was beginning to sound a lot like Woodsworth and other politician-preachers, and was drawing attention to himself, especially among the local farm leaders who were so desperately seeking action on their problems. They told Tommy that they and the labour groups, such as his own, the Weyburn Independent Labour Association, were working towards the same ends; shouldn't they try to get together? That seemed to make sense to Tommy, but he had no idea how to bring it about. So he wrote a letter to Woodsworth, in Ottawa, and J.S. wrote back to say that he had just received a letter from an alderman in Regina, M.J. Coldwell, who had raised many of the same issues that Tommy had and who was the president of the provincial ILP.

> He feels that the farmers' movement and the labour movement ought to join hands if they're going to be an effective force in Saskatchewan. I suggest you get in touch with him.[13]

Tommy did just that. In his memoirs, M.J. told the story of what happened next:

> Having nothing to do one Saturday afternoon, I took my car and my son Jack and we drove down to Weyburn, where I asked for the Baptist minister. I was shown a little house and I went there and knocked on the door, which was answered by a very attractive little lady, very young, who told me that if I went over to the little white church, I would find her husband in the library preparing his sermon. So I went over and saw Tommy Douglas for the first time. We talked about the Independent Labour Party, and Tommy agreed that he would try to form a branch of the Independent Labour Party there in the city.[14]

Thus was born one of the most effective political friendships in Canadian history.

---

[13] Douglas, *The Making of a Socialist*, 71.
[14] This is from M.J.'s unpublished memoirs, quoted in Stewart, *M.J.*, 95.

Tommy Douglas was twenty-eight at this time, M.J. Coldwell forty-four; M.J. became a mentor, to the extent that anyone could act in that role towards someone as fiercely independent as Tommy. They would remain friends and allies until M.J.'s death forty-two years later. The most immediate result of that meeting was a mass rally at the Weyburn exhibition grounds, organized by Tommy and his allies, which M.J. addressed on behalf of the Saskatchewan ILP in May 1932;[15] another result was that Tommy was, inevitably, pressed into accepting the presidency of the Weyburn Independent Labor Party, moving him into active politics, as opposed to speechifying.

Plan or Perish

These developments had not yet brought about the union of the labour and farm voices, but that was not long in coming. First, the Saskatchewan ILP met in downtown Regina, where Coldwell, re-elected president, told the delegates:

> The Labour Party cannot adopt the suicidal policies of those who want to see conditions get so bad that people will be goaded to revolt. Nor must we join those who wish to patch up a thoroughly worn out economic system. Neither brute force nor blind optimism are acceptable . . . In the face of all things that beset us, we must plan or perish.[16]

The ILP meeting was followed two days later by a united meeting with George Williams's increasingly militant farmers, who, now that they had opted to join the political world, were looking for a suitable ally. Williams was the most obvious choice to lead such a union, since his delegates far outnumbered Coldwell's ILP group. There were two barriers standing in his way. The first was that Williams had taken a trip to the Soviet Union not long before, which made a great many farmers uneasy — the collective farms of Russia were not their idea of the way to go.

---

[15] Douglas, *The Making of a Socialist*, 73.

[16] Stewart, *M.J.*, 95–96.

Williams's trip had been financed by the United Farmers of Canada, and he had written ten articles for them, which became a book called *The Land of the Soviets: A Western Farmer Sees the Russian Bear Change His Coat*. The book was unstinting in its praise of the Russian system.[17] The second barrier was that Coldwell, the public school principal, alderman, and intellectual — who had also become the kingpin of the teachers' union, and would soon be named secretary-treasurer of the Canadian Teachers' Federation — was certainly going to have a wider electoral appeal than Williams. George was a wonderful organizer, but a prickly leader. M.J. was a calm presence and a natural leader. George had been fired from the Farmers' Union of Canada for trying to steer it into direct political action before it was ready to take that step itself; he lacked both subtlety and patience. The delegates made their preference for Coldwell clear in their applause, and Williams withdrew his name from nomination. Coldwell became, by acclamation, the president of the new Farmer-Labour Party on July 27, 1932.

He began his new role with a solemn pledge to the delegates that this body would not betray their trust, as the Progressives had done when they drifted sideways into the welcoming embrace of the Liberals. However, Coldwell would not hold his new position long, because the new party was about to be swallowed by the odd conglomeration that would become the CCF.

Back in eastern Canada, a group of intellectuals, mostly academics, had formed the League for Social Reconstruction, in January 1932. The LSR was a sort of Fabian Society — with a dash of maple syrup — whose aim was to point the way to social and economic planning and a more equitable division of the nation's wealth. The members included such distinguished intellectuals as Frank Scott of McGill University; Frank Underhill of the University of Toronto; Graham Spry, long-time editor of the *Canadian Forum* (he had bought it from its bankrupt previous editor for one dollar); King Gordon, professor of Christian ethics at United College in Montreal; and Eugene Forsey of Ottawa, union organizer and gadfly. Many of the young men had some connection

---

[17] Tommy later complained that nobody got upset when the president of the Bank of Montreal went to Russia; but the president of the Bank of Montreal, for one reason or another, did not come home and write a book about what a good job Joseph Stalin was doing.

with Oxford or Cambridge, and a number of them had studied under John Maynard Keynes, the Cambridge economist.

The LSR had its beginnings in a discussion among Scott, Underhill, and Percy Corbett while they were walking up a mountainside in the Berkshires. Underhill wanted to initiate a third party in Canada that would not simply be swallowed by one of the mainline parties, as the Progressives had been. The others agreed. Underhill and Scott, on their return to Canada, began corresponding with friends in Toronto and Montreal, to get the process underway.[18]

At the founding meeting in January 1932, in Toronto, J.S. Woodsworth was made honorary president; clearly, the member for Winnipeg North Centre was not going to be swallowed by anyone. Frank Underhill, historian, political scientist, and something of a grandstander (Frank Scott called him "the most Shavian of the Canadian Fabians"), announced that what they needed was not more high-sounding and woollen-headed proposals, but some ringing declaration of practical principles to focus attention on what they were doing, and what they wanted to do. A manifesto, no less.

He wrote most of it himself, and the LSR adopted it as a policy statement. The central clause declared the LSR to be "working for the establishment in Canada of a social order in which the basic principle regulating production, distribution and service will be the public good rather than private profit."[19]

This working document was presented to Woodsworth in Ottawa, and he was obviously impressed. In March 1932, Woodsworth rose in the House of Commons to propose the establishment in Canada of a "Co-operative Commonwealth," which would reflect that same notion of a new social order:

> Whereas under our present arrangement, large numbers
> of our people are unemployed and without the means of
> earning a livelihood for themselves and their dependants;
> And whereas the prevalence of the present depression

[18] Frank Scott, interview by Walter Young, 13 July 1963, Walter Young Papers, University of British Columbia.
[19] Stewart, M.J., 97.

throughout the world indicates fundamental defects in the existing economic system;

Be it therefore resolved that, in the opinion of this House, the Government should immediately take measures looking to the setting up of a co-operative commonwealth in which all natural resources and the socially-necessary machinery of production will be used in the interests of the people and not for the benefit of a few.[20]

The CCF Takes Shape

The resolution, needless to say, was buried without ever coming to a vote, but its ideas went marching on. In May, the gaggle of parliamentarians on the left who called themselves the "Co-operating Groups" (others called them the "Ginger Group") met in William Irvine's office on the sixth floor of the House of Commons. They were a rather odd collection that included people such as Agnes Macphail, the militant farm spokesperson from Grey Southeast in Ontario; Ted Garland, one of the old Progressives; Humphrey Mitchell, a trade unionist; W.T. Spencer, a Conservative of the variety later dubbed "Red Tory"; A.A. Heaps, who had gone to jail for his support of the unionists in the Winnipeg Strike, and was now Woodsworth's fellow member from Winnipeg; Angus MacInnis, then generally described as a Marxist Socialist; and William Irvine himself, a political evangelist and, in monetary matters, an enthusiastic supporter of "social credit." The linchpin, of course, was J.S. Woodsworth, the charismatic figure who could persuade others to shelve, or split, their differences. He had prepared an agenda, which the meeting went through in an astonishingly short forty minutes, and which called for the creation of a new Commonwealth Party, with Woodsworth as temporary president.[21] The party would be organized in Saskatchewan by M.J. Coldwell; in Alberta by Robert Gardiner, president of the United Farmers of Alberta; and in Ontario by Agnes Macphail.

---

[20] House of Commons, *Debates,* 2 May 1932.

[21] MacInnis, *J.S. Woodsworth,* 263.

To advance this organization, all the bits and pieces, including the new Farmer-Labour Party of Saskatchewan, were invited to meet as the Western Labour Conference at the Calgary Labour Temple on August 1, 1932. This arrangement, whose formation Tommy watched with a fascination untainted by any notion that he would soon be a key player in it, was aimed at a pretty clear target: to create a new political movement in Canada. The delegates included a fair cross-section of Canadians, except for members of the business community, who were not likely to be impressed anyway. Grace MacInnis, Woodsworth's daughter, listed them this way:

> There were fifteen farmers, twenty construction work-
> ers, two lawyers, six teachers, one miner, one professor,
> six housewives, three accountants, six railway workers,
> three journalists, two steam engineers, one hotel keeper,
> one retired minister, one merchant, one motion picture
> operator, three nurses, two union executives, twelve
> members of Parliament and the Legislature, nineteen
> unemployed men and women.[22]

Tommy Douglas wasn't there; he was away in Manitoba, studying for his master's degree. Although his position on the Weyburn ILP meant that he was automatically entitled to be a voting delegate, he was not able to be in two places at once.

The convention lasted only one day, during which it gave itself a name, a president, and a platform. The name was chosen from a grab bag that included the "Canadian Commonwealth Federation" (Woodsworth's choice), the "National Party" (favoured by Clarence Fines), the "United Workers' Federation," the "United Socialist Federation," and the "United Workers Commonwealth." Coldwell favoured the "Social Democratic Party."

Two delegates suggested the "Co-operative Commonwealth Federation," a name very close to Woodsworth's original proposal, and John Fernstein

---

[22] Ibid., 266.

of Regina, one of its forwarders, proposed that the words "Farmer-Labour-Socialist" should appear underneath. This proposal was adopted, and the new party was, officially, the "Co-operative Commonwealth Federation, Farmer-Labour-Socialist." The CCFFLS, to pals.

J.S. Woodsworth was named president by acclamation. (One of the many ironies of the CCF — undoubtedly the most openly democratic party in the nation's history — was the number of times its leaders were chosen without significant opposition. On the other hand, it was perhaps not the most attractive post in Canada for anyone who wanted job security.) The program, which was drawn up by a committee chaired by Coldwell, was, by modern standards, terse — only eight pages long — and left no doubt as to what was proposed. It called for "a planned system of the social economy for the production, distribution and exchange of all goods and services." That was just to begin with. Banking, credit, and the financial system were to be socialized, along with the control of utilities and natural resources. There would be crop insurance, provided by government, along with insurance against illness, accident, old age, and unemployment. Health services would be socialized. Workers would have tenure in their jobs, and farmers on their farms. All "co-operative enterprises" would be encouraged as "steps towards the achievement of the co-operative commonwealth," and the federal government would accept responsibility for the unemployed and "supply suitable work or adequate maintenance."[23]

The new party would be quite unlike anything that had gone before; rather than a national unified body, it would be a federation, as Canada was a federation, and its members would belong to CCF clubs, organized wherever there was a need, demand, or option to form a club, such as in farm organizations or in trade union groups. The clubs would be directly affiliated to the central federation, but there would be a provincial organization, as well. The common thread for all of these member clubs would be some degree of adherence to the principles already adopted by the group in Calgary.

A rather ambitious program, to say the least, and it brought down

---

[23] Ibid.

roars of outrage from all of the nation's purveyors of conventional wisdom, who saw it as a milestone along the road to Soviet Bolshevism. To keep the kettle boiling, the convention delegates also set up a committee to prepare for another convention, in Regina in 1933, to bring all these groups back together, along with any others who showed interest, to prepare for the new political age.

The Regina Manifesto

The now famous Regina convention of July 1933 drew 131 delegates to Regina city hall to have another go at the party manifesto. Frank Underhill had reworked the earlier LSR manifesto at his summer cottage in Muskoka, and had circulated it to other LSR members for amendment and comment. Then the national executive of the new party went over it again before it was presented to the convention. The convention took place in Regina for the simplest of reasons: there was no money to pay expenses, and the Saskatchewan capital was close to the centre of the country. The delegates came by train and car, and some even turned up in "Bennett buggies" (these were automobiles that'd had their engines removed when farmers could no longer afford the gasoline to run them, and were now harnessed to a horse, or a pair of horses, to pull them). A few delegates hitchhiked.

Tommy did not register as a delegate, although, as president of the Weyburn Independent Labor Party, he certainly had a right to be there. He drove up to Regina only on the third and last day of the meeting, and sat in on the afternoon session as an observer. He was, after all, still convinced that the most important role he could play was in the church. However, the meeting was to prove a turning point both for himself and for Canada.

J.S. Woodsworth opened proceedings on the first day with a speech that was obviously gleaned in large part from the LSR manifesto, and that became the centre of debate over the period of the convention. There was a good deal of controversy as the delegates tried to position the party on the left of the political spectrum without falling over the edge. The Calgary convention had brought an unsurprising outpouring of editorial dislike and dismay from the nation's conservative media. Anyone who wanted fundamental change in the economic system was either a "Red" or a "dupe of the Reds." The adoption of the manifesto was bound to increase this flow of rage.

In brief, this document denounced capitalism as cruel and unjust, and called for an entirely new approach based on social planning, and public ownership of most of the important levers of power — including finance, transportation, and communications — along with nationalized health services, unemployment insurance, legal reform, and fairer taxes.[24]

It embraced and expanded on all of the major points of the original LSR program, while adding a few new points of its own (the original eight became fourteen). One of these dealt with external affairs, which had been completely neglected in the first version. It called on Canada to back the League of Nations and the International Labour Organization, but contained a couple of caveats. The first was:

> But we believe that genuine international co-operation is incompatible with the capitalist regime which is in force in most countries, and that strenuous efforts are needed to rescue the League from its present condition of being mainly a League of capitalist Great Powers.

And the second:

> Canada must refuse to be entangled in any more wars fought to make the world safe for capitalism.

This last was a sentence that would embroil the party in great controversy before long.

The Nudity Party?

Adopting the manifesto was no simple task, given the wide range of views assembled in Regina. The delegates represented, besides the

---

[24] Coldwell reproduced the Regina Manifesto as an appendix to his book *Left Turn, Canada* (New York: Duell, Sloan and Pearce, 1945). This summary is drawn from that source.

Farmer-Labour Party of Saskatchewan and J.S. Woodsworth's Ginger Group, the United Farmers of Alberta; the Socialist Party of Canada from British Columbia; the Independent Labor Party from Manitoba; the Canadian Labor Party; the Dominion Labor Party; and the LSR. Only one union, the Canadian Brotherhood of Railway Employees, was represented, and that by a single delegate, A.R. Mosher. The Brotherhood declined to affiliate with the new federation.[25]

There were many attempts to improve the work put forth by the framers of the program, one of which came from Ernest Winch, a BC Marxist, who wanted the new party to embrace public nudism. Possibly the vision of J.S. Woodsworth in the buff squelched this idea.

William Irvine tried to shoehorn in social credit principles, which were becoming increasing popular in his home province of Alberta with the regular radio broadcasts of William Aberhart, but few delegates could understand the theory (any more than did Aberhart; for him, it was a convenient club as much as a philosophy).

Many of the farm delegates objected to the word "socialization," which appeared in the manifesto many times, but Woodsworth insisted that it remain in the document. The BC delegation fought bitterly to delete the key phrase, "We do not believe in change by violence." They lost that battle, but won the addition of the final ringing sentence of the manifesto, hurriedly inserted at the convention by Frank Underhill, who thought the document needed a flashy finish.

> No C.C.F. Government will rest content until it has eradicated capitalism and put into operation the full programme of socialized planning which will lead to the establishment in Canada of the Co-operative Commonwealth.

This sentence would later become, in Coldwell's words, a "millstone around the party's neck,"[26] although that was not the reaction when it was read to the cheering convention in Regina.

---

[25] J.F. Conway, *The West: A History of a Region in Confederation* (Toronto: Lorimer, 1983), 115.
[26] Walter Young, *The Anatomy of a Party: The National CCF 1932–1961* (Vancouver: 1969).

The Regina Manifesto was clear and uncompromising. It was also a tough sell, as Tommy found out when he ran in a provincial election in June 1934. He did not run as a CCF candidate; the Saskatchewan membership insisted on clinging to the Farmer-Labour label until 1936, and he was officially the candidate of the Farmer-Labour Party (CCF). (His campaign literature, however, made no mention of the Farmer-Labour Party, instead proclaiming, "The CCF will protect our homes, our rights and human lives. Other parties will protect the millionaire and plunge us into war.")[27]

The provincial Conservatives were in very bad odour because of their inaction in the face of the Depression; meanwhile, the Liberals had nominated Dr. Hugh Eaglesham, a popular local doctor, and he was bound to win. Tommy had finally been persuaded to run because no one else would take up the task; he reluctantly agreed to take the nomination just so the party platform would get an airing.

He quickly found himself defending a land-use policy that had been passed at the Saskatchewan Farmer-Labour convention, then still under the sway of George Williams. The policy quickly became proof, in the eyes of many, that the left-wingers were bent on taking away the farms that remained in farmers' hands and turning them over to the state.

Actually, the policy was aimed at keeping the farms intact, but it was a little murky. The mortgage and trust companies would receive government bonds in lieu of the payments due to them on farmers' lands, or workers' properties in the city. The farmers would continue to occupy and till the soil, and they would pay as large a percentage of the principal as they could to the government. Meanwhile, the government would look after the mortgage and whatever credit obligations were held against the land, and the farmers and homeowners would occupy their lands and their houses without any fear of being evicted. Tenure would be on the basis of use rather than on individual ownership of the soil. That ownership would be vested in the government, but out of the control of mortgage companies, and the danger of eviction would be removed. The farmers could continue to till the soil on these terms as

---

[27] Campaign card issued in Radville, Saskatchewan, courtesy of "E. Crandall, Flour and Coal." Douglas Collection, Saskatchewan Archives, Regina.

long as they wished, and when they retired or died, the land could be continued on the use-lease system by their sons or daughters. Thus there would be complete security of tenure.[28]

That was the idea, anyway. It sounded to most of the electorate like something George Williams, its principal advocate, had brought back from his trip to Russia along with his postcards of the Kremlin. Williams had been asked to explain the proposal at the Regina convention but had refused to elucidate. Eugene Forsey, who thought the notion was hogwash, noted, "We were reminded that we were from the East," and that was that.[29]

This bizarre policy was blocked from becoming part of the Regina Manifesto only by the outrage of Agnes Macphail. That robust agrarian reformer from Ontario declared that preservation of the family farm was an absolute must with her group, and with all farmers. If the resolution then on the floor passed, she said, she would leave, and take the Ontario delegation with her.[30] As the Ontario group made up forty-five members, one-third of the voting delegates, this was a potent threat, and the resolution died. However, the Farmer-Labour caucus felt bound to back the proposal anyway, as part of the program of the United Farmers of Canada, and did so in both the provincial election of 1934 and the federal election of 1935.

Tommy defended the reform on the grounds that farmers "were already losing their farms" anyway, but, he acknowledged, "misrepresentation" of the issue made it hard to sell. "Everybody went around waving a title, saying that this is the title of your land that is going to be taken away by the Farmer-Labour party."[31] If the ownership of the land was to be vested in the government, which was the clear statement in the proposal, it is hard to see how this was a misrepresentation. The policy was to be implemented on a "voluntary" basis, it is true; but if you gave your farm to the state on the understanding that you would get it back when you had discharged all the accumulated debts upon it, you might be waiting till Judgment Day.

As if this clause were not enough to have hanging about the neck of

---

[28] Stewart, *M.J.,* 104.
[29] Pierre Berton, *The Great Depression* (Toronto: McClelland & Stewart, 1990), 207.
[30] Margaret Stewart and Doris French, *Ask No Quarter: A Biography of Agnes Macphail* (Toronto: Longmans Green, 1959), 169.
[31] Douglas, *The Making of a Socialist,* 76.

the CCF, the difficulty was exacerbated by the Catholic Church's 1931 encyclical *Quadragesimo Anno*, which declared, among other things, that private property was a right "that the State cannot take away." The archbishop of Regina, James Charles MacGuigan, weighed in with a declaration that all forms of socialism were contrary to the tenets of faith of the church.

Then there was Jimmy Gardiner, the "Relentless Liberal"[32] who had been premier of Saskatchewan from 1926 to 1929, and now, after a spell in opposition, was ready to rise again. Gardiner produced a campaign with lots of money; clever, meaningless slogans ("The CCF will take your earnings. The Conservatives will spend your earnings. The Liberals will increase your earnings."); and excruciating attention to detail. At one point, Gardiner ordered an investigation into a Sunday School pamphlet that mentioned the CCF but failed to criticize them.[33]

Tommy ran, he said later, "like a university professor giving a course in sociology." Still, he drew large crowds, especially when Woodsworth and Coldwell turned up in Weyburn. He addressed 120 meetings throughout the campaign, spoke in favour of crop insurance, and argued for a cut in interest payments and for the issuance of interest-free bonds. William Irvine had visited Tommy, and Tommy made Irvine's social credit policies part of his campaign. A Farmer-Labour government, Tommy declared, would issue provincial tokens to increase purchasing power — the central tenet of social credit — but he did not stress the land-use policy. He made a direct and forceful attack, however, on capitalism:

> The profit system has defiled whatever it has touched. And the profit system has touched everything. It has corrupted governments, debauched politicians, degraded morals, devitalized religion and demoralized human nature.[34]

Who could say fairer than that?

There was no money to run a real campaign, in any event, either in Weyburn or in the province at large. Clarence Fines organized dances

---

[32] The phrase belongs to the biography written by Norman Ward and David Smith, *Jimmy Gardiner: Relentless Liberal* (Toronto: University of Toronto Press, 1990).
[33] Ward and Smith, *Jimmy Gardiner*, 169.
[34] Quoted in *Weyburn Review*, 14 June 1934.

and whist tournaments, at twenty-five cents an evening, to pay the rent for the provincial office in Regina. The provincial secretary, Frank Eliason, reported that the party had managed to up its bank balance between May 1932 and May 1933 from $16.27 to $17.49, setting a mark for other parties to aim at in the matter of balanced budgets, but not providing much in the way of a slush fund for local candidates.

M.J. Coldwell, the provincial leader, spent a good deal of his own money running for a Regina seat in this election and wound up with a personal debt of $800. When some party members set up a Coldwell Fund to help defray his expenses, George Williams, who was now president of the provincial council of the party, asked for $2,000 to buy a car so that he could travel around the province, too. It was pointed out to him that M.J. had bought his own car (which cost a good deal less than $2,000). This was at a time when the phone company was threatening to cut off the party's telephone for non-payment. Williams did not get the money.[35] He would soon exact revenge.

On election night, June 19, the Anderson government was wiped out; the Conservatives did not win a single seat. The Liberals won 50 out of the 55 seats on 48 per cent of the vote, and the CCF, as it was now being called, won 5 seats, on 24 per cent. The CCF became the official opposition. The Conservatives won more votes than the CCF — 27 per cent — but Canada's singularly unfair first-past-the-post system, which would later work so often to the disadvantage of the CCF, worked this time in their favour, and left the provincial legislature Tory-less.

George Williams was one of the quintet of CCF winners. Tommy was not; he got 32 per cent of the vote, and only 16 per cent in the city of Weyburn. The Liberal, Dr. Eaglesham, won. Tommy noted ruefully, "Anybody who hasn't any more friends than I have in this town should carry two guns."[36]

After the votes were counted, the bruises began to show. M.J. Coldwell, badly defeated in Regina, suggested to Williams that it might be a good idea if one of the successful five were to resign and make way for himself, as party leader, to contest a by-election. Williams didn't think much

---

[35] Fines, "The Impossible Dream," 154.
[36] Whelan and Whelan, *Touched by Tommy*, 15.

of this; he wanted to be party leader himself. In a later memo to the provincial executive, he described the Coldwell proposal as "ridiculous."[37] Williams hastily called a meeting of the quintet and had himself named house leader, without ever discussing the matter with the provincial council.

Coldwell, rebuffed, prepared to retire to private life, but his allies on the provincial executive called a hasty convention that changed matters. This July 26 meeting adopted the name CCF (Saskatchewan Section) as its official designation, endorsed Coldwell as provincial leader, and named Williams house leader, which made him leader of the official opposition. However, the enmity between the two men would soon flare up again.

Tommy prepared to go back to what he regarded as his real work. He had done what was asked of him, but now he was busy with many other matters, including his first child, Shirley, born just before the campaign opened, and he wanted to go back to Chicago to finish his Ph.D.

Tommy was approached again in the fall of 1934, when it became clear that there would be a federal election in 1935 and that the Conservatives, in power in Ottawa, were about to face the same fate as their provincial counterparts, and for the same reason — their inability to deal with the Depression.[38] He decided not to run. The CCF(SS) had lost all four of the provincial seats that made up the federal Weyburn constituency and, although Tommy had gotten more than 15 per cent of the vote and thus hadn't lost his deposit, the other three candidates had. "I stuck to the position that I wasn't going to run."[39]

---

[37] Williams to provincial executive, memorandum, 12 December 1936, George Williams Papers, Saskatchewan Archives, Regina.

[38] Prime Minister R.B. Bennett finally came up with some radical reforms, introducing the legislation that gave Canada the Bank of Canada and the Canadian Radio Broadcasting Commission (forerunner to the CBC), among other things. But these reforms, mostly brought to him by his brother-in-law, William Herridge, a fervid admirer of Franklin Roosevelt, were in the nature of a deathbed conversion. His earlier view of the problems besetting Canada's economy were summed up in the following statement: "The people are not bearing their share of the load. Half a century ago people would work their way out of difficulties rather than look to a government to take care of them. The fibre of our people has grown softer and they are not willing to turn in and save themselves." (Quoted in Berton, *The Great Depression*, 32.)

[39] Douglas, *The Making of a Socialist*, 81.

That is, until two officials of his own church told him not to run. One was the superintendent of a Baptist church in western Canada, who had come to notify Tommy that he had talked to Tommy's congregation about the provincial election: "Your people don't mind it, and if they don't mind it, of course I'm not going to say anything about it, except this is to be the last. You're not to run again."[40]

The second official was the superintendent of the university church in Edmonton, who called to say that he knew Strathcona Church wanted Tommy as their pastor, and he strongly suggested that Tommy answer this call. When Tommy said that he had been pressed to run again, the superintendent said: "Leave it. If you don't leave it, and if you don't stay out of politics, you'll never get another church in Canada, and I'll see to it."

Tommy replied, "You've just given the CCF a candidate."[41]

---

[40] Ibid.
[41] Ibid.

Chapter EIGHT

Into Parliament He Shall Go

A lot of questions arose from the campaigns of our opponents. People asked if it was true we didn't believe in God and if it was true we were going to take the people's farms. Once, a woman with about five youngsters around her said to George Williams, "Is it true you're going to take all the children?" George said, "Certainly not." She said, "I thought it was too good to be true."

— Tommy Douglas, *The Making of a Socialist*

Canada's eighteenth federal general election, which took place on October 14, 1935, represented, according to the eminent historian Arthur Lower, "the huddling together of frightened people, uncertain of their way in the world."[1] It also represented, over much of the nation, a cat fight in a dark alley.

Mackenzie King, in the process of making an extremely successful career out of obscure and rambling pronouncements, ran under the proud banner "King or Chaos," and under a policy of having no policy. He had no more idea of what to do to overcome the Depression than did Bennett, who at least was stirred into spasms of action by the prospect of defeat, which, like the prospect of hanging, is famous for concentrating the mind. It was an interesting effort.

In 1934, Bennett's minister of trade and commerce, H.H. Stevens, had charged that large packing houses and other giant corporations were using their purchasing power to bully their suppliers, who in turn were forced to cut wages, adding to the economic woes of their workers and their families. Bennett rejected the charges, but when Stevens resigned, Bennett kept the matter from becoming public by forming a parliamentary

---

[1] A.R.M. Lower, *Colony to Nation* (Toronto: Longmans Green, 1946), 519.

Special Committee on Price Spreads and Mass Buying and making Stevens its chairman. The hearings of this committee soon made it clear that, if anything, Stevens's allegations had been far too modest.

A Miss Nolan, who worked in the sewing department of Canada's largest department store, Eaton's, talked about the results of a drop in the piece-work rates for making a dozen dresses — a drop from $3.60 to $1.75:

> *A:* Well, you had to work so hard, you were driven so fast, that it just became impossible . . . and you were a nervous wreck. The girls cried. It almost drove me insane.
>
> *Q:* Was that condition general, or did it happen only to you?
>
> *A:* It was general. All the girls were the same.
>
> *Q:* And did you break down by reason of it all?
>
> *A:* Yes. I went into hysterics several times and I had to go to the hospital and the nurse said, "What is the matter? You girls are always coming here."[2]

Miss Nolan was one of the people Prime Minister Bennett said were causing the Depression by not pulling their weight.

In the meat-packing industry, Stanley McLean, the president of Canada Packers, made headlines by telling the Stevens committee in a straightforward manner that his company's policy was to "buy cheap and sell dear." Throughout the Depression, Canada Packers had annual profits averaging close to $1 million, while its workers were paid as little as nineteen cents an hour.

In the tobacco industry, the committee heard, Imperial Tobacco, the leading firm, held off bidding for the 1932 crop, and other firms followed its lead. Within three weeks, the price dropped from forty cents a pound to twelve, and many farmers went under.[3]

Stevens made a brutally frank speech to a Conservative study club, blasting some of the business leaders who had appeared before his committee. The content of his speech found its way into the newspapers.

---

[2] Quoted in Stewart, *But Not in Canada,* 89.

[3] Ibid., 90.

Bennett demanded that he retract and apologize, but Stevens resigned instead. His committee was turned into a full-blown royal commission, with Stevens no longer in charge. The public had no doubt that this was a victory for the nation's industrial and financial interests, as that royal commission did what such bodies often do: it buried the scandals in unctuous ooze.

Meanwhile, to deal with the swelling hordes of unemployed who were now taking to the roads and railways, the government had set up labour camps, where what we now call "workfare" was put into practice. Men were paid twenty cents a day to labour on public works, some of which were quite useful, many of which were not — including one project that involved digging a large hole and then filling it in again.

The On to Ottawa Trek
On June 3, 1935, the rage the men in the labour camps felt over their low wages boiled over. They began to leave the camps in the BC interior and gather in Vancouver; from there, they would move eastward, amassing recruits as they went, until they could march into Ottawa and lay their grievances before their rulers. After giving many brave speeches, they piled onto boxcars and headed east.

Prime Minister Bennett was determined to bring the trek to a halt before it reached Ontario, much less Ottawa, although that is not what he said. What he said was that the federal government would not interfere with the trekkers unless asked to do so by a provincial government, since labour relations normally came under provincial jurisdiction.

On June 14, approximately 1,400 trekkers rolled into Regina, dismounted from their freight cars, formed into ranks of fours, and marched over to the football stadium, their temporary headquarters. Their behaviour was without blemish, but that didn't keep them from being branded as Reds, gangsters, and villains by the press and by municipal officials.

More than 5,000 people gathered to support the trekkers; some invited the men home to have a meal, or to stay overnight. The outpouring of local sympathy simply proved to national leaders that civilization was tottering on its foundations. Squads of RCMP and special police were moved in to block the protestors' path to the east.

However, Saskatchewan's Liberal premier, the relentless Jimmy Gardiner, affronted by Bennett's betrayal as much as by the federal government's move into an area of provincial jurisdiction, sent off a telegram to the national capital suggesting that the federal government should at least hear what the trekkers had to say.[4] As a result, eight of the protest leaders were summoned to Ottawa, where Bennett turned down all their demands, gave them a lecture on economics, and reviled them personally. Bennett called Arthur Evans, the leading strike spokesman, a thief; Evans called the prime minister a liar.[5] The leaders returned west in a rage.

On June 28, when a group of trekkers tried to proceed east by truck, they were stopped, and five of them were arrested. This led to a mass rally on July 1 in Regina's Market Square. It was here that the federal government decided to move in and arrest the leaders of the protest under a hastily framed Order-in-Council. This order made it illegal to belong to any "unlawful association," a term that was never defined. An unlawful association was anything the government said it was.

The attempt to make the arrests provoked a riot, during which a plainclothes police officer was killed. The trek was broken, and most of the strikers left the city to return to their camps. The police rounded up more than one hundred men, including all of the strike leaders. As none of the leaders had taken part in the riot, the charges against them were dropped. No one was charged under the Order-in-Council (which, it is to be hoped, would never have withstood a court challenge), but twenty-eight people were charged with rioting, and nine were eventually convicted.[6]

James Gray, a Canadian writing at that time for the American magazine *The Nation*, argued that the only rational explanation for the government's actions in the Regina Riot was that "Bennett, about to be booted into oblivion by an outraged people, was trying to escape from this fate by the dictatorship route."[7]

---

[4] Ward and Smith, *Jimmy Gardiner*, 182ff.

[5] James H. Gray, *The Winter Years* (Toronto: Macmillan, 1966), 155.

[6] Ibid., 20–22.

[7] James Gray, "Canada Flirts with Fascism," *The Nation*, 9 October 1935.

M.J. Coldwell, the CCF leader in Saskatchewan, was an active sup-porter of the On to Ottawa Trek, and brought some of the trekkers home for his long-suffering wife, Norah, to feed. Tommy was not on hand, but his sympathies were very much with the protestors, and he later cited the brutal suppression of their leaders as evidence that the capitalist system would always turn on workers if they tried to improve their conditions. Like the Winnipeg General Strike, the On to Ottawa Trek and its aftermath proved, even to the most complacent Canadians, that there was something fundamentally amiss in the economic system.

The Reconstruction Party and Social Credit

By the time the din of the Regina Riot was stilled, the Royal Commission on Price Spreads had reported, recommending steps to protect consumers against price gouging, and labourers against undue exploitation. These modest advances were turned into legislation that would have accomplished almost nothing, and H.H. Stevens, castigating the "utter inadequacy" of the bill, formed his own political group, the Reconstruction Party. Its aim was to "help reconstruct Canada's shat-tered national policy, to wage war with poverty, and to abolish involun-tary idleness."[8]

Reconstruction aimed to provide an alternative to socialism for Canadians who rejected the old-line parties — a 1930s version, albeit on a more modest level, of the Canadian Alliance party. It shared with the latter-day party its dependence on a single, somewhat flawed personality (H.H. Stevens) and a genuine sense of western grievance. It was quickly joined in the trenches by Social Credit, which, under Bible Bill Aberhart, swept to power in Alberta, virtually wiping out the United Farmers of Alberta. The Social Credit League quickly launched itself into the federal campaign, concentrating, naturally enough, in western Canada.

The War in Weyburn

In the riding of Weyburn, where Tommy Douglas — the fiery prairie preacher who at age thirty still looked twenty — was the CCF candidate,

---

[8] Quoted in J. Murray Beck, *Pendulum of Power: Canada's Federal Elections* (Scarborough: Prentice-Hall, 1968), 210.

the 1935 federal election was a mixture of about equal parts cat fight and uncertain huddling. With five parties in the field, and with no money in the CCF treasury, if Tommy was to win in Weyburn, he would have to do it on his own.

His first break came when he was approached by a man named Daniel C. Grant, who was currently unemployed but who said that he had had some political experience in various parts of Canada, which he did not bother to specify. He offered his services as chauffeur, cheerleader, and dogs-body. His last job had been a patronage appointment in the Labour Bureau for the Anderson Conservatives in Saskatchewan; when the Gardiner Liberals came in, he was fired. It later turned out that he had also worked for the Ku Klux Klan in the late 1920s, when that band of bigots was campaigning in Saskatchewan, ostensibly against the wickedness of brothels and gambling. Grant was a mystic, and amused his friends with teacup reading, fortune telling, palm reading, and numerology. He spent quite a lot of time working out when he was going to die, according to numerology. He was not much interested in the CCF, but he did want revenge on the Conservatives for firing him.

Tommy described him as "short, rather sharp-faced, with sort of a pug nose" and added that because Grant was always so well dressed, "he looked like an undertaker."[9] But Grant had a shrewd political sense. After he had helped decorate the hall for one of Tommy's appearances and made sure there were enough ushers and signs in the right places, he would melt into the audience. If he thought the questions after one of Tommy's speeches weren't provocative enough to bring out the best in the candidate, he would lob in a few himself. He also prodded Tommy to shorten and sharpen his speeches, and to make them less professorial and more downright political.

Clarence Fines composed Tommy's nomination speech, a speech that Tommy delivered on Saturday, June 15, at Cleland Hall in Weyburn. Fines, a shrewd and diligent researcher, had gone over Hansard for material on Edward J. Young, the Liberal candidate for Weyburn and the riding's sitting member, and had discovered that Young had made a speech on

---

[9] Douglas, *The Making of a Socialist*, 83.

February 9, 1933, saying that "the people of Canada must reconcile themselves to a lower standard of living." Fines injected this prominently into Tommy's address, and Tommy was nominated with an overwhelming vote. Like the candidates of the old Progressive Party, strong adherents to direct democracy, Tommy handed the chairman of the nomination meeting a signed letter of resignation, to indicate that the local CCF could force him out of Parliament if, once elected, he failed to act in accord with their wishes.[10]

Grant leapt on the key part of Fines's speech and advised Tommy that all his campaign literature should be aimed at one sentence: "The people of Canada must settle down to a lower standard of living — E.J.Young." Later in the campaign, Tommy spoke to a farmer near Estlin who couldn't say whether he would vote for him or not, "but I know who I'm not going to vote for; I'm not going to vote for that fellow who said we've got to settle down for a lower standard of living."[11]

Once nominated, Tommy submitted his resignation to the Calvary Baptist Church, but was asked to withdraw it and continue to preach on Sundays. He could resubmit it if he became an MP. In the meantime, he was free to campaign, with the best wishes of the Board of Deacons.

He also had, it turned out, the best wishes of the Social Credit organization in the riding, which turned out to be handy at the polls, not so handy afterwards. It was natural for the Socreds to move into Saskatchewan, where the same appalling conditions prevailed for most citizens of this province as for the citizens of Alberta. Moreover, as was the case in Alberta, in Saskatchewan the conviction was growing that there was nothing to lose by trying something new. Thus, the organizational methods honed to perfection by Social Credit members in Alberta might be expected to pay off here.

At this time, the CCF and the Social Credit League were essentially competing for the same votes. This was in the early days of Social Credit — before the party eventually abandoned its entire program — when it was known for its attack on the "Fifty Big Shots" of the financial elite and for its virulent dislike of the banks. The Social Credit of 1935 was a

---

[10] Reported in *Weyburn Review*, 22 August 1935.
[11] Douglas, *The Making of a Socialist*, 84.

vastly different party than the arch-conservative encampment it became after the discovery of oil in Alberta. (Historian W.L. Morton, on the subject of the Social Credit transformation, later wrote, "Social Credit provided an easy and sweeping reform, without Socialism. The Albertans turned to it, and, aided by the war boom and the oil boom, achieved utopia. If it be objected that the Albertan did not thereby achieve a new society, it must be admitted that he has attained a new complacency. If one must travel to nowhere, there is no more comfortable ride than on a tide of oil."[12])

Even without its monetary theory, Social Credit was a genuinely radical party, and up until it took on overtones of anti-Semitism, its proposed reforms — including, in particular, its apparently undying hostility towards the banks — were perfectly acceptable to many of the same people who plumped for the CCF. Indeed, the spouses of some members of the CCF association in Weyburn were Socred advocates.

M.J. Coldwell always believed Social Credit was an anti-democratic party, while Tommy Douglas thought Coldwell's approach too harsh, and wrote:

> Throughout my meetings, I have consistently taken the stand that Mr. Aberhart has taken an economically unsound position but that he has endeavoured to give the debtor a fair break in his debt adjustment legislation,[13] and that when those who have supported Social Credit come to realize its inherent weakness they will find a more comfortable home in the ranks of the CCF.[14]

Tommy, if he could, was going to cash in on the Socred vote.

Meanwhile, the Liberals were putting up dummy Socred candidates to split the vote. Tommy learned of this when he got a telephone call from E.B. MacKay, who had run against him for the Weyburn CCF nomination. MacKay said that he had been approached by two members

---

[12] Quoted in Shackleton, *Tommy Douglas*, 85.

[13] To keep the banks from simply foreclosing every time a farmer got behind in payments, the Credit of Alberta Regulation Bill required the licensing of all bank employees, and their activities were put under the control of the Social Credit Board. The legislation was later disallowed.

[14] Douglas to Coldwell, 6 December 1936, Douglas Collection, Saskatchewan Archives, Regina.

of the Liberal riding executive, who apparently thought he would be carrying a grudge. They offered him $1,500 immediately to allow his name to stand as a Social Credit candidate, with another $2,000 to follow the day his nomination papers were filed. When he explained that he wasn't a Social Crediter, they told him that this didn't matter; all he had to do was draw votes away from Tommy. When he turned them down, they told him he was very foolish, and persuaded another man, named Morton Fletcher, to run (Fletcher was appointed to a patronage job by the Liberals soon after the election).[15]

Tommy was outraged by this, but didn't propose to do anything about it. Dan Grant felt otherwise, and went charging off to Edmonton to talk to Premier Aberhart. The premier told Grant that if a genuine Social Credit candidate could be found for the Weyburn riding, he would denounce the Liberal "stooge," Morton Fletcher. Grant hotfooted it back to Weyburn and rounded up a gaggle of Social Credit supporters, or reasonable facsimiles thereof, for Tommy to address on September 28. Tommy told the group that while he could not stand as their candidate, he would welcome their support. The meeting's chairman had already read out a telegram from Colonel H.W. Arnold, the Social Credit organizer in Saskatchewan, which stated that there was no official Social Credit candidate in the riding[16] and that Tommy had the official support of Premier Aberhart. Morton Fletcher was left dangling.

George Williams had already written to Tommy, warning him that he would be better off "to frankly expose the fallacies of Social Credit than to try to compromise,"[17] but Tommy paid no attention. That was a mistake.

The Great Pamphlet Heist
The campaign of Weyburn's Liberal candidate, Edward J. Young, consisted mainly of wild statements that the CCF, if elected, would crush democracy, take away the family farm, and establish a Russian Soviet in Regina. He was very much on the right wing of the Liberal party, and had written a minority report on the Stevens Committee that not only endorsed the position of the nation's giant corporations, but used material

---

[15] Douglas, *The Making of a Socialist,* 87–88.
[16] Reported in *Weyburn Review,* 3 October 1935. The candidate chosen by the Liberals, Morton Fletcher, was not, in fact, ever recognized by the Social Credit party of Saskatchewan.
[17] Quoted in McLeod and McLeod, *Road to Jerusalem,* 62.

straight from the annual reports of Canada Packers and Simpson's Limited to defend them. When C.E. Burton, the head of Simpson's, made a speech in Regina, he suggested that Hitler had the right idea in dealing with the unemployed by imposing harsh discipline on them, and Young was quoted as saying that he agreed with Burton.[18]

Not surprisingly, Tommy was dying to lure Young into a public debate, but Young refused, repeatedly, to be drawn. Whenever Tommy had a meeting near one of Young's rallies, Tommy's meeting would be adjourned early, and then many of the crowd would swarm over to the other gathering. Tommy would listen to Young's extravagant statements and then stand up in the audience and challenge him.

Young was finally exasperated into agreeing to a debate, held on September 25 at the Weyburn Arena. That debate cost him the election. He had a weak, reedy voice, which could scarcely be heard in the jammed arena, while Tommy's resonant voice could be heard in every corner. Tommy made an unabashed bid for Socred votes by calling for immediate steps to increase purchasing power, before also calling for pensions at age sixty, public works to ease unemployment, and a national health plan.

Young attacked the CCF platform, which he said would bankrupt the nation, and waved aloft a pamphlet that he claimed proved the CCF intended to run all the farms in the province. This pamphlet had not been released by Tommy or the CCF. In fact, it had been stolen from the print shop where it had been produced. After the print-shop break-in, the RCMP had descended on the public school in McTaggart, a village in the riding, where Young's campaign manager, J.J. McCruden, was principal. At the school, the RCMP found copies of CCF literature. Faced with this, McCruden admitted to the break-in and theft. When Young suddenly began waving the stolen pamphlet in the air, Tommy demolished him. He told the crowd:

> Any man who would stoop to such methods is unfit to be a teacher of youth in this country! And any man who would make use of stolen property on a political platform

[18] Douglas, *The Making of a Socialist,* 85.

is unfit to represent the people of this constituency in
Parliament![19]

Young shook his fist at Tommy. McCruden, a rather larger man, threatened to knock his block off, but a band of Tommy's supporters promptly
intervened. It was a lively evening.

Young's campaign was doomed. Other Liberals might be able to cash
in on the backlash against Bennett, but not the candidate in Weyburn.
But on October 9, five days before the vote, Tommy was haled before
the provincial executive in the boardroom of the Hotel Saskatchewan in
Regina, along with his campaign manager, Ted Stinson, to explain why
he should not be repudiated as a candidate for collaborating with Social
Credit, against the express directions of J.S. Woodsworth.

The precedent was discouraging. Jacob Benson, the CCF candidate in
Yorkton, had been denounced by the party in September and stripped
of his status as an official candidate on the grounds that

> The policies of the CCF are clearly defined . . . and do
> not permit of collaboration on the part of any candidates
> with any other political party.[20]

Benson's crimes were that when he had been asked, "Will you agree to
support Social Credit members in the House?" he had answered, "Yes";
and that he had presented a signed resignation to the Social Credit executive (with the approval of the CCF riding executive).

Tommy had not signed any papers allowing the Socreds to recall him,
but he had certainly collaborated, and George Williams, the provincial
president and house leader, wanted his head on a platter. He nearly succeeded. "You have very successfully crucified the provincial organization," he told Douglas.[21]

It is hard to escape the feeling that Williams was more concerned
with getting back at his enemy, M.J. Coldwell, through Douglas,
Coldwell's protégé, than he was with the niceties of electoral politics,

---

[19] McLeod and McLeod, *Road to Jerusalem,* 62.
[20] *Leader-Post* (Regina), 25 September 1935.
[21] Special Executive Meeting of the CCF, 9 October 1935, CCF Papers,
Saskatchewan Archives, Regina.

but Williams did have a pretty good case. Tommy had not only accepted Socred support, he had sought it, and his backers had strung up at least one poster that read:

> VOTE DOUGLAS! Weyburn CCF–Social Credit Association[22]

Tommy's defence was belligerent, blunt, and ultimately successful. Confronted with the telegram from Colonel Arnold endorsing him as worthy of Social Credit support, he replied:

> I am the CCF candidate for the Weyburn federal con-
> stituency, and the Social Credit forces have the right to
> endorse me and a joint committee has the right to issue
> literature to repudiate this man Fletcher. I refused 100 per
> cent acceptance of Arnold's program. I refused to sign
> the Social Credit recall. All I did was promise to give
> Aberhart a hand. Whatever action the executive takes
> does not affect me.[23]

This was the word with no bark on it. Dump me, and I'll run anyway. He told the meeting that "Social Credit doesn't amount to a row of pins," and "You're wrong if you think I'm supporting a capitalist move-ment. I merely promised to give Social Credit a free hand, and support legislation to do so."[24]

Four of the five executive members were ready to vote to renounce Tommy; his only ally was Dr. John MacLean, a party stalwart and a close friend of M.J. Coldwell's. Coldwell, although a member of the execu-tive, was not at the meeting; he was at a party rally in Moose Jaw. MacLean persuaded the others not to take a vote in his absence. He warned them that if they did move against Douglas, Coldwell would resign. (Coldwell had said so, and had meant it.)

The executive meeting petered out. The very next day, the *Weyburn*

---

[22] Ibid.
[23] Ibid.
[24] Ibid.

Review carried a letter from Tommy headed "A Final Appeal." Obviously written some time before, it struck quite a different note from the scorn of Social Credit he had laid before the executive:

> I publicly place myself on record as being desirous that every possible opportunity be given Mr. Aberhart to work out his theories in Alberta, and furthermore that if elected, I am prepared to initiate and support legislation that would facilitate the workings of the Social Credit movement.
>
> There is no signed agreement between me and the Social Credit organization. I am the CCF candidate for this constituency who has been endorsed by the Social Credit forces, who have pledged me their whole-hearted support.
>
> [This] does not make me a Social Creditor any more than the Manufacturers' Association of Canada having endorsed Mr. Young makes Mr. Young a member of the C.M.A.[25]

Would Douglas have been dumped if this letter, specifically pledging to initiate "legislation that would facilitate the workings of the Social Credit movement," had appeared just before the executive meeting, instead of just after? Possibly. But it was apparent both that the cocky young candidate was not going to be fazed by the executive, whatever it did, and that M.J. Coldwell was not going to allow Tommy to be repudiated, nor — perhaps just as importantly — Williams to triumph.

In the end, Douglas went back to campaigning, and won the seat by 7,280 votes to Young's 6,979. The Conservative candidate got 1,557 votes, and Morton Fletcher, the Liberal lackey running as the denounced Social Credit standard-bearer, drew a miserable 362. (What did he care? He had a job.)

In 1985, when Tom and Ian McLeod were preparing their biography,

---

[25] *Weyburn Review*, 10 October 1935.

Tommy told them that he had, in effect, cobbled together a mock political party to attract Social Credit as well as CCF votes, and he made no
apology for it:

> Here was a mob of people, farmers, small businessmen,
> railway workers, who knew that something was wrong . . .
> and wanted to support something. And they didn't give
> a tinker's damn [sic] about all of the fine points.[26]

By this reasoning, no one should object to a modern NDP candidate
seeking the endorsement of the Canadian Alliance.

The CCF did rather well in the 1935 election, but as was to happen
so often, it was betrayed by the first-past-the-post electoral system. The
election concluded with the Mackenzie King–led Liberals winning a
smashing victory, tallying 173 seats — the greatest electoral victory in
Canadian history to that time. The Conservatives were reduced to 40 seats.
The fledgling CCF won 387,056 votes nationwide, more than twice as
many as the Socred's 180,301, but the Socreds came back with 17 MPs,
15 of them in Alberta and 2 in Saskatchewan. The CCF won 7 seats,
electing both of its Saskatchewan candidates: M.J. Coldwell in
Rosetown-Biggar, and Tommy Douglas in Weyburn. H.H. Stevens's
Reconstruction Party was dealt an even more brutal blow by the elec-
toral system: despite pulling in 384,095 votes, it won only a single seat
— Stevens's own, in British Columbia.[27]

Considering the somewhat dubious way in which Tommy scrambled
into his seat, it is remarkable how effective he proved to be as a member
of Parliament.

---

[26] McLeod and McLeod, *Road to Jerusalem,* 67.
[27] The Liberal tally was 1,975,841.

Chapter NINE

The Honourable Member

> *One of the most crying problems facing the Canadian people in all parts of this dominion is the tremendous one of public health. People need dental and medical and hospital care. We have all the facilities for rendering those services, yet there is not an hon. Member who does not know that people who have money can secure those services and people who have not money cannot, and are not getting them.*
> *An hon. MEMBER: That is not so.*
> — Tommy Douglas, in his maiden speech, and the response of another
> MP, 11 February 1936

A group of zealots at the annual meeting of the Baptist Union of Western Canada in Calgary celebrated Tommy's election to Parliament by trying to kick him out of his pulpit. These men preferred their preachers to be political eunuchs. William Smalley, the general secretary, quashed the idea. Just the same, Tommy would never again hold down a job as a preacher, although he remained on the reserve roll of the Baptist Union. He drew his last regular paycheque from Calvary in December 1935, but remained a member of the congregation all his life.

Under the heading of unfinished business, the CCF's provincial council in Saskatchewan took up the matter of the Socred seduction, which M.J. Coldwell, the provincial leader, kept ducking. George Williams sent Coldwell a strong telegram in which he complained that, as house leader in the provincial legislature, he was receiving complaints from party members that Tommy should be repudiated. Coldwell invited Williams to send along the complaints, but, as M.J. put it, "I didn't get any of the objections that George said were in, and therefore I never had to reply to them."[1]

---

[1] Stewart, *M.J.*, 121.

Finally, in December 1935, the provincial council took some action. A motion to expel Tommy was passed, but Coldwell forced the council to reverse itself and settle for a motion censuring the new MP. That done, Jacob Benson, who had gone a little further than Tommy in seeking Socred help, was welcomed back into the fold after pledging his loyalty to the party anew. Williams was disgusted at what he considered the misguided weakness of the council, but there was not much he could do about it. Thus ended what Clarence Fines called "a somewhat muddled and uncomfortable chapter in party relations."[2]

Tommy, Irma, and the infant Shirley went to Winnipeg to spend Christmas with Tommy's parents, Tom and Anne, and Tom managed to let his son know that he was pleased and proud, without actually coming out with words that might give the lad a swelled head. He said, "Now remember, laddie, the working people have put a lot of trust in you, you must never let them down."[3] It was their last meeting; Tom died suddenly of a burst appendix in January 1936, at the age of fifty-seven. Tommy went to Winnipeg for the funeral, and then went on to Ottawa to begin life as an MP.

Until Shirley was old enough to go to school, the family lived in an apartment in Ottawa during the session, and moved back to their small house in Weyburn for the rest of the time. When Shirley started to attend school at age six, Irma stayed with her in Weyburn, only going to Ottawa for formal occasions, like the opening of Parliament. Tommy roomed with M.J. Coldwell in these early years.

Tommy received $4,000 a year as MP, and although he kicked back 5 per cent of this to the party every year, and 10 per cent in election years — this became the custom for all CCF MPs — he still had a larger paycheque than he had ever received as a preacher. On top of the $4,000, he had a $2,000 tax-free expense allowance and a free railway pass. Even so, the costs of running two households, and the frequent gifts he gave to others, meant that by the time he left Ottawa to run for the premiership of Saskatchewan, he was in debt.

---

[2] Fines, "The Impossible Dream," 194.
[3] Douglas, *The Making of a Socialist*, 93.

Socialist Alley

Along the corridor of the sixth floor of the Centre Block of Parliament, ranging out from the men's washroom, were the offices of the seven CCFers who had been elected in the 1935 vote — "Socialist Alley," it was called. Besides J.S. Woodsworth, the party leader, the members were: A.A. Heaps of Winnipeg and Angus MacInnis of Vancouver, both returning MPs; Grant MacNeil and J.S. Taylor from British Columbia; and M.J. Coldwell and T.C. Douglas from Saskatchewan. Tommy and M.J. shared the office closest to the biffy (the *men's* biffy, of course — there was no women's; it would be decades before the House of Commons discovered that women MPs pee, too). By happy chance, the electors had served up some of the ablest of the party's stalwarts — the exception was Taylor, an enthusiast for astrology and numerology, whom even the kindly M.J. Coldwell described as "A very queer duck, indeed."[4] (Taylor soon jumped over to the Liberals.)

Agnes Macphail had won again, this time in Grey-Bruce, Ontario (her former riding of Grey Southeast had been abolished in 1933); but she had run as a United Farmers of Ontario–Labour candidate, not a CCF one, although the distinction soon blurred. She joined the CCF caucus, where she revered J.S. Woodsworth, fought with the sharp-tongued Angus MacInnis, and took a while to warm up to the members from Saskatchewan. She thought Coldwell was a bit too starchy, and Tommy a bit too brash.

Macphail, too, had an office in Socialist Alley, although she was not required to double up, as the men were. (This doubling up meant that anytime one member had a visit from a constituent, or from anyone else who wanted privacy, the other member would have to wander up and down the corridors or adjourn for a cup of coffee until the meeting was over.) Agnes used the public washroom.

There were no party research facilities and only one paid national organizer, Ted Garland, who travelled the country by rail, coach class, sitting up at night to save the cost of a sleeper. The MPs made use of the Commons' secretarial pool, but that was about all the help Parliament

---

[4] M.J. Coldwell, "Reminiscences," unpublished interviews by Clifford Scotton and Carl Wenass, Coldwell Papers, National Archives of Canada.

provided. Woodsworth's charming, brilliant daughter, Grace, acted as unofficial caucus secretary, keeping the minutes and stuffing envelopes, as well as arranging speaking itineraries for the members. Angus MacInnis had very cleverly married her in 1932. Tommy, like other CCF MPs, did most of his own research work, or drew on figures gathered by the League for Social Reconstruction, whose 1935 book, *Social Planning for Canada,* became an important part of every CCF member's kit.

In the summer of 1936, a young lawyer named David Lewis returned to Canada from Britain, where he had been a Rhodes Scholar, and presented himself in Woodsworth's House of Commons office, eager to help in any way he could. He soon became one of the dominant figures in the party, while pursuing a legal career so that he'd have something to survive on, since he received no pay from the party.

Lewis, brilliant, dynamic, tireless — and arrogant — was soon taking on more and more of the direction of the CCF, and the 1936 convention elected him to the CCF National Council, which promptly elected him national secretary, on August 6, 1936.[5] He still didn't get any salary. He persuaded the senior partner in his legal firm to give him a lean-to at the back of some property the firm owned on Wellington Street, across from the Parliament buildings, and this lean-to, with its sand floor (which became a mud floor every time it rained or snowed), became the CCF national office. For more than two years, 124 Wellington Street, sand (or mud) and all, remained the official CCF headquarters in Ottawa.[6]

Woodsworth's attitude towards these bread-and-butter matters was summarized in a letter he had earlier written to a Quebec follower, J.A. Martin, in 1932:

> If this is a genuine peoples' [*sic*] movement, it seems to me that the people themselves, all over the country, will have to take the matter up in their own localities. All we can do is to give a lead, then we must trust there will come to the front individuals and groups, who will rally the people in their various neighbourhoods.[7]

---

[5] David Lewis, *The Good Fight: Political Memoirs, 1909–1958* (Toronto: Macmillan, 1981), 116.

[6] Ibid., 118.

[7] Woodsworth to Martin, 22 December 1932, Woodsworth Papers, National Archives of Canada.

Which was all very well, of course, but to Lewis, Coldwell, Douglas, and others, it seemed useful to give the people a nudge, now and then, in the right direction. This was likely to require organizers, secretaries, and perhaps even the extravagance of a floor underfoot. Frank Underhill had also previously complained:

> I do feel very strongly that the movement must advance beyond the stage of being a collection of individual missionaries and must get more organization and more conscious direction at the centre.[8]

Woodsworth's reply had not been encouraging:

> I really think you hardly realize how weak we are throughout the country and how essential individual mission work is at the present time.[9]

Tommy and M.J. became the agriculture experts of the caucus, which, since one of them was a preacher and the other a teacher, drew a good deal of scorn from Jimmy Gardiner, who had given up the premiership of Saskatchewan to become Mackenzie King's minister of agriculture. Gardiner, a successful farmer as well as a politician, chided Douglas because he had never worked a farm. Tommy replied, "I can't lay an egg, either, but I know how to make an omelet."[10]

Once, when Tommy was trying to make a speech on farm matters, Gardiner led a chorus of heckling against him until Tommy said, "I don't want any more interruptions. If the Minister of Agriculture will sit up in his chair and dangle his feet, I'll go on with what I have to say."[11] Gardiner, like Tommy, was quite short, but unlike Tommy, he was quite sensitive on the subject; Gardiner never forgave Tommy for this crack.

The truth is that Douglas and Coldwell knew a tremendous amount about farm problems and spent a great deal of their time in farmers' homes. They made a formidable combination. They had a good deal in

---

[8] Underhill to Woodsworth, 12 July 1934, CCF Papers, National Archives of Canada.
[9] Woodsworth to Underhill, 2 August 1934, CCF Papers, National Archives of Canada.
[10] Shackleton, *Tommy Douglas*, 92.
[11] Douglas, *The Making of a Socialist,* 112.

common: both had come from Britain to Canada, and both were drawn to socialism as a way to right some of the appalling wrongs they saw about them. They were proselytizers, one as a preacher, the other as a teacher, although they had quite different styles. Douglas's humour was trenchant, an edged tool; M.J.'s was gentle, aimed more often at himself than at anyone else.

Douglas looked up to Coldwell, the older man — when they went to Ottawa together, M.J. was forty-seven, Douglas thirty-one — much as M.J. looked up to Woodsworth, who was then sixty-one. It was M.J. who urged Douglas to return to Saskatchewan and the provincial leadership, and he played an important role in both that event and the provincial election that made Tommy premier in 1944.

Tommy shocked M.J. only once, by telling an off-colour story on the platform. (M.J. was not averse to off-colour stories, only to telling them in public.) Tommy was trying to illustrate the closeness of the two old-line parties, whose pretended hostility covered a common purpose, and gave this parallel:

> When Noah first put the animals in the Ark, he told them that there was a shortage of room, so there could be no hanky-panky, and they all agreed. Then, when the storm was over and the animals were coming off the Ark, they came two by two, of course, until the cats came out, and there was a papa cat, and a momma cat, and a whole litter of kittens. Noah was dumbfounded, and the papa cat said, "I guess you thought we were fighting."

After Tommy told this story with M.J. on the platform, Coldwell announced that if Tommy ever did it again, he would leave the auditorium at once and let Douglas explain his exit to the crowd.[12]

In general, though, the two men seldom disagreed, and they formed the core of a bloc of politicians who were far more effective than their number indicated.

---

[12] Arthur Kroeger, interview by author, Ottawa, 17 June 1998.

A Dab Hand with Hecklers

Tommy was one of the bright young men of the House of Commons, and he soon drew the attention of the masses of Liberals on the other side of the chamber, whose heckles and catcalls Hansard usually reduces to its standard gibberish:

> Some hon. Members: Oh, oh![13]

He thrived on this, and always gave back as good as he got, sometimes better. Once, when the jeers opposite threatened to disrupt his flow, he cracked, "When you throw a stone into a pack of dogs and one yelps, he has been hit."[14] The Speaker asked him to withdraw the remark, deeming it unparliamentary, and Tommy complied.

In his capacity as agriculture critic, he formed an occasional alliance with the leader of the official opposition, R.B. Bennett, and, to his own surprise, found that he liked him:

> Before I had gone to the House I had thought of Bennett as a blustering bully. But at the House of Commons, I realized two things. First, he was probably one of the greatest orators and best parliamentarians the country ever had. In terms of carefully prepared statements that wouldn't commit yourself, Mr. King was better. In terms of an assessment of a situation and attempt to find an answer to it, Bennett was superior. Also, Bennett had a human side that he kept from the public. He was certainly very kind to Mr. Coldwell and me . . . In my opinion, he was a better Canadian than he was given credit for.[15]

---

[13] I once wrote a newspaper column that began "Hansard lies," and went on to compare the official record's "Oh, oh" with what was actually said in the House, usually something uplifting like "Aw, shuddup!" Stanley Knowles, ever the defender of Parliament, wanted me brought before the bar of the House and censured, but could gain little support for this laudable aim. I stick to my story: Hansard lies.

[14] House of Commons, *Debates*, 14 January 1939.

[15] Douglas, *The Making of a Socialist*, 95.

When Bennett, embittered and deserted, as he felt it, fled Canada in 1939 for an estate in Surrey, England, only three men went down to the Ottawa railway station to see him off: Howard Green, the Conservative MP for Vancouver South; Ernest Perley, the Conservative MP for Qu'Appelle; and Tommy. Tommy remembered:

> The man who had been fawned and flattered by all the politicians was completely ignored when he left. He said he left Canada betrayed by his friends and deserted by his party. He felt very bitter about it, and I think it was a great pity.[16]

Mackenzie King, the man who replaced Bennett as prime minister, on the other hand, Tommy held in contempt, quoting Agnes Macphail's description of him as "a fat man full of words."[17]

During his first session, Tommy spoke sixty times, on everything from Ethiopia and the League of Nations to unemployment relief and the Weyburn post office. This was far more often than a newcomer — and a young newcomer at that — is supposed to speak in his early years, but Tommy and the tiny CCF caucus, going up against the overwhelming Liberal majority, were trying to carve their initials in marshmallow, never an easy task.

Throughout this session, the CCF members kept hammering away at social policy, farm policy, and unemployment; the main effect was to place arguments for reform on the record for later leverage. As the costs of providing relief grew, such aid came to be accompanied by a rich tradition, still with us, which holds that most of the money spent on welfare goes to ne'er-do-wells, welfare cheats, and foreigners. The Ontario government of George Henry sent relief inspectors out to track down the rascals; one of the inspectors reported that in Hamilton, the supervisor of relief, one Sam Lawrence, was "a labour man . . . even a Red." He was committing the unpardonable sin of distributing relief "according to individual circumstances," rather than following guidelines that limited assistance

---

[16] Ibid., 96.
[17] Ibid., 94.

to a risible amount. Being a Red, Sam had "foreign friends," who were "well stocked with all they asked for." None of these things could be proven, but who needed proof when everybody knew that foreigners living in Hamilton were getting allowances for family members "probably living in Central Europe"?[18]

As in our own modern demonization, these unsubstantiated anecdotes were enough to convince a wide sector of the taxpaying populace that government support was simply being thrown away, so there was little sustained pressure for its expansion — except from the larger and larger army of victims, whose voices were generally ignored.

Aside from closing the relief camps, which had become a nuisance, and adding a little more cash to programs offering direct relief, the King government did very little throughout the Depression. For King, charity was the cardinal Christian virtue, so there was no need to take government action until public agitation reached the point where his own political survival hung in the balance. The Liberal party had a medicare proposal in its platform as early as 1919; it would be implemented in 1964. That, it seems, was the proper pace at which to introduce these radical changes.

Most Canadians, at least the comfortable ones, tended to agree with him; they wanted solutions, but not radical solutions. In this atmosphere, the CCF became particularly vulnerable to the manoeuvres of the Trotskyites and other far-left factions, whose belligerent statements were always given good play by the press. The original formation of the party didn't help; because of its federal nature, the national office couldn't enforce discipline (David Lewis made it clear that he would have moved with swift brutality against the interlopers). Only the provincial parties could act. The CCF were under attack from the left by Communist Party members, who constantly tried to penetrate the CCF clubs, take over their executives, and then promptly shut the door to anyone who disagreed with them.

The Communists and Trotskyites became experts at sitting; they would send a small group to a CCF club meeting and out-sit everyone

---

[18] Struthers, *How Much Is Enough?*, 83.

else. As others drifted off, the infiltrators would ram through resolutions that were likely to embarrass, if not destroy, the host club. In London, Ontario, where I grew up, solemn burghers who joined the CCF for its economic policies — they held pretty good social events, too — would find themselves at evening's end suddenly confronted with an invitation to join the comrades across the sea in the Soviet Union in a movement to crush the capitalist under the heel, and otherwise turn the city over to the more rigorous forms of class warfare.

It worked, sometimes, in some places. In British Columbia, for example, the CCF spent much of its energies in internal debate as to whether it was better to try to regulate the hours and wages of the workers or usher in the New Dawn by some firmer action, such as stringing a few capitalists up on the lampposts.

In Ontario, the increasing infiltration of Communists led the United Farmers of Ontario, the heart and soul of the CCF in the province at the time, to march out in a body, led by Agnes Macphail. This came about after a number of incidents, which included the London CCF Council passing a resolution to join the Communists in defence of Rev. A.E. Smith, leader of the local Communist Party (and the man who had once helped Tommy), who had been charged with sedition by the federal authorities. The provincial council had specifically rejected passing any resolutions to support Smith, but the London body had rammed through one of those end-of-the-meeting resolutions to join the protest, and that was that. Smith had spent much of his time attacking the CCF, and Woodsworth, for various sins, and the party officialdom was not anxious to come to his defence (even though the charge of sedition was, like so many such charges at that time, based on airy nothing; if you were against the government, you were seditious).

Agnes Macphail, as the provincial president, was horrified by the way the Communists had managed to take over CCF clubs (Woodsworth described the CCF organizations as "a happy hunting ground for cranks and Communists"), and she set out to chuck the left-wingers out of the party, because their views were nowhere near in accord with the Regina

Manifesto. She soon discovered that she could not do it. Because there were no individual memberships at the provincial level, the only way to get rid of troublemakers, if their own affiliated CCF organizations would not reject them, was to expel the whole organization. In disgust, she instead took the United Farmers out of the CCF. J.S. Woodsworth then stepped in, and the Ontario CCF was dissolved and reorganized, with individual memberships.[19]

Ontario — and this is a point that is often missed in discussions of the CCF — was always the largest sector of the party in terms of members and votes. In the 1935 federal election, for example, the CCF got 127,927 votes in Ontario, almost twice as many as in Saskatchewan, although the former did not produce any MPs. Canada's first-past-the-post system made it almost impossible to elect a number of members commensurate with the ballots cast for the party, but that did not make the province any less important to the CCF as a whole. When Ontario was in trouble, the CCF was in trouble.

On the other side, the government was using its considerable powers to get into and destroy any left-wing groups, including the CCF. The RCMP provided *agents provocateurs*, who, when they couldn't get the evidence of wickedness they needed, often made it up. This was a time when you didn't even have to be a Red to be investigated, rebuked, and threatened; it was enough if you were not sufficiently anti-Red. In 1930, a peculiar group of idealists formed the Toronto chapter of the Fellowship of Reconciliation, which had taken on the awesome task of sorting out all international misunderstanding. The Toronto members applied for a permit to hold a meeting at the Empire Theatre in Toronto, which was first promised, and then withdrawn when the head of the city's Red Squad called on the manager and pointed out to him that these were dangerous people. A group of sixty-eight professors at the University of Toronto were foolhardy enough to write a letter to the Toronto newspapers in protest against this attack on free speech. That drew an editorial in the Toronto *Globe,* which wanted to know, "Why is the cause of a group of revolutionary agitators to be preferred to the welfare

---

[19] Stewart and French, *Ask No Quarter,* 177–78.

of a loyal, Christian nation?" The newspaper wanted the profs fired, as did the university chancellor, Sir William Mulock, but the Board of Regents balked.[20] The nation seemed to be running out of tolerance, crouching in fear before imagined demons, and anyone who represented democratic socialism could easily be smeared as a Bolshevist, Red, and home wrecker.

Tommy was relatively easygoing about the interlopers — his hero, M.J. Coldwell, saw them as a much greater menace — but their presence in the party made life that much more complicated, and explaining the party program that much more difficult.

Spanish Eyes

In 1936, after the House rose, Tommy was sent to the World Youth Congress in Geneva as one of three "chaperones" for a delegation from the Canadian Youth Congress.[21] (In addition to all his other work, Tommy had been elected president of the Co-operative Commonwealth Youth Movement and had a key role among the party's younger members.) Some of the Spanish delegates to the youth meeting asked the MPs to visit Spain, where the revolution — or, as Tommy called it, "the counter-revolution" — had broken out. He visited several cabinet ministers in Madrid, and found them, far from being the Communists they were alleged to be, "to the right of centre . . . We would have thought of them as Lloyd George Liberals."[22]

He also visited the front, talked to priests who were fighting alongside the government troops, saw German and Italian planes flying overhead, and concluded:

> There isn't any doubt that without the financial aid from the big interests of Spain, surrounding countries, and even the United States, and without German and Italian planes, munitions and tanks and troops and technicians, Franco could never have defeated the government of Spain.[23]

---

[20] Stewart, *But Not in Canada*, 64.
[21] Douglas, *The Making of a Socialist,* 106. The other two MPs were Paul Martin, later to become Liberal minister of health, and Denton Massey, a Conservative MP who had, Tommy reported with awe, "the biggest Bible class in the world, two thousand members."
[22] Ibid.
[23] Ibid., 107.

Britain's Labour Party was then backing Neville Chamberlain's policy of non-intervention, in Spain or anywhere else, and Tommy was appalled. However, the intervention he pressed for at this time was from the League of Nations — although, after the disaster of Ethiopia, that made very little sense.

During that three-month trip, he also went to Nuremberg, to see the annual festival put on there by Hitler:

> It was frightful. I came back and warned my friends about the great German bombers roaring over the parade of self-propelled guns and tanks, Hitler standing there giving his salute, with Goering and the rest of the Nazi bigwigs by his side. There was no doubt then that Hitler was simply using Spain as a dress rehearsal for attacks on other nations.[24]

Tommy came back to Canada convinced that Germany had to be stopped, and made a number of speeches in Saskatchewan calling for "a system of collective security" to curb Germany. He received threats from the *Deutscher Bund* in the province, which was pro-Nazi.

George Williams had suggested these lectures as a means of raising money, and encouraged Tommy. Williams, by this time, was convinced that war was coming and that Canada should stand at Britain's side. However, both Woodsworth and Coldwell were declared pacifists, so the position Tommy took in the House was somewhat murky. This was not surprising; having seen the results of fascist aggression in Europe, he was much closer in his views to Williams (and to David Lewis, who had been horrified by what he had seen on a visit to his native Poland) than to Woodsworth and Coldwell. But they were the men he admired and liked; the kindest thing he could say about Williams, the prickly pear of CCF politics, was that he was a "splendid organizer."

When Parliament reassembled in 1937, Woodsworth proposed a resolution that called on Canada to "remain strictly neutral" in case of war,

---

[24] Ibid., 108.

no matter which nations were involved. Douglas spoke in support of this resolution and called for "economic sanctions," but not military ones, to be enforced, somehow, by the League of Nations. More practically, he proposed immediate government control of nickel exports, which were going to help arm Canada's enemies.[25] The CCF National Council debated this issue at length and concluded that in the event of war, "finance and industry should be automatically conscripted."[26] If this was a pacifist stance, it was an odd one. Coldwell, in the House, followed Woodsworth in giving it his own spin. He did not believe in making preparations for war because: "I do not believe in war and I conscientiously object to it."[27]

Right up until the eve of war, the party, and its tiny caucus, continued to be divided by the arguments about armaments and war. Tommy could, and did, speak eloquently about war profiteers, the need to curb arms shipments, and the wickedness of the capitalist class in general, but he was never a pacifist, and the party's confusions were as painful to him as to others.

On February 23, 1937, King Gordon, a member of the national executive who shared Coldwell's views, was scheduled to speak under CCF sponsorship at a peace rally in Regina. Williams, now the provincial leader (Coldwell was in Ottawa as an MP), not only refused to share the platform with him, but released a statement to the press explaining that "the CCF had never discussed pacifism and had no declared policy in connection with it." The proper place to sort out the dispute was not on a public platform, he said, but within the councils of the party.[28] But despite endless meetings aimed at doing just this, the matter was not resolved until the Second World War was actually under way.

Nevertheless, the party did keep up a constant barrage on the subject of the coming war — a growing threat that Mackenzie King simply refused to recognize. When Germany violated the Versailles Treaty by marching into the Rhineland in 1936, he summed up official government policy this way:

> The attitude of the government is to do nothing itself and if possible to prevent anything occurring which will

---

[25] House of Commons, *Debates,* 4 February 1937.
[26] Minutes of CCF National Council Meeting, 30–31 January 1937, CCF Papers, National Archives of Canada.
[27] House of Commons, *Debates,* 15 February 1937.
[28] Agnes Jean Groome, "M.J. Coldwell and CCF Foreign Policy, 1932–1950," master's thesis, University of Saskatchewan, Regina (1967), 37–38.

precipitate one additional factor into the all-important discussions that are now taking place in Europe.[29]

The first ten words might have made a suitable epitaph for King.

Over and over again, Tommy attacked the Canadian manufacturers who were making fortunes by re-arming Germany and arming an expansive and aggressive Japan. Tommy contended, among other things, that it was the influence of Standard Oil of California that led to the embarrassing Riddell affair. Dr. W.A. Riddell, Canada's delegate to the League, advocated oil sanctions against Italy when Mussolini invaded Ethiopia. King disavowed his own envoy. What sanctions the League did attempt to impose did not include bans on oil supply, and the sanctions failed. In the House, Tommy noted that "oil sanctions are much further away than when they were first suggested," and went on to ask:

> Why is that so? Is it because the oil interests have too much influence on the powers of government? Is it because those people who make their profits have a great deal more weight in the councils of governments than have the dictates of humanity?[30]

The War over Pacifism

The CCF National Convention in Toronto, in August 1936, called on the party to press for legislation that would allow Canada to remain neutral in any future war, even one involving Britain,[31] and Tommy backed that resolution. Woodsworth was finally moved to support the view that there ought to be an international police force, a body that could take up arms against a tyrant like Hitler who attacked another country,[32] but he would never back the idea of Canada participating directly in a war.

Although Tommy had tremendous admiration for pacifists, and appeared before the War Relations Board in defence of many conscientious objectors, he declared that he was never himself a pacifist, for three reasons. First, "I think

---

[29] Quoted in Kenneth McNaught, "The 1930s," in *The Canadians, 1867–1967,* ed. J.M.S. Careless and R. Craig Brown (Toronto: Macmillan, 1967), 269.

[30] House of Commons, *Debates*, 11 February 1936.

[31] Records of the National Convention, Toronto, 3–5 August 1936, CCF Papers, National Archives of Canada.

[32] House of Commons, *Debates,* 3 April 1939.

that any absolute creed is always an oversimplification"; second, "one not only has the rights but the responsibilities of a citizen"; and finally,

> If you accept the completely absolutist position of the pacifist, then you are saying that you are prepared to allow someone else who has no such scruples to destroy all the values you've built up. This is what I used to argue with Mr. Woodsworth . . . if you came to a choice between losing freedom of speech, religion, association, thought, and all the things that make life worth living, and resorting to force, you'd use force. What you have internationally is what you have within a nation. You must have law and order, and you must have the necessary military means to enforce that law and order.[33]

As the German juggernaut rolled over Europe, Coldwell reluctantly came to the same view, as did every other member of the caucus, except its most important member, the leader, J.S. Woodsworth.

Wars, said Woodsworth, were basically capitalist spasms, driven by arms sales, and they never, ever achieved the just peace that was always the claim for either launching one or replying to force with force. The Regina Manifesto had not made the CCF a pacifist party; it had, rather, insisted that Canada stay out of any future *imperialist* wars, and party members who were increasingly dismayed by the tone of the statements made by Woodsworth, as George Williams was, had a point. The Canadian people had gone far past the argument that mere international pressure could bring Germany to heel.

The CCF National Council had already shifted ground, and instead of opposing the government's defence expenditures because they were defence expenditures, MPs were instructed to oppose them because they were based on the wrong policy. No money should be spent to prepare for Canadians to send an expeditionary force overseas; but it was all right to spend money to defend our own shores.

---

[33] Douglas, *The Making of a Socialist,* 104–5.

Britain declared war against Germany on September 3, 1939. The CCF National Council met in the cafeteria on the fifth floor of the House of Commons in emergency session, and debated the issue for two days. In the emergency meeting, chaired by Coldwell (Woodsworth, who was by that time already in very poor health, sat by his side), George Williams was the only one who argued for full military participation in the war.[34] Woodsworth not only pleaded the pacifist cause, but made it clear that if the party voted against him on this, he would have to resign.

Coldwell, as chairman, did not speak, but had already moved to a view very close to the one finally accepted by the council. Frank Scott of McGill argued that the coming conflict was, at heart, a battle between capitalist nations. "The war springs out of Europe's conflicts . . . I am not interested in a victory as between two sets of gangsters," he said, but then he went on to move to support Canada's participation in a war. The logic — the inescapable logic — of this position, was thus put by British Columbia's Angus MacInnis, Woodsworth's son-in-law:

> If a bandit enters a building with a shotgun we send the police to get him. We do not leave him alone because he is a product of Canadian capitalism. Hitler may be a product of European capitalism, but that does not mean you should let him dictate to the whole world.

MacInnis proposed a motion that rejected any coalition with the Liberal government and declared that there should be no conscription, no Canadian expeditionary force overseas, and no restrictions on Canadian civil liberties during wartime. Finally, while Canadian arms could and should be sent to Britain, the arms industry should be controlled by the government.

In the end, the council voted fifteen to seven for the MacInnis proposal on the evening of Thursday, September 7. (For supporting this proposal, Tommy was later castigated by Carlyle King, the leading

---

[34] This famous meeting is discussed in full in David Lewis's *Good Fight,* M.J. Coldwell's "Reminiscences," and Grace MacInnis's biography of her father. Tommy made very little reference to it in *The Making of a Socialist,* and it appears that he was not that active in the debate, probably because he was truly torn between his own views and his loyalty to Woodsworth, as were many others.

Saskatchewan pacifist, as an imperialist and a warmonger.) Woodsworth announced that he would have to resign as leader and as a member of the party, since he could not accept the official party position. But the council refused to accept this resignation, and the next morning it was agreed that Woodsworth would be the first speaker for the CCF in Parliament later that day, but that he would speak only for himself. The official position would be put by Coldwell. David Lewis later wrote:

> I know of no other political organization that would have insisted on retaining as leader a man who totally rejected a crucial policy of the party. It was unwise politically, but it was profoundly human.[35]

When J.S. Woodsworth rose in the House to speak the case for pure pacifism, he was received in respectful silence, except for one cry of "Shame!" from an unidentified backbencher. Woodsworth stated:

> While we are urged to fight for freedom and democracy, it should be remembered that war is the very negation of both. The victor may win, but if he does, it is by adopting the self-same tactics which he condemns in his enemy.[36]

J.S. was in terrible shape physically when he got up to speak, as the result of a stroke. His wife had written out notes for him in crayon, with the letters a couple of inches high, using several sheets with a few key words on each. He could hardly see them, and Tommy passed them to him one by one. By the time he sat down, he had effectively relinquished his leadership of the party to M.J. Coldwell. The *Vancouver Province* noted, "The old leader, honoured and respected in all corners of the House, spoke what may well be his party valedictory."[37] Actually, Woodsworth addressed Parliament once more, four days later, when he attacked war profiteering and proposed that before Canada thought once more of

---

[35] Lewis, *The Good Fight,* 174.
[36] House of Commons, *Debates,* 8 September 1939.
[37] Quoted in MacInnis, *J.S. Woodsworth,* 304.

conscripting her young men to send them off to war, the nation should conscript wealth, including "bank accounts and property of every kind."

The CCF stance of demi-virginity in regard to the war did not last long as Hitler walked through Denmark, Norway, Belgium, and Holland in early 1940. Williams kept trying to convene meetings at the federal or provincial level to promote a more belligerent stance, but he was frustrated by the majority of members at both levels who wanted to shy away from a topic that showed such a fundamental division in the ranks.

After the fall of France, when Britain stood alone against Hitler, the party decided that Williams had been right all along and, in the end, moved to wholehearted support of not only the war, but even conscription.

Tommy joined the 2nd Battalion of the South Saskatchewan Regiment, and went back to Weyburn to train. (It was not hard to combine the duties of MP and soldiery at a time when the House of Commons sat more briefly than it does today.) He rose quickly from corporal to lieutenant and then to captain, and became an instructor, but he never adapted well to the army's disciplinary methods. One of the permanent force lecturers, who laid down the laws of strategy and tactics to recruits under Tommy's command, insisted on moving the group from place to place, for what appeared to be no reason. When Tommy asked for a reason for all this shuffling about, he replied that it was "to confuse the enemy."

"If you want to confuse the enemy," Tommy suggested, "why not give them one of your lectures?"

Tommy learned that the Winnipeg Grenadiers were to be sent to Hong Kong as part of the expeditionary force to that doomed place, and volunteered to go with them, but his gimpy knee kept him from being accepted. A friend of his from Weyburn who was accepted, died in Hong Kong.[38] From then on, Tommy divided his time between training duties in Weyburn and his parliamentary duties in Ottawa; the time, that is, that he could spare from his constituency work, his party work, and his family. His family, alas, came last.

Tommy became an effective critic of the government's war policy, and a defender of civil liberties in the teeth of the hysteria that so often

---

[38] Douglas, *The Making of a Socialist,* 130.

overtakes nations in times of war, but he did not — though he was later to claim that he did — object to the federal government's brutal treatment of Japanese Canadians.

The Liberals Win Again

When King called a snap election in March 1940, the Liberals, unsurprisingly, came back with an even stronger majority than in 1935 — 183 seats — and the CCF, with a slightly smaller proportion of the popular vote than in 1935 (8.5 per cent in 1940, 8.7 per cent in 1935), picked up one more seat. It now had 8 seats nationwide, but of these, 5 were in Saskatchewan (where both Tommy and M.J. Coldwell won easily); the others were in Nova Scotia, Manitoba, and British Columbia.

The heart of the nation was still a wilderness, and, almost eight years after the CCF's founding, the party appeared to be going nowhere. Tommy was an effective backbench MP, increasingly well known for his wit, his passion, and his hard work. He had shown, in the long debate on the party's position on the war, not only that he was no dreamer, like Woodsworth, but that he could keep on friendly terms with people on all sides of this issue without abandoning his own basic ideas (although, admittedly, without making them any too clear to Woodsworth). He and George Williams, in letters, were now "Dear Tommy," and "Dear George."

Coldwell, though, remained bitterly antagonistic towards Williams, whom he once described as "the most cunning individual with whom it has ever been my misfortune to be associated . . . I have made up my mind that I will be no party to placing George H. Williams in the premier's chair."[39]

During the 1938 provincial election, Williams, who ran the party almost single-handedly and seldom consulted anyone else, had decided that the Liberal government could not be defeated, so the CCF ran candidates in only thirty-one ridings. Moreover, he made a deal with both the Conservatives and the Socreds to "saw off" a number of seats. That is, the CCF would not run candidates in certain ridings, so as not to divide the vote, and the other parties would return the favour. The result

---

[39] Fines, "The Impossible Dream," 238.

was that the CCF won 10 provincial seats in 1938, but its share of the popular vote dropped from 24 per cent to 19 per cent. This did not bode well for the future. Moreover, many loyal CCFers were upset and disillusioned that Williams, who had tried to drive Tommy from the party for flirting with the Socreds, was himself, if not exactly flirting with other parties, standing by to hold the door for them in selected ridings.

Williams held both the party presidency in Saskatchewan and the position of house leader; he controlled party membership and finances, as well as making all decisions on policy. Because of his dual role, he was overworked, and because he rarely called executive or provincial council meetings, the party's internal communications were fragmented, and membership began to fall. It was time to make a major change.

When the House of Commons reassembled after the March 1940 federal election, the CCF caucus held a strategy meeting on the second floor of the Commons building. The meeting had barely begun when Woodsworth suddenly said to Coldwell, "I've had a stroke! I've had a stroke!" The right side of his face was contorted, and he was taken to hospital. He remained paralyzed from then until his death in March 1942.[40] Coldwell was immediately named House leader, but from that moment he was effectively the party's national leader, and in a position to bring about a major change in his home province. Sometime in 1940 (he never said when or exactly how he came to this decision), he decided that the best way to block Williams was to send back to Saskatchewan his attractive young colleague, Tommy Douglas.

Soon after Coldwell took over the federal helm, he, Tommy, and the other Saskatchewan MPs had a meeting in which it was decided that, at the very least, the party presidency should be separated from the political leadership. In Saskatchewan, the president, as had been the case in the past, should look after organizing, and the leader should speak to policy issues. This view was embodied in a document that was presented to the Saskatchewan council one day before a provincial convention in the summer of 1940. Although it was unsigned, Williams was convinced that it was "the work of T.C. Douglas, and an attack on my leadership."[41]

---

[40] Stewart, *M.J.*, 142.

[41] McLeod and McLeod, *Road to Jerusalem*, 102.

That was the end of chumminess between dear Tommy and dear George Williams managed to get the document shelved so that it would not appear before the convention, and soon after the convention he suspended executive and council meetings. Next he announced that he had joined the 11th Hussars and was leaving for Europe as a quartermaster. However, he would not resign the party presidency, and left behind a bitter letter claiming that Coldwell and Douglas were working to get rid of him (which was perfectly true, but it seemed a little odd to announce such a complaint on the way out the door).

In July 1941, Tommy, with Coldwell's urging and backing, returned to Saskatchewan to contest the party presidency, a job then, as now, compatible with being an MP. Tommy would cover himself by not resigning his federal seat. Neither he nor Coldwell then realized that they were grooming the former Baptist preacher not for the presidency, but for the premiership.

The Student Preacher: Tommy at Carberry, Manitoba, in 1927. He got $8.00 a Sunday for sermons.

CREDIT: Saskatchewan Archives Board

Brandon University today looks much as it did when Tommy was a student there.

CREDIT: Walter Stewart

Tommy was active in debates and dramatics. He is in the middle row, third from the right, in this photo of a 1929 college musical called "East is East and West is West."

CREDIT: McKee Archives, Brandon University

Tommy always looked younger than his years, so he assumed a grave countenance for this campaign portrait in 1944. He was thirty-nine.

CREDIT: Saskatchewan Archives Board

Calvary Church in Weyburn, where Tommy preached, lies saved from the wrecking ball by the townsfolk. It now serves as a church-cum-theatre. Very apt.

CREDIT: Walter Stewart

Tommy, Irma, and Shirley Douglas in the living room of their home in Weyburn in 1944.

CREDIT: Saskatchewan Archives Board

The news of his election as premier came to Tommy on the telephone in Weyburn.

CREDIT: Saskatchewan Archives Board

The premier walked to work from this house on 217 Angus Crescent in Regina.

CREDIT: Walter Stewart

The premier wears a suit posing with cabinet members at the Matador Co-operative Ranch. The others are, from left, J.C. Nollet, L.F. McIntosh, T. Johnstone, and J.S. Stury.

CREDIT: Saskatchewan Archives Board

In 1946, Tommy presented Saskatchewan's first health card to a pensioner.

CREDIT: Saskatchewan Archives Board

Tommy shares a grin with adopted daughter Joan in a family portrait with Irma and Shirley in 1948.

CREDIT: Saskatchewan Archives Board

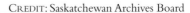

C.M. Fines, left, was Tommy's prop and stay — and sometimes his cross to bear. At right in this 1951 photo is C.C. Williams.

CREDIT: Saskatchewan Archives Board

The premier hams it up at the Saskatchewan Golden Jubilee celebrations, Hudson Bay, Saskatchewan, in 1955.

CREDIT: Saskatchewan Archives Board

This is how many of us remember Tommy best, hands on hips, firing one-liners at a convention. This was in 1954.

CREDIT: Saskatchewan Archives Board

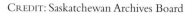

Tommy's mentor and friend was M. J. Coldwell. Here, outside the Commons in Ottawa in 1971, they talked about old times.

CREDIT: Saskatchewan Archives Board

Another old friend, Stanley Knowles, in the front row at right, turned up for the fiftieth reunion of the class of 1930 at Brandon in 1980.

CREDIT: Saskatchewan Archives Board

Chapter TEN

Prairie Fire

It would be honest, looking back on it now, to say I didn't think there was any prospect of forming a government at the next election when I accepted the leadership. But I thought it might be possible to give the movement a shot in the arm and to see it through the next election.

— Tommy Douglas, *The Making of a Socialist*

The July 1940 convention of the Saskatchewan CCF party gave the lie to the notion that absence makes the heart grow fonder. John Brockelbank, the provincial house leader (but not, of course, the leader of the party outside the house), nominated George Williams, who by now was stationed in England, for the presidency, but the meeting voted, by a margin of three to one, for the present Tommy over the absent George. Since Williams had always asserted that the leadership and the presidency were one and indivisible, Tommy assumed that he was now the leader. So did Clarence Fines, who had become his vice-president, and so did the party newspaper, *The Commonwealth*. But the provincial MLAs, Williams's supporters to a man, rejected this idea, and pronounced the leadership vacant until after the next convention.

This was no small matter. When Fines introduced Tommy at a meeting as "the next Premier of Saskatchewan," the caucus howled its outrage and demanded a retraction. But if Tommy was not the leader, and the CCF were to win an election, who would be premier? Answer came there none.

Tommy and Clarence Fines accepted the uncertainty, but paid very little attention to it, and indeed went ahead as if the matter were unimportant.

They began to reorganize the party, launched a fundraising campaign (under the redoubtable Sandy Nicholson, one of the five Saskatchewan CCF MPs, a mild-mannered but hard-working United Church minister), and established a network of committees to prepare the CCF for power.

Tommy ranged across the province, beating the bushes and raising the hopes, as well as lightening the wallets, of party stalwarts. During one of these rallies, at Fir Mountain, his chair collapsed under him and dumped him onto the platform. He got up, rubbed his butt, and pronounced, "Mr. Chairman, that is just where Mr. Gardiner's Liberals give me a pain."[1]

By the time of the 1942 convention, he was the unquestioned leader of the provincial party in everything but formal title, and that was soon settled. While Williams was again nominated in absentia, he was again defeated in absentia. The same meeting split the presidency from the leadership, and Clarence Fines was quickly made the new president.

Williams sent a letter to the 1943 convention, indicating his willingness to serve as leader/president again, but Clarence Fines kept the letter in his back pocket, and Tommy's only competition on the convention floor came from John Brockelbank. It was no contest: Tommy was elected party leader in a walk. He then moved swiftly to mend fences, offering Williams, in the case of a CCF victory, any cabinet post of his choice, and nominating Brockelbank as party vice-president.

The new leader was quickly showing the qualities that would serve him so well in the years to come, and which were, as we have seen, the product of his background and training. He was aggressive, surely, but he could also be patient; he was a tireless worker, but also knew how to delegate authority; he had a clear set of principles, but he could be persuaded to compromise, and on occasion, he could even be slippery. He was a tough opponent, but a ready friend; once a battle was over, he was eager to heal the breach and get on with the job. Finally, like every successful leader, he had a pretty good knack for picking the right people for a job, as he did with Fines and Brockelbank.

---

[1] McLeod and McLeod, *Road to Jerusalem*, 105.

He was also lucky. When he first came back to scout the leadership job in Saskatchewan in 1940, it was scarcely worth having. This was Canada's poorest province, still bearing the weight of debt and despair left over from the Depression. The party was broke, as usual, and its membership was sagging. The Liberals had been comfortably in power since 1935, using a patronage machine built by Jimmy Gardiner with brutal efficiency. While Gardiner was no longer premier, he was still, as the federal minister of agriculture in Mackenzie King's administration and minister responsible for national organization, very much in charge. The premier, William T. Patterson, was Gardiner's handpicked choice, and if Patterson was "heavy and lethargic" — in the all-too-accurate phrase of Mackenzie King[2] — it was not of much matter. The voters were surely not going to go back to the depression-dealing Conservatives, any more than they would opt for the oddness of socialism.

However, between 1940 and 1944, the nation underwent a sea change. As the war dragged on, an increasingly important sector of the electorate began to feel that, when it ended, if ever, Canada could not simply go back to the old ways of doing things. If the Conservatives had earned contempt for their helplessness in the face of the Depression, the Liberals had done very little more. It was the war that brought the economy back, not Mackenzie King.

In Ottawa, the CCF, despite the small size of its parliamentary group, assumed a more and more important role as the critic and conscience of the House, especially on social issues. This was boosted in turn by the party's growing strength in the provinces, and the two strains reinforced each other. The Liberals were pushed to take over CCF initiatives for fear of losing votes. By September 1943, the CCF had become the official opposition in Ontario and, for the first time, led the Liberals in a national Gallup Poll — with 29 per cent support nationally versus 28 per cent for the Liberals and 27 per cent for the Conservatives.[3] The CCF was now anything but a small, regional group of gripers.

---

[2] Quoted in Ward and Smith, *Jimmy Gardiner*, 284.
[3] Hugh G. Thorburn, "Conservatism, Liberalism and Socialism in Canada," in *Party Politics in Canada*, ed. Hugh G. Thorburn (Toronto: Prentice-Hall, 1967), 70.

Sweden Shows the Way

Reform was in the air. In England, Sir William Beveridge's white paper entitled *Social Insurance and Allied Services* was handed to the government in 1942. It proposed a post-war social security system that would cover every British citizen "from the cradle to the grave." It would be funded, in the main, from taxes, and it would provide a "social minimum" of income, health, housing, and education for all.

The Swedes had already adopted a similar scheme — under a Social Democratic government — that threw in motherhood benefits, marital loans, and subsidies for school lunches. There was even a tax on state construction expenditures to finance the acquisition of art for Swedish public buildings.[4]

A copy of the Beveridge Report was brought to Canada in 1943, and Leonard Marsh, a social sciences professor at McGill University, was commissioned to prepare a document on "Social Security for Canada," which he did, recommending many of the same reforms. King used this to block what he called "the threat of defections from our own ranks in the House to the CCF." Within weeks, the Advisory Council of the National Liberal Federation had met and drafted a fourteen-point program of reform, including improved pensions, unemployment insurance, and a vastly increased government role in the economy. King told his diary, "I think I have cut the ground in large part from under the CCF."[5]

But he had scotched the snake, not killed it, and when it became clear that, as usual, what he meant was to announce new initiatives, not enable them, a certain restiveness became apparent. In Saskatchewan, the Liberals, who stayed as far away from the public as possible, and used the war as an excuse not to hold an election for six years, were as heavy and lethargic as their leader. C.M. Dunn, a member of the Patterson cabinet, put his finger on the real problem: "The great mass of the people (believe) the Liberal Party is on the side of big business . . . and has no longer the coinage to be the champion of the common man."[6]

---

[4] Samuel Martin, *An Essential Grace* (Toronto: McClelland & Stewart, 1985) 54.
[5] J.W. Pickersgill, *The Mackenzie King Record, 1939–1944* (Toronto: University of Toronto Press, 1960), 1:601.
[6] Quoted in Ward and Smith, *Jimmy Gardiner*, 284–85.

Small businesspeople, farmers, and what Dunn called "the non-English" were shifting their old allegiance away from the Liberals.

Tommy was back and forth between Ottawa and Regina, readying the troops, and Clarence Fines, John Brockelbank, and M.J. Coldwell were all working furiously on the provincial campaign. By the time Tommy officially resigned his House of Commons seat on June 1, 1944, the election was only two weeks away, but the CCF was already primed to win.

His job throughout the campaign was essentially a simple one, although not an easy one. He had to convince the electorate that most of what they were being told by the province's newspapers and radio stations was simply untrue. Some sample headlines from the time catch the flavour of the problem: "Socialism Leads to Dictatorship," "All Opposition Banned if CCF Wins Power," "CCF Government Would Take Away Farms," "CCF Government Would Destroy the Credit of the Government."[7] This last one was really rich; the Saskatchewan government had been virtually bankrupt for years, and hadn't been able to borrow on its own credit since 1932.

The day before the election, the Liberals took out full-page advertisements in all the daily newspapers with screaming headlines that asked: "Would You Like to Pay 20% Sales Tax on Everything?"[8] Of course, there was no such tax in contemplation. Tommy had to persuade the public that he was not, in fact, the dupe of Soviet Russia, a ravening monster who would take away their farms (but not, alas, their children).

Canada's corporate leaders, affrighted by the CCF surge and affronted by the election of Joe Noseworthy, an unknown school teacher and the CCF candidate in the Toronto riding of York South, over Arthur Meighen, the newly-minted Conservative Party chieftain,[9] formed a committee to beat back the Socialist hordes.

Its members included the presidents of Noranda Mines, Imperial Oil, International Nickel, and Massey-Harris. Simpson's Limited offered its catalogue service as a distribution system for propaganda. Meighen and Charles Dunning, a former Saskatchewan premier, were the spokesmen,

---

[7] Quoted in Fines, "The Impossible Dream," 358.

[8] *Leader-Post* (Regina), 14 July 1944.

[9] Although Mackenzie King hated Meighen, the Liberals did not run a candidate in this by-election, as a courtesy to the new party leader. When King was told that Meighen might be defeated in a Tory stronghold, he dismissed the report as "sheer nonsense." Pickersgill, *Mackenzie King Record*, 341.

but the voices were those of the companies, who warned that, if the CCF won, anyone who advocated free enterprise would be regarded as "guilty of treason."[10] Nationally, this scare campaign did the CCF a great deal of harm; but in Saskatchewan, it was hard to sell.

Tommy, Coldwell, and Agnes Macphail, who came out from Ontario to join the battle, were all seasoned campaigners, and about as respectable a trio as you could put together. Moreover, the scare campaign backfired when the mortgage and trust companies sent land agents around to tell farmers in Tommy's own riding (part of his federal Weyburn riding, the provincial constituency was also known as Weyburn) that if the province dared to go CCF, before it could pass any legislation, they would foreclose on mortgages. Tommy promptly promised to "put a blanket moratorium across the province in order to protect the farmers."[11]

He set up a shadow cabinet, divided the province into groups of constituencies, and set everybody to work organizing from poll to poll. He ranged up and down the province, conducting open air meetings and indoor rallies, and, at the end of a long day, writing and delivering radio broadcasts, which were the most effective medium in this campaign, and a way to get around the undiluted hostility of the newspapers:

> I wrote a lot of broadcasts at night until two or three o'clock in the morning in the hotels after a meeting was over. Then I would rush in and do a broadcast, and get on the road again. Many times I'd ride half the night, get a few hours sleep, write a broadcast, record it, and then get on the road.[12]

The set speeches always started with a spate of jokes, but the broadcasts were serious, straightforward expositions of the reforms the party would make, from protection for farmers, and encouragement for the co-operative movement, to better labour laws and hospital insurance. Since it was not possible to know in advance when one of his radio speeches would be

[10] McLeod and McLeod, *Road to Jerusalem,* 108.
[11] Douglas, *The Making of a Socialist,* 152.
[12] Ibid., 153.

played, the party set up a telephone system to pass along the word when to listen. Shades of Paul Revere, except that instead of "The British are coming!" the message was "Tommy is coming — on the radio."

Farm ownership became the key issue of the campaign, and in the end, the rural folks believed they had a better chance to hold on to something with Tommy than with the mortgage companies and their representatives in government.

Tommy had no secretary, although the provincial office was able to have his speeches typed at any hour of the day or night, and he had no one to protect him from what he called "the politician's greatest cross," that is, the hordes of well-meaning people who wanted to press a meal on him when all he wanted was to sleep.[13]

Election day, June 15, 1944, was a clear, sunny day, which the CCF took as a good omen, because it meant there would be a heavy turnout. And there was. Tommy spent the day in Weyburn with Irma and Shirley, between visits to local polls to make sure the scrutineers were on the job. The party had set up an elaborate telephone network to feed results into the Weyburn committee room, and very soon after the polls closed, it was reporting a trend that pointed to an overwhelming victory. Tom McLeod, who had worked as an organizer in the riding, remembers that Shirley Douglas, then ten, kept running in and out, asking, "Is my father premier yet?"[14] By 10 p.m., he was, in all but formal terms.

When the counting was done, the CCF had won 53 per cent of the vote, and 47 of the 53 seats in the legislature. Clarence Fines had predicted 48 seats, and party insiders thought he was dreaming; Tommy's highest guess was 35 seats. After the obligatory victory parade down Main Street and a celebration at the Legion Hall, Shirley went to the microphone and said, "It's been a great victory for all of us."[15]

It was also a great shock to the Liberals, who proceeded to make the changeover as nasty as possible.

Building a Cabinet, and Cutting Its Pay

Tommy took his family to Carlyle Lake, in the southeast corner of the

---

[13] Ibid.
[14] Thomas McLeod, interview by author, Victoria, 6 May 2001.
[15] Shackleton, *Tommy Douglas*, 127.

province, where they spent their vacations. He was not on vacation, though; with the help of Clarence Fines he was planning his cabinet and his first term. One of his early appointments was that of Tom McLeod, who had studied economics. McLeod became "Economic Adviser to the Executive Council," as well as a researcher, personnel adviser, and planner. Another was that of Eleanor McKinnon, the daughter of a well-known Liberal, one of the elders at Calvary Baptist Church. Tommy had met her when she was secretary to the superintendent of the Weyburn Mental Hospital. He explained that he wanted her to move to Regina to help him, but only with her father's permission, of course. She was at his side for forty-two years, a completely unflappable, absolutely dependable secretary, manager, and guardian of the gate, deflecting the inevitable cranks who besieged the new premier's office.

Archibald McNab, a colourful character, and the Lieutenant-Governor, swore in Canada's first socialist government on July 10, 1944, in a crammed legislative chamber. Tommy's mother, Anne, was there, in a formal gown.

In selecting his cabinet, he overlooked the fact that most of the caucus had backed Williams against him, and gave many of them places. George Williams became agriculture minister (although poor health kept him from assuming office, and he died not long after) and John Brockelbank got municipal affairs. Fines became the provincial treasurer. The cabinet size was increased from nine to twelve. The three new departments were the department of social welfare, the department of co-operatives, and the department of labour. Tommy announced these changes to his caucus, along with a suggestion that the pay for a cabinet minister be cut from $7,000 a year to $5,000, to avoid charges of extravagance. The caucus voted in favour, without knowing who was going to be in the cabinet. His own pay, before he deducted his tribute to the party, was $6,500, roughly $65,000 in today's purchasing power.

Clarence Fines arranged the details for the change of power. Premier Patterson was friendly enough, but when the CCFers took over the former government's offices in the legislature, they found that thousands of files had been taken away, presumably to cover up activities that the general public did not wish to hear about. In the premier's office, the filing cabinets that had contained departmental correspondence were completely barren. Tommy had to contact the Prime Minister's office for a copy of the agenda of an upcoming federal–provincial conference; all correspondence relating to it had been taken away.

Later, a couple of files that had avoided destruction turned up; one of them contained detailed instructions to agricultural land agents on what threats to use on farmers if they seemed likely to want to vote for the CCF.[16] Another referred to a racket by which the Liberals were making a rake-off on purple dye, used to colour the gasoline sold for farm operations, which was tax free. A firm called Acme Dye Company (and no, it was not a supplier to Wile E. Coyote) bought large quantities of dye from the manufacturer and resold it for about two and a half times the purchase price to the government of Saskatchewan. But the Acme Dye Company was a phantasm, it only existed on paper, and the profits apparently disappeared into the coffers of the Liberal party.[17]

When Tommy, who had taken on the health portfolio as well as the premiership, went to ask his predecessor, Dr. John M. Urich, for suggestions and a report on what was going on in the department, Urich told him, "You made all the promises and know all the answers; go ahead and see what you can do."

Tommy replied, "I'll just give you a tip that we plan to do more in the next four years than you've done in the last twenty-five."[18]

But where was the money to come from? The province had the highest per capita debt in the nation, and a budget of about $40 million, perennially in deficit. It had kept going by continually rolling over its old bonds into new ones, at higher interest, an approach that Clarence Fines called "tin-cup deals."[19] But with the CCF in power, the lending institutions might well decline to drop the required coins in the cup, and there were persistent rumours that the CCF would be forced to default on the debt. In the jittery days after the swearing-in, that might well have happened, if not for the long-headedness of Clarence Fines, the

---

[16] Douglas, *The Making of a Socialist,* 163.

[17] Ibid., 164.

[18] Ibid., 157.

[19] Fines, "The Impossible Dream," 381.

provincial treasurer. When the head of the Regina office of a major brokerage firm came to see Fines about a week after he took over the treasury portfolio to ask if he, personally, would ever buy Saskatchewan bonds, Fines replied, "Certainly." Then he went to a bank and borrowed $15,000, which he used to buy $5,000 worth of bonds from each of three of the major brokerages. Very soon, despite the confidentiality that is supposed to attend these matters, word was out on the street that the provincial treasurer was buying provincial bonds, and bond prices rose.[20] When he bought them, each $100 bond was selling for $92; that is, the bonds were selling at a 6 per cent discount, because they were seen as a shaky deal. He sold them two years later for a profit of $3,000. He was then accused by the Liberal opposition of taking advantage of his position as treasurer to make a personal gain.[21] Fines simply told them to follow his example and buy provincial bonds.

A special session of the legislature, which met from October 19 to November 10, authorized the issue of new bonds to develop provincial resources; it was oversubscribed by 30 per cent, mostly by ordinary citizens. That special session passed seventy-six bills, a staggering total, including three that led to endless problems: the Mineral Taxation Act, the Farm Security Act, and the Local Government Board (Special Powers) Act.[22] The first aimed to increase the taxes on mineral lands that were not being developed, but merely held for future gain. The other two blocked arbitrary foreclosures and set up local government boards to adjudicate the claims of bondholders against municipalities that had run into financial difficulties. The Farm Security Act, fulfilling the key promise of the campaign, protected the quarter section around a farm home from foreclosure and suspended mortgage payments during years of crop failure — defined as any year in which, because of circumstances beyond his control, the farmer received less than six dollars per acre planted to grain. It also suspended interest payments during those years.

---

[20] Ibid., 381–82.

[21] McLeod and McLeod, *Road to Jerusalem,* 187.

[22] Other bills covered, partially or completely, new programs to establish an economic advisory board, collective bargaining, holiday pay for labour, socialized health services, free hospital and medical care for the mentally incompetent; free medical care for old-age pensioners; co-operative farms for war veterans; larger school units; crop failure insurance; increased pay for teachers; rural electrification; and a government purchasing agency; and there was a bill to allow the government to enter the insurance business, a precursor to provincial auto insurance.

In 1946, many farmers received less than three dollars per acre; this was not an academic matter.

The Dominion Mortgage and Loan Association and the Canadian Pacific Railway (which held huge lands in Saskatchewan as part of the original construction deal) petitioned the federal cabinet to disallow all three laws, and the provincial Liberals backed them, declaring that the legislation was "confiscatory." Saskatchewan was told it had three weeks to show why the laws should not be disallowed, and Douglas went on the radio — private radio, since the CBC would not carry his message — to deliver what might be called a vintage Douglas harangue. In part, he said:

> We have just finished a war which was fought, we were told, for the preservation of democratic institutions. It would appear that the war is not finished. We have simply moved the battlefields from the banks of the Rhine to the prairies of Saskatchewan.
>
> If corporations can have these laws disallowed then there are no laws passed by a free legislature which they cannot have set aside. Where then is our boasted freedom? Why elect governments if Bay Street and St. James Street are to have the power to decide what laws shall stand and what laws shall fail?[23]

After a warning to "those who are moving heaven and earth to have this legislation disallowed" that it was not passed by a "government of tired old men who are merely holding onto the spoils of office with a hope of finding a final resting place in the Senate," but by "a government fresh from the people," he went on to invite his listeners to make their views known to the federal government.

They did, by the thousands, and soon the federal government decided not to disallow the legislation after all. The companies then took the route they should have taken in the first place, and submitted the laws to

---

[23] The complete text is carried in "The Case Against Disallowance: The People vs. the Financial Interests," in L.D. Lovick, ed., *Tommy Douglas Speaks* (Victoria, BC: Oolichan Books, 1979), 90ff.

the courts, which, years later, gave the companies most of the relief they were seeking.

But the political fallout from this scrap did not take years: it immediately became clear to most of the people of Saskatchewan that Tommy was indeed on the side of the underdog and the Liberals on the side of the top dog.

Going Against the Grain Deal
Another early battle with Ottawa showed how blunt the Ottawa Liberals could be when they were dealing with junior governments of the wrong political persuasion. The Patterson government had made an arrangement with the federal government under which farmers were advanced money for seed grain on the joint guarantee of the provincial government and the federal government. The money was advanced by the banks, and with interest the farmers were pledged to pay about two dollars a bushel for grain which, it turned out, they could sell for only about fifty cents a bushel.

When the CCF took office, the federal government suddenly demanded payment of $16.5 million, about half the total Saskatchewan budget at that time, although no such demand had ever been made to the previous provincial government, which had been involved in similar arrangements with Ottawa for years.

Since the farmers couldn't come up with the entire amount, the province was called upon to make good the shortfall. Tommy said his government was due to pay only 50 per cent, because it had only guaranteed that share, and he would pay that, over time. The federal finance minister, J.L. Ilsley, then seized any monies due to Saskatchewan under the federal–provincial tax-sharing arrangements, and the province was suddenly deprived of badly needed funds.

After months of agonizing bargaining, a deal was reached under which the province issued non–interest-bearing treasury bills to the federal government, and used the proceeds to pay the banks. The notes were not paid off by the province until 1957, but the federal payments were restored. Tommy was convinced that Ilsley was sympathetic to the provincial plight, but that Jimmy Gardiner was able to persuade the cabinet to take a hard line. In any event, the deal that was finally struck went through on a day when Gardiner was providentially absent from Ottawa.[24]

Once again, the end result was that most Saskatchewan farmers were convinced that the silliest thing they could ever do was to vote Liberal, and it was many years before they did so in any appreciable numbers.

Tommy and Irma bought a comfortable, modest house on Angus Crescent in Regina, within walking distance of the legislature. Every day, Tommy walked to work and home again, about six blocks. He worked long hours, often until one or two in the morning, and saw little of his family except during their vacations at Carlyle Lake. Irma made the home a refuge for him and would not allow anyone to disturb him there.

In 1945, to provide a companion for Shirley, the Douglases adopted Joan, who was three years younger than Shirley. From the first, she was treated as if she had always been a member of the family, and most of Tommy's friends had no idea she was adopted. Even his closest friends were never given any of the details. (Tom McLeod, who was as close to Tommy as anybody, covered Joan's arrival in his biography with a single phrase: "a second daughter joined the family in 1945." He explains, "That's all I knew.")[25]

The Man Who Said No
The heart of the government, early and late, consisted of Tommy and Clarence Fines. Tommy was the activist, the doer, the familiar face and voice. Fines, who was philosophically much more conservative, was the man who said no. Grand schemes were all very well, he would say, but where was the money to pay for them? The result was that, under his stern and steering hand, the CCF, far from committing the gross economic follies expected by its fondest enemies, delivered seventeen balanced budgets in a row, constantly decreased the provincial debt, and turned the fortunes of the province around completely.

---

[24] Douglas, *The Making of a Socialist,* 171.
[25] Thomas McLeod, interview by author, Victoria, 6 May 2001.

Another key figure, because of his keen political antennae, was John Wesley Corman, a former mayor of Moose Jaw and the only lawyer in the cabinet (we call those the good old days); he thus became the attorney-general by default. Tom McLeod remembers:

> He spent a good deal of his time reading newspapers. He read every weekly newspaper in the province every week, and the result was that if you wanted to put a street light on a street in Stoughton, he could tell you exactly how many votes it would bring you.[26]

Jack Douglas, the chief provincial organizer, who had also acted as M.J. Coldwell's campaign manager in the federal seat of Rosetown-Biggar, handled the patronage portfolio — highways. Up until that time, all the road-building in the province was subcontracted through the hands of local reeves, municipal councillors, or well-to-do farmers who had shown themselves to be loyal to the party (i.e., Liberal) cause, and tenders were not called. Douglas was given the job of getting rid of all these contracts and putting them out for completion to the lowest bidder. According to Tom McLeod:

> The money the government saved in scrapping the old sweetheart deals — on highways, printing, construction, supplies — went a good ways towards paying for the CCF's new programs.[27]

The most important of the new government's initiatives was embodied in the Saskatchewan Health Services Act, passed in the autumn of 1944. This first bold step towards a complete medicare system was actually built on a foundation laid down in many areas of the province when the Liberals were still in charge. In January 1945, all old-age pensioners, blind persons, mother's allowance cases, and wards of government received a card entitling them to free medical care, hospital care, dental

---

[26] Ibid.

[27] McLeod and McLeod, *Road to Jerusalem,* 123.

care, eye care and glasses, and medication. The CCF also implemented legislation that the Liberals had passed, but never implemented, to provide free care for all cancer patients.

Tommy always had in mind a complete medicare program — much more complete, in fact, than we have today — but he agreed with Fines that it could be put into place only as the province could afford it, and the Health Services Act was what the province could afford.

It was a bold beginning, but it was only a beginning.

Patronage Peters Out

Another of Tommy's main campaign promises was to take politics out of the civil service, and Canada's first Civil Service Commission did just that. He promised that "no one would be fired who had done the job properly," but several hundred bureaucrats decamped anyway. Tommy's explanation was that these bureaucrats were patronage appointments and had not been doing the job properly. At least some of them may have been people who assumed that Tommy's promises were no more durable than any other politician's: every provincial election so far had been followed by a blood-letting and the appointment of the new government's pals; the CCF would probably be the same. But it wasn't. In the long term, one of the finest collections of civil servants the nation had ever assembled was drawn to Saskatchewan. They made Tommy's job not so much easier, as possible.

Another campaign promise that was speedily fulfilled permitted civil servants to form unions to deal with their employer, the government, and if they chose, to engage actively in politics (as long as they didn't do so on government time). This was also a first in Canada; it was modelled on legislation in New Zealand. It proved a mixed blessing. The unions instantly did what unions do best, and pressed for ever-larger pay-cheques, which didn't help the budget.

Tommy was running a government that not only kept most of its promises, but implemented them early and never drew back. It was an astonishing, rivetting performance, and journalists from all over Canada, as well as the United States and Britain, came to Regina to see what they almost always called "the Socialist Experiment" in action. Not many of them noticed that it was not really a socialist experiment, if socialism means that the major means of production are in the hands of the state. In Saskatchewan at this time, the major means of production were in the hands of farmers, and Tommy fought to keep them there.

The new social welfare department would not send out cheques to the unemployed if it was possible for them to work. "We were not interested in paying able-bodied people merely because they weren't able to find work," said Tommy.[28]

"Relief" was gone, and in its place were two classes of people eligible for "social aid." Those who were too old or too handicapped to work received support automatically, but anyone who couldn't find a job elsewhere would be put to work clearing roads, fencing pastures, installing phone lines, or working in community pastures — what is today called "workfare" and is roundly condemned by every respectable left-winger.

The mixed economy that was being built in Saskatchewan did not have much resemblance to the Red Dawn promised in the texts; it was, by and large, a pragmatic government. If an insistence on balanced budgets, work for welfare, and value for money is seen as characteristic of rabid socialism, it was, even as its critics claimed, rabidly socialist. Today, we would call it "moderately reformist." The Governor General, Lord Tweedsmuir, twitted Tommy and M. J. Coldwell, when they went to see him some time earlier, for being too timid. "You're just left-wing Tories," he said, "dishwater socialists."[29]

A Wartime Trip

In 1945, Tommy took a trip overseas to visit Saskatchewan personnel stationed in Europe, and especially those in hospital. During a visit to the South Saskatchewan Regiment in Germany, the jeep he was travelling in was hit by a truck. He and the driver were both thrown out of the vehicle, and Tommy injured his knee. The osteomyelitis that had bothered him so much as a boy flared up again, and would bother him for the rest of his life.

---

[28] Ibid., 174.
[29] Douglas, *The Making of a Socialist,* 110.

On VE Day, Tommy was in Manchester, England. Shortly thereafter, he went up to Glasgow to revisit old haunts, and found himself seated, at one of the innumerable banquets, next to Donald Gow, the president of the Scottish Co-operative Wholesale Society, who asked him if he had ever been in Glasgow before. When Tommy said that he had gone to the Scotland Street School, Gow exclaimed, "You're not wee Tommy Douglas who used to play inside left for our football team?"[30] Guilty as charged.

Japanese Canadians

Another incident in 1945 shows Tommy in quite a different light than we have seen so far, and it is worth exploring to demonstrate the complexity of his character. The background is this. In March 1942, the King administration had passed legislation that allowed the government to establish the British Columbia Security Commission, with the power to remove Canadians of Japanese origin from the "protected area" of British Columbia. No Canadian of Japanese origin had been, or ever was, found guilty of or even charged with any act of sabotage, but that didn't seem to matter. The neat part was that the property of the 23,000 Canadians who were deported to camps in the interior of British Columbia, or to farms in Alberta, Saskatchewan, and Manitoba, was seized and sold for rock-bottom prices to their former neighbours at public auctions. Many of the displaced Canadian citizens were put to work on road-building projects, and were paid a net salary of $7.50 a month.[31]

These measures were discussed in the House of Commons on March 4 and May 18, 1942, when the government was pleased to report that, so far, "202 persons of the Japanese race" had been detained, in addition to those being removed. None of these was ever charged with anything. There is no record anywhere in the House of Commons *Debates* of 1942, 1943, or 1944 that Tommy ever said anything against either the legislation or the treatment of Japanese Canadians. There is every chance that he was not in the House on any occasion when the subject was discussed.

---

[30] Ibid., 215.
[31] Stewart, *But Not in Canada*, 70ff.

Just the same, it is a fact that he never objected to the treatment of these people, although he would later frequently claim that he had done so.

In July 1944, the government introduced an amendment to earlier legislation that had denied all Japanese Canadians the vote. The amendment said, in effect, that Japanese Canadians who had been able to vote before the passage of the original legislation would be able to vote again, as would Japanese Canadians who had served in the armed forces. Thus, Japanese Canadians would be divided into two classes for electoral purposes, and only a tiny group of them would be allowed to cast a ballot.

During the three-hour debate on this measure that took place on July 14, 1944, Liberal Arthur Roebuck said, "I am apprehensive when we touch something that even smells of racial discrimination and I oppose it with everything that is in me." Clarence Gillis, the CCF MP from Cape Breton, said, "Make no mistake about it, when you start interfering with the liberties of any one class of people, the time is coming when you are going to interfere with all." And Stanley Knowles, Tommy's pal, and at this time the CCF MP for Winnipeg North Centre, said that any legislation of this sort was a "violation of the basic traditions of Liberalism." An extensive exposé of the treatment of Japanese Canadians was laid out in a pamphlet by Grace and Angus MacInnis, called "Oriental Canadians — Outcasts or Citizens?"

Tommy said nothing. It was a federal matter, and not something for him to comment on, perhaps.

On March 22, 1945, when this issue was still very much at the fore (the federal government was now in the process of using Orders-in-Council to deport Japanese immigrants and even Canadians of Japanese descent to Japan; in all, 3,964 people were hustled out of Canada and dropped into that war-torn nation),[32] W.D. Wilkins of Shaunavon, Saskatchewan, dashed off a letter to his premier in which he said he had recently spent four months in British Columbia:

> I have had the opportunity of seeing what the Japs have actually done here. Without a doubt, they are anything

---

[32] Ibid.

but loyal citizens. They were fully prepared to receive their countrymen when they arrived, and they expected them to overtake our country.

I am convinced they are the big interest friend [*sic*], as they would work anywhere for starvation wages, during hard times. The white man had to stand in line for hours to see the boss, but the Japs would walk right by and go to work. It is not that they do better work, but, because they live like dogs or worse, they can make headway on the lowest wage.

. . . British Columbia does not want them, they asked for them, and had a good reason for doing so, now they want to push them on the rest of Canada.

We must not forget that if we take on a thousand Japanese today, we will have several thousand in the near future. No doubt we will have a very great number of our boys come back, badly shot up by the Japs, and I feel it is the duty of every individual Canadian here at home to see that no disloyal alien or enemy stands in the way of the progress of these boys on their return.[33]

This letter seemed to invite a short, rough response, or something like what Tommy would write a thousand times during the medicare battle to those who disagreed with him: "Thank you for bringing your views to my attention."

Instead, for reasons that remain unclear, Tommy wrote back:

I appreciate the point of view expressed, and *I think that what you have said with regard to the Japanese themselves is quite true* [italics mine]. Unfortunately there are a number of Canadian born Japanese who do not speak Japanese, and who have never been in Japan. We may blame previous governments for bringing the Japanese

[33] Wilkins to Douglas, 22 March 1945, Douglas Collection, Saskatchewan Archives, Regina.

here, but, now they are here, I do not see how we can do otherwise than try to make good citizens of them. Sending back to Japan those who speak the Japanese language is one thing, and sending back Canadian Japanese who do not speak the language will be another thing entirely. It certainly is a very complicated problem, and I only hope our people will try to deal with it from a humane point of view.[34]

I have read this letter half a dozen times, and I cannot help but make the following conclusions: (1) that Tommy, at this time, agreed that the Japanese as a people live like dogs or worse; (2) that it was regrettable that they were allowed to come to Canada in the first place; but (3) that was the fault of previous governments; (4) that we should not send back to Japan those Japanese Canadians who speak no Japanese; and (5) that he presumably would not have objected to deporting Canadian citizens of Japanese ancestry if they spoke their native tongue. Later, he would deplore the way these people had been treated and hold himself out as their champion. But he was not their champion when it counted.

Given Tommy's lifelong defence of civil liberties, it must be that this letter is an aberration — inexplicable, but damning.

---

[34] Douglas to Wilkins, 3 April 1945, Douglas Collection, Saskatchewan Archives.

Chapter ELEVEN

One Good Term Deserves Another

We recognize that no one can build an island of socialism in a sea of capitalism. Within the limited jurisdiction of a provincial government, we can lay the foundations of a co-operative commonwealth, and begin to set up public, co-operative, and private ownership in our provincial society.

— Tommy Douglas, 1944

When Tommy went to call on the Lieutenant-Governor, the Hon. Archibald Peter McNab, he found, instead of a creature of regal mien, a short, rotund man who looked like a cab-driver or a plumber. The Premier, with due ceremony, passed over the list of appointees to his cabinet and intoned, "Your Honour, I now have the names I would like to submit."

His Honour tapped the Premier on the arm and responded, "Just call me Archie." After that, Tommy recalled, "We got along famously."[1]

Archie had been a Liberal MLA and the minister of public works, but he was a man of modest means because he gave away almost everything he earned to charitable causes. One of the many oft-told stories about him concerns the time in 1939 when King George VI and Queen Elizabeth were his guests at Government House. After a long state dinner, Archie invited His Majesty to take off his coat, and, although it was strictly against proper protocol, he did so. A footman promptly spirited the garment away. Not long afterwards, the king announced that it was time for Their Majesties to retire, so Archie pottered off to find his coat. The king followed behind him, so silently that Archie had no idea that he was there when he bellowed at the footman, "Where in hell's the king's coat? The bugger wants to go to bed."[2]

---

[1] Douglas, *The Making of a Socialist*, 197.
[2] Ibid., 198.

When Archie died in 1945, Tommy wired Prime Minister Mackenzie King to suggest that there was no need to replace him; the duties of a Lieutenant-Governor could be carried out more cheaply by the Chief Justice. This would mean a substantial saving to the province, especially since it would mean that Government House, with its staff of cooks and butlers, footmen and maids, could be closed. The Prime Minister replied, "very properly," Tommy said, that the appointment of a Lieutenant-Governor was a matter for the federal, not the provincial government, and no change was contemplated. Two other Liberals followed Archie, one of them William Patterson, the premier Douglas had defeated, and who had denuded his own office on departure. They got along fine.

Tommy managed to save most of the money he meant to get out of Government House, anyway. It was leased to the Department of Veterans' Affairs for the sum of one dollar per annum, and the viceregal envoy was housed in splendid, but rented, digs. This kind of practical and non-ideological thinking permeated the Douglas regime as it went about the business of restructuring the province. It was not at all orthodox socialism; the CCF used whatever means were to hand, from government ownership and crown corporations to private enterprise. The rhetoric was always more socialist than the performance, but that made little difference to its critics.

The government of Ontario had provided its citizens with a publicly owned electrical system in 1906, in exactly the same way that the government of Saskatchewan did four decades later: by taking over existing companies and putting them together under a crown corporation. Yet nobody seriously accused the Conservative government of James P. Whitney of leftward leanings. What people wanted in Ontario, as they let the premier know in a Grand March on the Ontario legislature on April 11, 1906, was "Cheap Power!" Exactly what Saskatchewan farmers wanted. Adam Beck, the man who planned and launched Ontario Hydro, spoke in words that would have affrighted Tommy or, if not so much Tommy, certainly his sidekick, Clarence Fines. "Nothing is too big for us!" Beck roared, "Nothing is too expensive to imagine. Nothing is visionary."[3]

---

[3] Quoted in Walter Stewart, *Uneasy Lies the Head: Canada's Crown Corporations* (Toronto: Collins, 1987), 88.

The authorities gave Beck a knighthood. Tommy got the raspberry. It was agreed by all the best people that he was a dangerous radical. If not actually a stooge of Joseph Stalin, he must be a naive blunderer who would lead his province down a sinkhole of debt.

What Tommy and his government actually did was throw up thousands of miles of blacktop (when Tommy took office, there were fewer than 150 paved roads in all the province); they brought electricity to homes that had seen nothing but coal oil and candles; they put water and sewer systems in municipalities where backhouses held sway; they built hospitals and schools and introduced the most advanced labour legislation on the continent.

In his first term, Tommy also established an auto insurance plan, financed by a six-dollar yearly premium paid by every driver, to cover cases where non-insured drivers had caused an accident. It was established as a social welfare measure to rescue from poverty people who had suffered injuries for which they could receive no compensation, but it soon expanded into a full-blown, state-run insurance plan. Tommy promised that it would never make money; every dime would be ploughed back into more coverage or lower premiums. It turned out that private auto insurance was so swollen with bureaucracy and inefficiency, to say nothing of profit, that a state-run plan could do the job far more cheaply than the private sector. Tommy's auto insurance plan was another in the string of firsts established by his government in its first term, and it brought down the wrath of the insurance firms all across the land. Not because it worked so badly, but because it worked so well. (And still does.)

Of course, all this activism proved that Tommy was a communist; either that or a maniac. But that is not how his own constituents saw him. They saw him as a reformer, who gave them good roads, cheap electricity, and flush johns. Saskatchewan old-timers remember, as one of the finest sights ever seen, the funeral pyres of the outhouses on the rural landscape as socialism tightened its iron grip on the countryside during the late 1940s.

To pay for the most muscular government the continent had ever seen, Tommy developed provincial resources, although nearly always through programs developed by private enterprise. The Saskatchewan government made sure it got a fair share of the take.

King's Cunning
The activism of the CCF government in its first term demonstrated the lassitude and ineptitude of the federal government, the one level of government that had the resources to fund ambitious new programs. When Mackenzie King told his diary that he thought he had dished the CCF by promising to implement the social security reforms brought forward by Leonard Marsh's report in 1944, he didn't mean that he meant to *do* anything; he felt, correctly as it turned out, that all he had to do was promise.

The only part of the "cradle to grave" coverage King introduced as a result of the Marsh study was the Family Allowance Act, passed in 1944, which could be puffed at the next election. He also had the Cockfield Brown advertising agency produce a series of pamphlets offering "womb to tomb" security — old-age pensions, health insurance, unemployment assistance, and housing subsidies. The Liberal party slogan was "Vote Liberal and keep building a new Social Order in Canada."[4]

On the hustings, King sounded like a social crusader:

> The world is not going to stand for a few millionaires and poverty side by side ... The great natural resources which God has given to all the people are not going to be controlled by a privileged few while great multitudes walk the streets in search of employment.[5]

M.J. Coldwell, the CCF national leader, couldn't have put it better. And King went on to say that he had offered Coldwell a post in his cabinet because, while Coldwell might have the right idea, he would need a cabinet team to do the work.

---

[4] Beck, *Pendulum of Power*, 248.
[5] Quoted in *Chronicle* (Halifax), 6 June 1945.

All these promises did their magic, and King won the 1945 election handily. Then he put the entire program away and forgot about it.[6]

However, that election did produce twenty-eight CCF MPs, eighteen of them in Saskatchewan (along with two Liberals and one Tory); Tommy certainly had the mandate and the muscle to mount his program of reform. But he would soon be attacked, tooth and nail, by the Liberals.

The Hate Campaign

The CCF was done permanent, long-term damage by a hate campaign conducted all across the country that wafted its poisoned tendrils back into Saskatchewan. This outpouring of deceit and slander was launched even before McCarthyism reared its ugly head in the United States, and continued for at least thirteen years, roughly from 1944 to 1957.

The CCF had been moderating its policies from 1933 on, and by war's end was officially embracing the idea that Canada's economy was, and should remain, a "mixed economy" rather than the state-planned model envisioned by the Regina Manifesto. The Manifesto was trotted out on special occasions for uplift rather than guidance, although it was not officially replaced until the Winnipeg Declaration of Principles in 1956.

Ironically, the CCF's more moderate approach, precisely because it made the party more electable, inspired what Cameron Smith called "the most vicious and concentrated campaign ever undertaken against a political party."[7] Supported by huge donations from chambers of commerce and boards of trade, and by the help of most of Canada's large corporations, including its banks and trust companies, the campaign portrayed the CCF as dictatorial (a wonderful irony since, at this time, the CCF was the only political party in Canada to hold open conventions; the Liberals' last convention had taken place in 1919). And not only dictatorial, but communistic and crooked.

A typical note was struck by Fred Gardiner, the reeve of Forest Hill, then an independent village within Toronto, who rumbled that "Socialistic rule in Canada would mean musclemen and gangsters, who understand mob organization and the handling of machine guns."[8]

---

[6] Blair Fraser, *The Search for Identity: Canada, 1945–1967* (Toronto: Doubleday, 1967), 18–19.

[7] Cameron Smith, *Love & Solidarity* (Toronto: McClelland & Stewart, 1992), 99.

[8] Ibid.

In Ontario, the government of George Drew established a political police office in 1943 on the second floor of a garage on Surrey Place, just down the street from Queen's Park. Ontario Provincial Police Captain William J. Osborne-Dempster was put in charge, provided with funds never authorized by the legislature, and set to work as a political spy, complete with code name: he was called "D.208," and signed his reports to the deputy commissioner of the OPP, "Yours to command, D.208."

This "Special Branch" did not appear in the public accounts of Ontario, although that was a legal requirement. Osborne-Dempster set up files on all CCF members of the legislature, and on anyone who levelled any criticism against the government, free enterprise, or international finance. These people were seen as either communists or the dupes of communists, and they included not only Edward B. Joliffe, the Ontario CCF leader, but B.K. Sandwell, editor of *Saturday Night* magazine, Mitch Hepburn, the former Liberal premier, and David Croll, a prominent Liberal senator.[9] Copies of reports purporting to link all these left-wingers with communism were fed not only to the provincial Conservatives, but to two peculiar propagandists, Gladstone Murray and M.A. Sanderson. Murray, who had been general manager of the CBC until 1948, when he was asked to resign for failure to account for funds he had received,[10] was hired by the Canadian Chamber of Commerce to mount an anti-socialist campaign. He received generous payments from many of Canada's prominent corporations and used them to produce propaganda and pamphlets.

Sanderson, known to intimates as "Buggsy," although his first name was actually Montague, was the manager of the Reliable Exterminator Company, but spent much of his time attacking socialism because the resultant publicity apparently increased the sales of bug spray. He used the D.208 reports as the basis of a huge, crude advertisement directed at CCF candidates in the 1944 Toronto municipal election. The ad, headed "This Is the Slate to Rub Out on New Year's Day," contained the flat assertion that all CCFers were communists. Since it was illegal at that

---

[9] Stewart, *But Not in Canada*, 167ff.

[10] Reg Whitaker and Gary Marcuse, *Cold War Canada: The Making of a National Insecurity State, 1945–1957* (Toronto: University of Toronto Press, 1994), 274.

time to be a communist, the CCFers sued for libel. As there was no evidence to validate Sanderson's charges, a "special jury" that consisted entirely of businessmen found for the plaintiffs, and awarded them each one dollar in damages. In the meantime, all of them were defeated in the election.

Alvin Rowe, an OPP constable working under Osborne-Dempster, became more and more concerned about the activities of the Special Branch, which were clearly outside the law, and took his worries to Agnes Macphail, who in turn took them to Ted Joliffe, the Ontario CCF leader. Joliffe consulted the CCF national leader, M.J. Coldwell, who worried that revealing the material might do more harm than good, but Joliffe disregarded this advice. On May 24, 1945, in the middle of a provincial election, he went on the radio to charge that the Ontario government had set up a secret police force, that Premier George Drew knew about it and sanctioned it, and that it was being used to harass the legitimate opposition to the Conservatives, including Liberals and CCFers. All of this was true. However, he chose to call the Special Branch "George Drew's Gestapo," an emotive term that blew up in his face.

Canadians simply would not believe that a government of theirs would condone, much less engage in, such activity, even though Joliffe, well primed by Alvin Rowe's files, was able to produce dates, incidents, and copies of D.208's reports. Premier Drew, unable to dismiss the charges out of hand, denied that he had a role in any of the alleged activities, or indeed any knowledge of them, and promised a royal commission to look into the matter, which put it out of the way for the rest of the election. The Conservatives won that election, and the Ontario CCF was decimated.

In due course, a royal commission was established under Mr. Justice A.M. LeBel, a prominent Liberal, with Joseph Sedgwick, a prominent Conservative, as commission counsel. The commission's terms of reference were carefully drawn to exclude prying into the activities of the Special Branch; it was only allowed to consider whether the premier had had any responsibility for its establishment. Drew went into the witness box in due course and perjured himself. He said that Joliffe's entire charge was a "deliberate lie," and Mr. Justice LeBel swallowed this account whole. LeBel concluded that there was no direct link between Drew and the Special Branch, and therefore Joliffe's charges were groundless. He also concluded that Osborne-Dempster's role was not to make life difficult for the legitimate opposition, but to investigate communism, although D.208 never once submitted a report on communism as such.

His Lordship also found that, while Osborne-Dempster's reports were frequently misleading and often outright false, they were not intentionally so. Gladstone Murray testified that he had never received the secret reports of D.208, nor had he ever used them. LeBel believed Murray, despite other testimony, and proclaimed that it was simply not credible that large corporate interests, in the persons of Gladstone Murray and Buggsy Sanderson, would be in the business of purchasing palpable falsehoods. Therefore, he said, it hadn't happened. He found, finally, that the payments that supported the Special Branch were illegal; that, at least, was undeniable. But no action was ever taken in the matter.

The chief witness against the government, Alvin Rowe, died in a plane crash after the hearings, and the transcript of the hearings disappeared. No one seemed to find this odd.

It was not until 1980, when David Lewis was writing his autobiography, that at least part of the truth was established as fact. Two dogged researchers, Dr. Alan Whitehorn and David Walden, were helping Lewis gather material, and they dug into the private papers of both Drew and Murray. What they found was that Drew had a direct, personal, and long-lasting relationship with Gladstone Murray, in flat contradiction of his own account before the commission; that the D.208 reports were indeed used in precisely the way that Alvin Rowe had said they were used; and that, as Lewis wrote, "The head of the Ontario government had given false testimony under oath."[11]

Too late. In the election that took place in Ontario ten days after the Gestapo charges were first levelled, the CCF plummeted from 21 seats to 8, while the Liberals became the official opposition, with 11 seats, and the Conservatives won a thumping, 66-seat majority.[12]

---

[11] Lewis, *The Good Fight,* 274.
[12] *Parliamentary Guide,* 1946.

Federally, as well, the incident did inestimable harm, convincing many swing voters that the CCF was a party of desperation that would resort to anything to crawl to power. Political scientist Murray Beck, an even-handed commentator, noted that "the politically inept E.B. Joliffe" had hurt the CCF cause nationwide because "his charges that the Premier maintained his own private Gestapo backfired badly."[13] So they did, although the charges happened to be true. In the federal vote, while the CCF claimed 28 seats, none was in Ontario, where the party had to break through if it was to be a national force.

The Liberals combined with the Communists during that 1945 vote, and were happy to do so. The national director of the Liberal Federation noted, "We're glad of co-operation; we're for co-operation, not coalition." David Lewis called this "an unholy alliance between the Liberals, who had no principles, and the Communists, who had no ethics."[14] No blame was attached to the Liberals for these alliances, which saw them making saw-off deals with the Labour Progressive candidates (as the Communists called themselves while it was illegal to be communist) in a number of ridings to avoid splitting the vote.

The CCF itself certainly had some communist sympathizers, and indeed, Communist members, but it spent a good deal of time and effort trying to weed them out. For this Tommy and the CCF were pilloried on the left as "reactionary" at the same time that Liberal Walter Tucker, a Saskatoon lawyer and member of Parliament for Rosthern, lambasted them for being "in the pay of Moscow." Hard to beat that for chutzpah, but Tucker was only warming up.

"Tucker or Tyranny"

The 1948 election was not only one of the most important in Saskatchewan's history, but also one of the nastiest. The stakes were, after all, immensely high for the Liberals. If the CCF upstarts — who had lunged into office not because they were popular, but because the Patterson government was unpopular — could be defeated in 1948, the whole nightmare might go away. Tommy could go back to his pulpit, and life in

---

[13] Beck, *Pendulum of Power*, 250.
[14] Smith, *Love & Solidarity*, 106–7.

the boardrooms, of not merely Saskatchewan but all of Canada, could return to its familiar and comfortable (for some) groove.

To bring about this happy end, the Liberals rounded up a massive war chest, lined up the radio and newspaper moguls (not that they needed much lining up; they were as anxious to crush the socialists as anyone else), and prepared to usher Walter Tucker into the premier's office.

Tucker, up to this time, had a reputation as a progressive. He was a family man with nine children, and had been a gold medallist in law school. He was also a large man, in all directions —he looked quite a lot like Oliver Hardy, but did not have Ollie's sense of humour. Tucker had been groomed for the post of Liberal leader by Jimmy Gardiner, who then subjected him to an endless series of suggestions, proposals, and commands. He even told the Liberal leader where to put filing cabinets in the party's two-room headquarters in Regina.[15]

However, although he didn't know it, Gardiner faced a fundamental problem in his dealings with Tucker. Gardiner was convinced that because he himself was interested only in federal matters, so were the voters of Saskatchewan, whose moods and habits, he believed, were as familiar to him as the back of his hand. He advised Tucker to make much of the creation and actions of the Canadian Wheat Board, for example, while Tucker wrote to a friend, "This . . . is a provincial election, and I saw no point to arguing Federal matters."[16]

Tucker's platform, from beginning to end, consisted of one note: Tommy Douglas was dangerous, and to re-elect the CCF would bring the return of Chaos and One Night. Those were not his words, because he could never put a coherent thought in a short sentence, but that was the nub of the thing.

The two men had met before, had debated before, and were on moderately friendly terms. That didn't last long. They met in debate not long after Tucker's election as provincial leader, at a joint picnic (such joint party clambakes were common at the time) at Crystal Lake, near Yorkton. Once the crowd of 3,000 had golloped down 800 gallons of ice cream, gone for a swim, lined up for airplane rides, conducted a

[15] Ward and Smith, *Jimmy Gardiner*, 301.
[16] Ibid., 304.

singalong, and otherwise disported themselves, the serious business of the afternoon took place.

Tucker, large and rotund, and Tommy, neither of these, clambered up onto the bed of a truck trailer, and went at it, hammer and tongs. Tommy laid out a number of the things his government had done, from special funding for the financially strapped education system to protection against foreclosure for farmers. And, he threw in, the government had increased support for single mothers. This caused Tucker to riposte that the Liberals had introduced mother's allowances to Saskatchewan when Tommy was "just a little fellow."[17]

Big mistake. Tommy replied: "I am still a little fellow. Mr. Tucker is big enough to swallow me, but if he did, he would be the strangest man in the world. He would have more brains in his stomach than he does in his head."[18]

The *Regina Leader-Post* opined the next day that this crack was undignified. Which it was. Funny, though.

Tucker, stepping hastily away from that one, went on to charge that the man really in charge of the province was not Tommy at all, but George Cadbury, the urbane economist who had come over from England to serve as chairman of the Economic Planning Board, the province's central policy-making body on the financial side. Cadbury was a scion of the English chocolate company, a Quaker, and a gentle man of impeccable manners and wry humour. He was also very tall and distinguished looking. Watching him walk down a hallway with Tommy gave the onlooker insight into the comedic possibilities of Mutt and Jeff. However, on a summer day at a picnic where almost no one knew him, he could be made to appear a left-wing villain, and the embodiment of the excesses of the Labour Party in Britain. (At that time run by Clement Attlee, whom Winston Churchill once described as "a sheep in sheep's clothing.")

Moreover, Tucker rumbled, the CCF was being backed by the Communists, "financially and otherwise." For this, Tucker was roundly booed.

---

[17] Which happened to be untrue; they were introduced three years earlier, as we have seen.

[18] Tommy's later recollection improved this to "he would be a biological monstrosity." The version given here is the way it appeared in both the Regina *Leader-Post* and the Saskatoon *Star Phoenix* of 14 July 1947.

It didn't get any better. The Liberal slogan became "Tucker or Tyranny." (Tommy claimed he had run into a farmer who said he didn't know this fellow Tyranny, but whoever he was, he had to be better than Tucker.)

Outside money, none of it from the Communists, poured into the province before and during the election. The Canadian Insurance Underwriters Association set up a public relations office in the Saskatchewan Hotel to warn the people about the perils of public auto insurance (this was before the underwriters' own handbooks began to show that auto insurance for similar policies was 20 per cent cheaper in Saskatchewan than anywhere else in Canada), and business leaders from coast to coast called on the people of the province to restore sanity by banishing the socialist hordes back to the wilderness.

Ugly rumours were circulated. One said that Tommy had made $3 million selling a brick plant to the province. Another, which must have driven Tommy into a blind rage, touched on his daughter Shirley, who was then eighteen.

The Douglas papers in the Saskatchewan Archives contain two large scrapbooks of clippings that Tommy's secretary, Eleanor McKinnon, assembled from the provincial newspaper coverage of this campaign. Every article that mentioned the campaign appears to have been included. Eighty-seven pages of this material contain statements made by Tucker or news coverage of his comments. One page consists of rebuttals by Tommy. To get around this clear bias, Tommy used small radio stations — the party even bought one to make sure it had some chance to get on the air — weekly newspapers, and the party's own organ, *The Commonwealth*.

A typical sample of the news coverage, even before the election broke out, began, "Dangerous and retrogressive summed up the reaction of most civil servants to the government's action." This referred to the CCF introducing legislation that allowed civil servants to take part in politics on their own time.[19] (Under the Patterson government, civil servants were active in politics on government time, albeit without the

[19] *Leader-Post* (Regina), 5 April 1947.

sanction of law.) However, the reporter was apparently unable to track down any actual civil servants to comment on the legislation, although there were then 5,000 of them at hand. Instead, the reporter talked to Walter Tucker, whose powers of telepathy enabled him to pass along what the bureaucrats were thinking. According to this source, the civil servants knew that the only members of their tribe who would be allowed to politic were those who backed the government.[20]

A sampling of headlines from the province's overwhelmingly dominant dailies, the *Star Phoenix* of Saskatoon and the *Leader-Post* of Regina (both owned by the Sifton family at the time), conveys the flavour: "Communist Tendencies Denounced"; "CCF Trying to Control Veterans"[21]; "Tucker Warns Red Faction Moving In"; "CCF Hidden Hand Is Revealed — Tucker"[22]; "CCF Doing Better Job for Stalin's Kremlin than Any Communist, Walter Tucker States"; "Tucker Sees Similarities Between CCF and Reds."

Besides carrying whatever false charges Tucker cared to levy against the CCF, and systematically freezing Tommy out of their columns, the two newspapers went to work with their own hatchets. The Saskatoon *Star Phoenix*, for example, more in sorrow than in anger, pronounced that "All CCFers may not be Communists, but whether they know it or not they are working for the Communist Party."[23] Joining in on the fun, the *Leader-Post* invited the leader of the Liberal Party in Saskatchewan to contribute a number of articles presenting the claims of his party for election on June 24. In these articles, Tucker referred constantly to "Mr. Douglas and his Communist supporters," and in the final article, on the eve of the election, he accused Tommy of running a "smear" campaign,[24] which may have puzzled his readers, who had scarcely heard a word from the premier, either smear or cheer, during the entire exercise. Also on the election eve, the *Leader-Post* ran a fawning article by its chief political correspondent, Ken Liddell, flatly predicting a Liberal victory. It was headlined, with that even-handedness we all recognize as the hallmark of great journalism, "Sincerity Is Walter Tucker's Hallmark."[25]

---

[20] Ibid.

[21] This referred to legislation giving war veterans free thirty-year leases on farmland. A private member's bill to accomplish this had been talked out by one Walter Tucker, MP for Rosthern. Go figure.

[22] The hidden hand, needless to say, stretched all the way from Moscow.

[23] *Star Phoenix* (Saskatoon), 3 April 1948.

[24] *Leader-Post* (Regina), 23 June 1948.

[25] Ibid.

In case the journalists were not getting the good word across, near the eve of the election the Liberals ran full-page ads in the two newspapers, under the "Tucker or Tyranny" rubric, that carried the monster headline "Do Not Let These Socialists Deprive the Farmer of Ownership of His Land."

To guard against the Red Menace thus revealed, the Liberals and Conservatives made deals to mount a joint candidate in many ridings: "Liberal-Progressive" was the tag.

A Case of Libel

The Liberal smear campaign dominated the 1948 Saskatchewan election, and poisoned the atmosphere to such an extent that Tommy lost his temper and got himself into a libel suit involving Walter Tucker, which put a huge strain on both himself and Irma.

A woman named Parania Warrows of Fish Creek, in Tucker's riding, complained to Tommy that her parents had, many years earlier, been deprived of their land by a company called the Rosthern Mortgage Company. Tommy referred her to the local mediation board, set up by his government to look into these matters, and the mediation board thought there was something suspicious in the circumstances. The parents, a Ukrainian couple, had apparently signed off on the ownership of their land to the mortgage company, but neither of them could read or write English.[26]

The man who acted as translator for the couple had apparently persuaded them that by signing a quit claim for the property they would be assured of keeping it, when, of course, the opposite was the case. Instead, another man bought the property from the mortgage firm and, on the basis of the signed quit claim, foreclosed on the couple — even though they insisted that they had made all payments under the mortgage — and took possession. The couple thought they had a case in law, and had launched a suit, naming the mortgage company and the translator as defendants. They contended that the foreclosure had been obtained "in fraud of the plaintiffs," and wanted the property restored and damages paid.

---

[26] There is an extensive file on this libel suit in the Douglas Collection, Saskatchewan Archives, Regina. This account is drawn from that file, which includes clippings, letters, and legal documents.

The defendants said that there was no fraud, that the transaction was perfectly legal, and that the plaintiffs had surrendered the land willingly by signing the quit claim, although it was never evident why they would do so.

This case was making its desultory way through the courts when the matter landed in Tommy's lap. He saw at once that the secretary to the mortgage company was none other than Walter Tucker, and since Tucker was making so much noise about the danger of the CCF taking away farms, he raised the issue in a speech at Caron, west of Moose Jaw, in which he said that "the danger lies in mortgage companies like the Rosthern Mortgage Company of which Mr. Tucker is the secretary . . . He took people's farms up in the Rosthern district under very suspicious circumstances." He added that the family involved was suing Tucker's firm "for allegedly depriving by fraud these people of their property."

Tucker promptly announced that he was suing Tommy for $100,000, and Tommy just as promptly announced that the case was a "bluff." But it wasn't.

Irma was distraught. "Where in heaven's name are we ever going to get $100,000?" she asked. Tommy told her not to worry, but in fact, he was deeply worried himself. The case not only took his mind off the election, it cost him thousands in legal fees, and he had very little financial leeway.

When the suit came to court, at Prince Albert in October of 1949, Tucker made no denial of the facts as presented by Tommy, but rested his claim on the fact that Tommy had made the statements out of malice, to hurt Tucker's reputation.

He was asked by Tommy's counsel, Everett Clayton Leslie: "These statements are true, then?"

"Yes."

"Then why did you object to Mr. Douglas making these statements in a community where everybody knew whether or not they were true? Don't you think the people of Rosthern knew about this?"

Tucker replied, "Not too many knew, and this is not the kind of thing that you want broadcast around."

On this basis, a jury speedily found in favour of Tommy, and the judge ordered Tucker to pay the costs of the trial. Tucker appealed, and a Court of Appeal ordered a new trial based on an argument that the first judge had misdirected the jury. *Tucker v. Douglas*, reported in 1950, also took away the award of costs against Tucker.

Tommy appealed this decision to the Supreme Court of Canada, which held, on December 17, 1951, that Tucker had a proper grounds for appeal on the issue of justification. That is, there was no question that the statements made by Tommy were correct; the only issue was whether he was justified in making them in the way he did.

By this time, it had become apparent that the case was doing Tucker a good deal of harm politically, in a province where even being associated with a mortgage company was enough to condemn someone in the eyes of the farm population, and the case just faded away. Tucker still had, in law, every right to pursue it.

Tommy felt afterwards that the libel case hurt Tucker. It certainly hurt Tommy, at least in the pocketbook: the unsatisfactory outcome meant he had to shoulder his legal costs, although some of his supporters stepped in to help defray some of these expenses. His final comment on the case indicated how distasteful the whole matter was to him: "The Scottish way of thinking is, if you're in court, there's something wrong. Decent people stay out of court."[27]

The Permanent Socialists

The CCF won the 1948 election, but were cut from 47 seats to 31, while the Liberals and Liberal-Progressives (a title dropped immediately) won 19 seats. The Socialists were not a sometime thing, then, but a permanent power, at least in Saskatchewan.

Inevitably, the atmosphere of the campaign led to a sour and savage legislative session. One day in the House, Tucker called Tommy "a stinking skunk and a dirty little thing."

---

[27] Douglas, *The Making of a Socialist*, 262.

Tommy noted, "I certainly resent that 'little.'"[28]

Tommy was now becoming a national figure because of, or in spite of, the intense media coverage of the province. He introduced reform after reform, from a voting age of eighteen, another first on the continent, to an expansion of oil exploration. Tucker had claimed that as long as there was a CCF government in charge, "there will never be a barrel of oil produced in Saskatchewan." By 1958, there were 3,600 oil-producing wells in the province; oil had become a significant source of provincial income.

By that time, the CCF had won four provincial elections in Saskatchewan (in 1944, 1948, 1952, and 1956), each time by a majority. It had had its share of mishaps and scandals, but was generally recognized, within provincial boundaries, as a moderately efficient, pragmatic, progressive government. If it was no longer the prairie fire, if its socialism was diluted by experience, it was still far and away the Canadian province most open to reform.

At the same time, it balanced the books. Every year. If there is such a thing as respectable radicalism, that is what Tommy provided. Inevitably, though, as session succeeded session in the handsome Saskatchewan legislature, the emphasis was more on respectability and less on radicalism. The province still led the nation in labour legislation (although there were still bitter battles with, and within, the public service unions); it was still more interventionist than other governments; it was still the only province in the country that seemed to pay much heed to the needs of its farming population; it was still leading the nation in social policy. But it remained in power not because of ideological purity or party doctrine, but because enough people in the province thought it provided them with good government.

---

[28] Ibid., 265.

Chapter TWELVE

T.C. Douglas, Mink Rancher

I'm more of a radical than when I took office for one very obvious reason. In 1944 I thought these things could be done, and today I know they can be done.

— Tommy Douglas, 1958

The 1948 provincial election, while it cost the CCF some seats, allowed it to settle into power in Saskatchewan; not to relax, exactly, but to get on with the job. Too much had been attempted in the first term, and the process of digesting some of these moves was barely underway. The question of protecting farm tenure was still before the courts, and the Saskatchewan government would lose one of the main cases. But no one was talking any more about the imminent disappearance of the socialist hordes; they were in place for at least another four years.

At this point, Tommy was very little changed from the youthful preacher who had first gone into politics. He still looked years younger than anything reported on his birth certificate (he was forty-four, and looked about twenty-four), and was excitable, enthusiastic, quick-tempered, and demanding.

At home, he was busy paying off a mortgage (the house on Angus Crescent cost $6,000, plus another $150 for a garage; Tommy sold his little cottage in Weyburn for $2,000 and took out a mortgage to cover the rest) and, thanks to his daughter Shirley, looking after young boys again. Shirley came home from Sunday school one day and announced that the superintendent was begging for someone to look after some of the more obstreperous boys, who had more time and energy than could be readily absorbed in the contemplation of scriptures.

Very soon, Tommy was supervising eight boys between the ages of twelve and fourteen, a group that expanded quickly to more than forty. They met three times a week: on Saturday for bowling, on Sunday for Sunday school, and one night a week: for a trip to the RCMP barracks, where there was an athletic centre at which they could swim, play basketball, and box.[1] (If Tommy had had a son, he might have turned him into a pretty fair fighter.)

On the hustings, he had become such a consummate campaigner that a Liberal MLA complained, "Douglas doesn't have to kiss babies. Babies kiss him."[2] As the head of a government that was constantly opening new offices, factories, and other ventures, he finally got his picture into the newspapers — cutting ribbons. One of the better stories this occasioned has a Regina housewife struggling to open a jar of preserves, giving up, and declaring, "I ought to call Tommy Douglas. He's opened everything else in the province this week."[3]

He knew what was going on among the backbenchers and senior civil servants because he made it a habit always to have his lunch (usually the same lunch: one egg, poached or fried, on whole wheat toast) in the legislative cafeteria. This left him open to the personal lobbying that is so much a part of politics; it also ensured that nothing moved on the shores of Wascana Lake (the widened river had been dignified with an upgraded name to render it suitable as a site for the provincial parliament) without his knowledge.

He was developing into a first-rate leader, able to select, promote, and train first-class talent. He was willing to give his ministers a free hand, and then back them when they got into trouble, a loyalty that would prove costly when, as inevitably happened, he made the wrong choice in the first place.

His labour minister, for example, Charles Cromwell Williams, though no relation to George Williams, was almost as troublesome at times. A railway telegrapher and sometime mayor of Regina, he was of very little use either as an administrator or as an even-handed advocate of labour within the cabinet.

---

[1] Douglas, *The Making of a Socialist*, 234.

[2] Robert Tyre, *Douglas in Saskatchewan: The Story of a Socialist Experiment* (Vancouver: Mitchell Press, 1962), 49. Tyre worked for the Regina *Leader-Post* and later, briefly, as a public relations officer in the Industrial Development Office. He displayed a visceral hatred of Tommy, mainly because of his conviction that "Socialism is an alien way of life in Canada." Still, he found that Tommy was "a spellbinder."

[3] Ibid., 48.

Williams was popular and charming, but not swift. David Lewis said of him:

> I was not impressed with Williams as Minister of Labour. In my lengthy report to the premier,[4] I urged that "unless Charlie is given the necessary underpinning, you are likely to have more trouble in the future." I added, "I have never met a man more willing, nicer or more decent than Charlie. At the same time, I have seldom met a man less adequately equipped for an important job such as he has."

Williams was a member of the Trades and Labor Congress. His appointment immediately drew the ire of its then rival, the Canadian Congress of Labour, and the local CCL demanded that Tommy fire him. He refused. Williams was still in his job when Tommy left his in 1961, but much of his work had to be done by his deputy ministers, most notably Ken Bryden, a brilliant economist and later a significant force in the Ontario CCF. Bryden was the "underpinning" Lewis had asked for, and he was the one who recommended Bryden to Tommy. For Tommy to keep a man so palpably incompetent as Bryden in his portfolio — which meant that Tommy himself had to step in on the political side when things went wrong — says more about Tommy's loyalty than about his political savvy.

The Socialist Entrepreneur

Tommy was seldom blindsided by events except when they sprang from his own actions. In these cases, he seemed to be ruled by a combination of trust and naïveté that left him open to proper censure, which he never quite seemed to understand. It was Clarence Fines, his confidante, friend, and pillar of strength, who most often got him into trouble.

Not having enough to do as premier, Sunday school teacher, father, husband, and (inevitably) spokesman for the CCF not only in his own

---

[4] Lewis, *The Good Fight*, 473. The "lengthy report" was a long, hectoring letter in which he told Tommy exactly where he had gone wrong, and what to do about it. Even Lewis recognized that some might see "presumption, if not arrogance on my part," in the corrective missives he fired off from time to time. Not to worry. "I don't ever recall being inhibited by a person's 'station in life.'" He had raked Tommy over the coals when he was a lowly MP, and didn't mean to stop just because he had become a premier.

province but across the country (he was always extraordinarily open to wandering journalists for interviews, and never betrayed the slightest impatience when asked the same questions he had already answered a score or more of times), Tommy decided that he needed a hobby. (He played golf, but only a few times a year, and golf is more of a penance than a hobby, anyway.) He also needed money. Fines put these two needs together and came to Tommy with the suggestion that they go into the mink ranching business.

They got hold of a little bit of property on the edge of the city, whacked together a bunch of cages, bought a score of adult minks, and waited for the money to roll in: "The old mink ranchers of the province always tell about the time Fines and I tried for four solid hours to breed a mink by putting two males in the same cage!"[5]

The ranching venture did not go well, in part because the partners hired a real mink rancher to do most of the caring for the animals, and "he seemed to have considerable difficulty keeping our mink separate from his own."[6]

It never occurred to Tommy that, if this had turned out to be a growth industry, he would have been selling furs, in time, through the co-operative the province had set up to encourage the fur industry, and would have been open to charges of conflict of interest. The advantage of failing, at a cost of about $1,500 between Fines and Tommy, was that they at least avoided this difficulty.

Fines was a true entrepreneur, while Tommy was never more than a dabbler and an innocent. Fines also paid very little attention to either propriety or common sense in his dealings, and Tommy was never able to choke him off. In 1950, Fines invested $1,250 in a drive-in movie theatre on Pasqua Street, where it meets the Trans-Canada Highway, and persuaded Tommy to put $500 into the same investment. When the story broke that the premier, a Baptist minister, was part-owner of a drive-in, the opposition had a good deal of fun with it, instantly dubbing the place the "Premier's Passion Pit." Tommy insisted that he had hoped that there would be boxing matches before the movies came on,

---

[5] Douglas, *The Making of a Socialist,* 233.
[6] Ibid., 234.

along with performances by local musicians and actors: "a very good community affair."[7]

Fines and Tommy had invested in the drive-in through Morris Shumiatcher, the irascible but brilliant Regina lawyer who was, for a time, a government adviser. The problem was that the major shareholder in the Sunset Drive-In was a Regina businessman named Phil Bodnoff. It later came out that Bodnoff had obtained a $75,000 mortgage from the Saskatchewan Government Insurance Office (SGIO) to purchase two movie theatres in Weyburn. Fines was the minister responsible for the SGIO; he was also a member of the board that approved the loan for his business partner. The Liberals, not surprisingly, leapt on this revelation and demanded an inquiry. Fines agreed to allow the matter to go before the Crown Corporations Committee in 1952. There, the Liberals argued that the government appeared to be lending money to its friends. Worse, it seemed that the premier and the provincial treasurer stood to gain personally in these transactions.[8]

Fines, waving copies of the cancelled SGIO cheques to show that they had been deposited on behalf of the Weyburn properties, and had nothing to do with the Sunset Drive-In, protested that neither he nor the premier had done anything wrong. Tommy said much the same thing in his appearance before the committee: "I make no apology for investing in any local venture that can be of assistance to the community."[9]

It is not hard to imagine what Tommy would have done with a defence like that had he been on the other side. But the committee, formed on the basis of representation in the legislature, contained a CCF majority, which had no difficulty finding that nothing much was wrong with the premier's adventures in the "passion pit." Tommy then discovered something that should have occurred to him long before:

> This taught me a lesson that as a politician you can't just do the things you would normally do as a citizen, because somebody will try to make a mountain out of a molehill. I made up my mind that I would never at any

---

[7] Ibid., 186.
[8] *Star Phoenix* (Saskatoon), 29 February 1952.
[9] Ibid.

time try to dabble in any kind of business, because inevitably any business will have something, directly or indirectly, to do with government.[10]

Tommy mostly kept to this resolve, though much later he did become a director of an oil company. But he was not in government at the time, and had not been for decades.

Clarence Fines, on the other hand, didn't seem to get it; he dabbled in commodity markets, gold mining, and resort properties at the same time that, as the cabinet member responsible for the provincial securities commission, he had a privileged relationship with the investment houses. No one could ever show that he took advantage of insider information; nevertheless, there is only one word for such a violation of the common-sense rules of conflict of interest: idiocy. It was later revealed that, as minister responsible for the Liquor Board (Fines was the pooh-bah of the CCF government, responsible for too damn much), he had not only accepted hospitality and small gifts from liquor interests, but had received a donation of $1,500 from an agent of Alberta Distillers, which was forwarded to party coffers.[11] This was more than idiotic; it was improper.

A Put-Up Job

The incident that very nearly brought Fines, Tommy, and the CCF government to real grief had all the earmarks of a put-up job. On March 10, 1953, Walter Tucker, the Liberal opposition leader, rose in the House to read a sensational affidavit into the record. It was the sworn statement of one Joseph Oliver Rawluk of Regina that he and his wife had been involved, along with Morris Shumiatcher, in an insurance firm, Financial Agencies Limited, which had had some dealings with the government before sagging into bankruptcy. Phil Bodnoff was a shareholder and director of the company. Rawluk claimed that, in the course of this business, Fines and the managing director of the SGIO, a man named Mike Allore, had demanded kickbacks on the award of insurance business to this firm.

---

[10] Douglas, *The Making of a Socialist*, 235.
[11] This did not come out until the McLeods found the evidence in Clarence Fines's personal papers.

If true, the charges were not merely damaging, but smacked of criminality. Tucker would not table the Rawluk affidavit, but instead proposed that it be laid before a committee of inquiry to be set up by the Crown Corporations Committee. Fines, who was in the legislature at the time (neither Tommy nor George Stephen, the government's expert on procedure, was present) immediately agreed to this proposal as the fastest way to clear his name.[12]

Tommy saw the trap at once. If there was evidence to back the charges, the government was in serious trouble; if not, and the committee said as much, it would be accused of a whitewash. It was a lose-lose proposition.

The committee hearings went on for a month. Rawluk proved a very frail reed upon which to lean. He had first sworn out his statement in the offices of a member of the provincial Liberal executive early in 1952, and then spent most of a year trying to sell it, either to the Liberals or to anyone else who would pay him for it.[13] He finally gave it to Walter Tucker, who, instead of bringing it immediately to public notice, waited several months, until he could drop his bombshell in the legislature. It also turned out that Rawluk had sold insurance policies without registering them with the SGIO, as required by law; had written cheques on behalf of his company that had bounced; and had been stripped of his franchise and sued, successfully, by the SGIO for non-payment of premiums.[14] Neither Rawluk nor Tucker nor anybody else had a scrap of reliable evidence to present to show that Fines had ever demanded a kickback, or that it had ever been forthcoming.[15] Moreover, despite Tucker's claim that it was Rawluk's fondest wish to make his complaints public, Rawluk testified that he was there "against my will."

The committee found that "Mr. Rawluk must be regarded as wholly unworthy of belief," and that his charges were "unwarranted and unfounded," when it reported on April 11, 1953. The Liberals, unsurprisingly, said the whole thing was a whitewash and demanded that a judge be appointed to overturn the work of the committee. Tommy refused, pointing out that, after sitting on the matter for nearly a year, Tucker had

[12] McLeod and McLeod, *Road to Jerusalem*, 188.

[13] *Report of the Standing Committee on Crown Corporations*, Regina, April 1953, Douglas Collection, Saskatchewan Archives.

[14] Ibid.

[15] Rawluk trotted out a story that he had once had a ride in Fines's car, and left $100 on the front seat. That was it.

chosen to lay it before a legislative committee instead of asking for a judicial inquiry; he couldn't now ask for a new game with a new umpire.

Then the Liberals moved for an amendment to the motion accepting the committee report. This amendment — which was not properly an amendment at all,[16] although it was accepted for debate — demanded that the report be set aside and replaced by a 16,000-word summary from the Liberals, the contents of which amounted to a simple statement that "the charges against Allore and Fines have not been disproved."

Tommy unloaded on the opposition in a two-and-a-half hour speech in which he summarized all the evidence, dismissed the notion that Allore and Fines had to prove their innocence, proved it anyway, and then asked that any Liberals who actually believed Rawluk stand in their places and say so: "Come out of the bushes and let's see the colour of your liver!"[17]

No opposition member rose to challenge Tommy, the vote proceeded without further ado, the amendment was defeated, and life went on.

Walter Tucker resigned as opposition leader soon after, and went back to being member of Parliament for Rosthern, in due course rising to a position on the legal bench. Fines did not resign, because he felt to do so would give some credence to the charges. He left politics only after Tommy moved back into the federal arena. Then Fines left his wife and moved to Florida to live comfortably on his investments. He died there after writing his account of the CCF rise to power.

The nasty brawl showed Tommy in a number of lights. He was a brilliant debater, which no one ever doubted; he was loyal to his friends, even when they had ceased to deserve it; he was honest. However, much of the mess might have been avoided if he had brought Fines to heel years earlier. The formula "For Pete's sake, Clarence, stop this stuff!" might have done the trick. But Tommy had been unable to do so.

The CCF owed Fines a debt of gratitude; there was no doubt about that. He not only ran the provincial finances brilliantly, but his presence on the

---

[16] Because its effect, if passed, would have been to render the main motion void; it is unclear why the Speaker ever accepted it in this form.

[17] Saskatchewan Legislature, *Debates and Proceedings*, 14 April 1953.

front benches assured business interests that a real free enterpriser — some might have said far *too* real a free enterpriser — was in charge of the cash flow. But Tommy let Fines get away with exactly the kind of behaviour that would have drawn his withering scorn had it come from the other side of the House.

Years later, Tommy noted winsomely that Fines had come to him with a proposal to set up an exclusive franchise for the distribution of propane gas for the entire province:

> I don't think there's any doubt we'd have made a million dollars quite comfortably. But I came to the conclusion then, and I hold it even more tenaciously now, that any man who is in public life is wise to sever himself from any business connections for his own sake, for the sake of his party, and above all for the sake of his colleagues.[18]

Tommy would have done well to have reached this conclusion before he ever ranched his first mink.

Uneasy Lies the Head that Owns the Crowns

The charge most often laid against the Douglas government was that it was socialist. That seemed to be enough to condemn it in the eyes of the media and the business community. Certainly the CCF described itself as socialist, always carefully injecting the adjective "democratic" to sort it out from other brands of socialism.

Here is how *Webster's New Collegiate Dictionary* defines "socialism":

> n. **1**: any of various economic and political theories advocating collective or governmental ownership of the means of production and distribution of goods. **2a**: a system of society or group living in which there is no private property; **b**: a system or condition of society in which the means of production are owned and controlled by the state. **3**: a stage of society in Marxist

---

[18] Douglas, *The Making of a Socialist,* 235.

theory transitional between capitalism and communism and distinguished by unequal distribution of goods and pay according to work done.

The CCF in Saskatchewan was socialist under the first definition, never under either of the others. But any government that applies an income tax to its people and delivers any form of social assistance is distributing goods; any government that owns any of the means of production is, according to this definition, socialist. When the Conservative government of R.B. Bennett set up the Bank of Canada in 1934, when the Liberal government of Mackenzie King created thirty-two crown corporations to sell wool, harvest timber, make tools, refine uranium, and build ships, among other things,[19] it was certainly sliding down the slippery slope. The United States, when Ronald Reagan was in charge, owned 24,000 government enterprises.[20] (They no longer count them, so it is hard to work out today's total.) The Tennessee Valley Authority, headquartered in Knoxville, Tennessee, is larger, in terms of assets, employment, and revenue than any other government corporation on the continent except another U.S. government corporation — the post office.

Governments wind up owning the means of production and distribution, by and large, *faute de mieux*. The Cape Breton Development Corporation (Devco), a far larger enterprise than anything the CCF owned in Saskatchewan, came into being because of the failure of private enterprise. The Dominion Steel and Coal Company, after years of making money, began to lose it. They pulled out in 1967, leaving 6,000 Cape Breton families without any visible means of support. The federal Liberals, socialists to a man, stepped in to save the jobs (and the votes that went with them), and, over the next thirty years, spent $1.6 billion to keep the corporation going. Before long, Devco found itself in oyster farming, fishing, sheep breeding, beef production, maple syrup, boat construction, wool milling, food processing, metal casting, lumber milling, and door making. Not profit making, though; never profit making. It went into the tourist industry and financed a steam railway, a

---

[19] Stewart, *Uneasy Lies the Head*, appendix VII.
[20] Ibid., 64.

golf course, beaches, marinas, and restaurants. Some of these were good and suitable projects and some were not; what they all had in common was that, without government help, it is unlikely that any of these job-creating ventures would ever have seen the light of day.

Somehow, this proved to the nation's editorial writers that government enterprise is no good, and private enterprise is wonderful. When the Chrétien government finally pulled the plug on Devco, the *Toronto Star* huffed that the workers of Cape Breton (where the unemployment rate still hovers around 20 per cent) "would be far better off today had Ottawa not tried to shield them from economic reality for the past 30 years."[21]

Actually, $1.6 billion spread over thirty years looks like a pretty good investment, when the alternative was to walk away and let Cape Breton be depopulated. Ottawa spends about $25 billion every year in subsidies to private corporations. Why is this "an investment in opportunity," while keeping Cape Bretoners in good jobs is shielding them from economic reality? In one tax ruling, Revenue Canada allowed the Bronfman interests to transfer assets out of the country tax-free, a deal that cost about $800 million, or half of what it cost to keep thousands of men and women working for three decades. Was that a better deal?

What distinguished the CCF under Tommy Douglas was that they went into government enterprise with their eyes open. They believed in planning, and they adopted plans. They believed in government enterprise where necessary, and private enterprise where necessary, and mixed enterprise where that made sense. They never proposed or performed a slate of plans in which all the major elements of production and distribution belonged to the state. They simply believed, like the Conservatives of Ontario when they set up Ontario Hydro, that there are conditions under which state ownership is either the best or the only way to get something done.

When the CCF came to power, about 80 per cent of Saskatchewan's gross provincial product came from agriculture, mainly wheat.[22] It had the nation's highest per capita debt and second-lowest per capita income. Outside investment in the province ranged between poor and pitiful. Between 1936 and 1946, census figures showed, about one quarter

---

[21] *Toronto Star*, 2 June 1999.
[22] This was the figure used in the 1941 census.

of the population moved out of the province, a trend that promised to leave the place to the gophers before long, if something wasn't done.

The CCF government's Economic Planning Board quickly steered the province into commercial ventures in insurance, power generation, and telephones, all of which made, and continued to make, profits for years. Joe Phelps, the minister for natural resources, was a much sturdier socialist than Tommy, and vowed to carry out the "eventual and complete socialization" of all provincial resources, the ambitious goal of the first Planning Board.[23] Warned that he might be pushing on faster than the province could abide, Phelps would shout, "Never say whoa in the middle of a puddle!" and would plunge ahead.[24]

Nobody seemed to notice that, while Phelps was indeed setting up all sorts of government-owned ventures, the premier had slipped away to talk to oil barons in London, New York, Toronto, and Chicago, and was persuading them to come to Saskatchewan, where, he promised them, they need never fear they would be taken over by the government. To offset the constant drum roll of press notices warning them off, he wrote a public letter promising that any corporations that invested in the provincial natural resource sector (aside from power and natural gas, which he told them were "natural monopolies" reserved for the province) would be left free of interference. As long as they paid the necessary royalties, as under any other jurisdiction, they would be able to operate exactly as they chose.[25]

By 1958, the province had outside investment in the oil industry of $2 billion. The annual production from the mineral sector increased almost ten-fold from 1945 to 1958, from $22 million to more than $200 million. Royalties from natural resources grew from $1.5 million to $25 million. Although agriculture had grown both in acreage planted (by more than a million acres) and in average farm production, it was no longer providing most of Saskatchewan's income: it had dropped from more than four-fifths of the gross provincial product to just over a third.[26] Public and private investment in the province stood at more than $600 million annually (higher, per capita, than the national average), and

---

[23] Economic and Advisory Planning Board, *Four-Year Plan, 1947,* Douglas Collection, Saskatchewan Archives, Regina.

[24] McLeod and McLeod, *Road to Jerusalem,* 167.

[25] Douglas, *The Making of a Socialist,* 296.

[26] Statistics Canada, *Canadian Economic Observer, Historical Statistical Supplement, 1995/96.*

the unemployment rate was lower than that of either Alberta or Manitoba. The Planning Board's diversification scheme had worked.

The principle — not the one Tommy pushed on the hustings, but the one he outlined to Chris Higginbotham, with whom he recorded his life story — was this:

> Let me remind you that we believe in a mixed economy of public ownership, co-operative ownership, and private ownership. The problem was deciding which businesses belong to each category. There were some things we did, not because they belonged in the public ownership category, but because there was no one else to do them.[27]

Thus, when no one else would undertake to develop the massive deposits of sodium sulphate at Chaplin (where, to this day, the white alkaline deposits make a wintry landscape along the Trans-Canada Highway in the middle of July), the province built a plant that quickly paid for itself. Then it built another plant, at Bishopric, and that was soon turning out a profit, as well.

Common sense was the real criterion, not ideology. Jimmy Thomas, a minister in Britain's Labour government, once noted, "The trouble with socialists is that they let their bleeding hearts go to their bloody heads." Tommy quoted him with approval. Socialism was fine, and he applauded it, but it wouldn't do to lose sight of the fact that, as Clarence Fines kept reminding him, these things had to be paid for.

The Wrong Box

The investments that got the CCF government into trouble, because they received such huge and hostile media attention, were in a woollen mill, a shoe factory, and a box factory. In every case, the government was reluctant to step in, and only too happy, when the time came, to get out.

The province had given itself, under the Crown Corporations Act, the right to expropriate a private company under certain limited circumstances. It was used only once: to take over a small box factory in

---

[27] Douglas, *The Making of a Socialist*, 284. In point of fact, although he never would, Premier Ralph Klein of Alberta could say the same.

Prince Albert. The employees were being paid about twenty-five cents an hour, on average, when they organized themselves into a union. For more than a year, their employer refused to recognize the certification granted by the Labour Relations Board, and the Board then issued a court order requiring him to comply. Tommy phoned the owner and asked him to come to Regina to talk about the matter. The man said he couldn't come until about three weeks later, and then used this grace period to transfer ownership of the factory to his sister, to whom the court order did not apply. Then he fired every employee in the place.

At this point, the province expropriated the plant, negotiated an agreement with the employees, and then offered the place back to the owner. He refused the offer and took the province to court, where he was awarded about twice what the factory's books showed it to be worth. The province was left with a box factory it didn't want, and didn't know how to operate, which lost money for about four years before it was finally closed.

This debacle proved to the outside world that the government of Saskatchewan was the foe of private enterprise. To people inside the province, it proved that the CCF would not allow any employer simply to tear up the collective bargaining process.

The mainly hostile press coverage had an unintended side effect: it helped persuade a number of young and able people who were anxious to be in on a socialist experiment (in the current term) that Saskatchewan was the place to be. Allan Emrys Blakeney, a brilliant young Rhodes scholar from Nova Scotia, was drawn to Saskatchewan in 1950 for just this reason, and after one meeting, Tommy offered him a job.[28] For $275 a month, Blakeney became the secretary and legal adviser to the major provincial crown corporations, little dreaming that he would wind up as premier himself.

While he worked mainly with the crowns, which, decade after decade, made (and continue to make) millions for the province, in such a small administration he had a bird's-eye view of almost everything that went on. He admired the way Tommy Douglas and Clarence Fines "worked the good-cop, bad-cop routine":

[28] Allen Blakeney, interview by author, Saskatoon, 24 October 2000.

> Some grand scheme would be presented to Tommy and he would be very supportive, and then he would turn to Clarence, and the first thing you knew, it had been turned down on the grounds that, however laudable it was, we just couldn't afford it at this time. I can't prove it, but I swear that it was all worked out beforehand. Tommy would say yes, and Clarence would say no, and that was that.[29]

The crowns, under the guidance of talents like Blakeney's, were a success, both electorally and financially, and before long the government of Saskatchewan was in the chemical business, the fur trade, bus lines (because no private entrepreneur would take on the task of serving outlying areas), the brick business, fish marketing, and, in the north, the operation of trading posts. (The 15,000 people in the north of the province were entirely at the mercy of the Hudson's Bay Company, and often found, at the end of the year, that between the low prices paid for furs and the high prices charged for everything else, the foxes were not the only ones getting skinned. From the very beginning, the government intended to develop this as a co-operative business, which is what it became, in time.)

The acid test in measuring the genuine spirit of socialism of the CCF under Tommy Douglas was, of course, the land-use policy, which had been hanging about the party's neck in the 1930s. It disappeared without a trace. The party Tommy headed always ran as the defender of "the family farm as the basis of rural life."[30]

This abandonment of principle, if you like, caused Peter R. Sinclair, writing in the *Canadian Historical Review,* to comment:

> Changes in the CCF's land policy were possible in Saskatchewan because almost nobody in the party adopted a doctrinaire position that would have involved abandoning the ideal of the family farm as the basis of rural life. Therefore, the adjustment of the party to a pragmatic reformist position was relatively painless.

---

[29] Ibid.

[30] The phrase appeared in the 1944 platform, and every platform thereafter.

Basically, CCF members accepted small-scale capitalist production and only flirted briefly with a socialist solution to the agrarian crisis of the thirties.[31]

Sinclair called his article "The Saskatchewan CCF: Ascent to Power and the Decline of Socialism," a combination that a cynic might be forgiven for saying was no coincidence.

It is just possible that the CCF was kidding itself, as well as the outside world, in laying so much emphasis on the purity of its socialism. It always wanted to be seen as a movement, not a party. But when the bell rang for an election, it looked like a duck, walked like a duck, and quacked like a duck. It was a far more active and interventionist government than in other provinces at that time, but that's all.

Wimpy in Winnipeg?

In 1956, when, after years of internal bickering about exactly how socialist it should be, the CCF got around to revising its vision of the world in the Winnipeg Declaration of Principles, the words "socialism" and "socialist" were notable mainly for their rarity. It was a repeat of the Regina Manifesto in some ways — the goal was still the establishment of a co-operative commonwealth, put in place through democratic socialism — but the language was much less strident and menacing, and the approach to reform was quite different. Gone were the massive nationalizations and state planning apparatus of the earlier document; the new declaration stated that a CCF government would apply public ownership only where it was necessary to break the stranglehold of private monopolies and facilitate social planning. Private business was welcomed, and encouraged to make a healthy contribution to the development of the national economy.[32]

The Winnipeg Declaration was immediately attacked as a shift to the right to appease the newly united labour movement, which, under the Canadian Labour Congress (CLC) banner, was officially launched in April 1956. This was a fair enough criticism; the CLC was certain to

---

[31] Peter R. Sinclair, "The Saskatchewan CCF: Ascent to Power and the Decline of Socialism," *Canadian Historical Review* (December 1973), 433.

[32] Leo Zatuke, *A Protest Movement Becalmed: A Study of Change in the CCF* (Toronto: University of Toronto Press, 1964), 63.

become a major element in CCF circles. Claude Jodoin, who became president of the new body, agreed with the CCF national secretary, David Lewis, that the CLC would commit itself to supporting the party. This labour link was bound to be an element in the party's thinking, whether it offended purists or not.

Maclean's magazine sniffed that with its new statement of principles, there was no reason for the party to exist anymore. (Since *Maclean's* had never seen much need for the party, this was probably a criticism most CCFers were willing to live with.)

Times had changed. Canada in 1956 was a very different country than it had been in 1932, and the Regina Manifesto, in this new world, would have been the equivalent for the party of having a large "Kick me" sign painted on their leader's backside. The rolling, sonorous statements of the Manifesto were more quotable than they were persuasive.

Anthony Crosland, a minister in the Labour cabinet in England, had recently published *The Future of Socialism*, which argued that public ownership was not a necessary adjunct to economic reform because most large companies are run by their managers, not their owners; that Marx was passé; and that private profit, rather than a blight, was to be encouraged in order to increase the tax revenues that any socialist government would need to extend public programs and social planning.[33] Significantly, Crosland was a keynote speaker at the CCF convention. The Winnipeg Declaration sounded more like Anthony Crosland than it did like J.S. Woodsworth. One reason it was treated with editorial scorn by the nation's media was unquestionably that it made quite a lot of sense — and made it more difficult to attack the reforming CCF as a gaggle of hotheads.

Tommy had always been a reformer, never a hothead. He tended to describe the government he ran as socialist because he was comfortable with the term, and uncomfortable with the inequities and iniquities of unbridled capitalism. (Bridled capitalism, he could live with.)

To see real socialism at work — in the sense of government taking an activity that has been entirely a private industry and making it into one

---

[33] C.A.R. Crosland, *The Future of Socialism* (London: Jonathan Cape, 1956).

that is mainly a public industry, both for efficiency and because it is the right thing to do — it is necessary to look at something now embraced, at least on all ritualistic public occasions, by every government of every stripe in Canada: medicare.

_____

Chapter THIRTEEN

Strong Medicine

I think your greatest and enduring accomplishment was the intro-
duction and putting into effect of Medicare in Saskatchewan. Without
your program as a successful one in being, I couldn't have produced
the unanimous report for the Canada-wide universal health recom-
mendations in 1964. If the scheme had not been successful in
Saskatchewan, it wouldn't have become nation-wide. Generations to
come will be your debtors.

— Emmett Hall, in a letter to Tommy Douglas, 1971

Without Tommy Douglas, Canada would not have a universal medicare system (or what's left of one) today. Without Tommy Douglas, Canada's medical system would undoubtedly look very much like the system in place in the United States. The role of government would be, as it is in the United States, to put up some money for those citizens who can prove that they are sufficiently poor to qualify.

Many people may believe that the Liberals would have produced a universal medicare system even without the example the CCF set in Saskatchewan, but then, many people believe that Elvis is still alive. The Liberal Party of Canada put a medicare program into its platform in 1919, but once he won the party leadership, Mackenzie King did what he did best and tucked away the promise in case he might ever need it again. (He didn't have to worry about a subsequent party convention calling him to task because, once elected, he never allowed another party convention to take place.) When the Liberals at last got around to push-ing the program through, forty years later, it was mainly to dish the NDP and to win the 1965 election (at which it was only partly successful).

Left to its own devices, the Liberal government would probably have produced a health insurance plan, but the operation of the system might well have been left entirely in private hands.

The same Liberal convention that promised a federal–provincial scheme for insurance against "unemployment, sickness, old age and other disability" also promised the nation a system of proportional representation.[1] The logic of this electoral reform is less heart-wringing, but just as cogent, as the argument for universal health care, but no province fought for it the way Saskatchewan fought for medicare, and we still don't have it.

Canada's governing parties almost never undertake real reform, reform that is likely to upset their private enterprise financial backers, until and unless they believe that they will be hurt more for not doing the right thing than for doing it. Medicare was no exception.

Otto Shows the Way

The earliest record of joint action to provide medical services on this continent, according to the *Report of the Royal Commission on Health Services*, was a contract signed in 1665 between seventeen residents of Ville Marie (Montreal) and a master surgeon. In 1883, St. Joseph's Hospital in Victoria, British Columbia, offered a plan under which, for one dollar a month, individuals could have their doctor's visits, hospital admission, and medicines covered. That same year, in Glace Bay, Nova Scotia, a colliery offered medical and hospital coverage as part of a collective agreement with its workers. Soon after that, a few hospitals, such as Medicine Hat General Hospital in Alberta and the Hotel Dieu in Chatham, New Brunswick, offered prepayment plans.[2]

In Europe, the idea of a collective arrangement to cover the expenses of illness or accident was much more fully advanced. When Germany emerged as an imperial power under William I in the 1880s, his Iron Chancellor and man of all work, Otto von Bismarck, shoved through a bewildered Reichstag a series of astonishingly liberal reforms. Among them were compulsory old-age insurance and compulsory sickness

---

[1] R. MacGregor Dawson, *William Lyon Mackenzie King: A Political Biography 1874–1923* (Toronto: University of Toronto Press, 1958), 319.

[2] Chapter 1 of *Report of the Royal Commission on Health Services* (Ottawa: Queen's Printer, 1964).

insurance, funded by employer and employee jointly. Bismarck was moved less by the lot of the poor and middle classes who might be stricken with illness than by the need to outflank the socialists after the scribblings of that troublesome wretch Karl Marx became widely circulated.[3] But whatever his motives, his initiatives were soon noted elsewhere.

France passed a National Law for Free Medical Assistance in 1893, under which anyone who could not afford to pay for medicine or for hospital care was treated at no cost. In Britain, the 1905 Royal Commission on the New Poor Law suggested that, in the case of those whose needs could not be covered by private charities, hospital fees should be paid by the state. (Of course, Sidney and Beatrice Webb, in their minority report, went much further, asking that state social services be provided to everyone, not just the poor, to insure against illness and misfortune.)

The Laggard Liberals
By the time the Liberals in Canada got around to advocating universal health insurance — at the convention in 1919 that made Mackenzie King their leader — the reform was not exactly revolutionary. The Liberal proposal recognized that the British North America Act had assigned health to the provinces, and was essentially a plan to persuade the provinces to take part by offering funding assistance from the central government — the solution finally adopted.

Nothing prevented any province that wanted to initiate health insurance coverage from doing so. Nothing except the adamant opposition of the medical establishment, that is. The nation was carpeted with provincial hospital associations, physicians' groups, and private insurance companies, all of which wanted no part of any state-run plans. They preferred prepaid plans of their own (although they would welcome any cash contributions the state might choose to make to support these). In the mid-1930s, when the British Columbia government of William Patullo called a province-wide referendum to test the waters on a medical insurance plan, 59 per cent of the voters plumped in favour. However,

---

[3] Emil Ludwig, *Bismarck*, translated by Eden Paul and Cedar Paul (London: George Allen & Unwin, 1927), 550–51.

the province's doctors soon let the premier know they did not approve and would not co-operate, and the scheme died without subsequent issue. In Newfoundland, the Cottage Hospital and Medical Care plan of 1935 offered insurance to the indigent, but Newfoundland was not part of Canada at the time, and no other eastern jurisdiction showed the slightest inclination to copy Newfoundland. In Quebec, a plan was put forward tentatively in 1942, but was allowed to languish and die when it became clear that the medical establishment would greet it with hostility.

The only province in Canada where any substantive progress had been made was in Saskatchewan itself, and this factor undoubtedly helped the CCF in the 1940s. They were not starting from scratch. In 1914, one Saskatchewan town, about to lose its only doctor, put him on salary and kept him. Two years later, the Union Hospitals Act allowed local municipalities to set up hospitals where townsfolk could receive treatment paid for by the community. Land taxes paid for this service in a handful of towns. In 1939, this coverage was extended by the Patterson government to permit a tax of not more than $50 per family to finance such schemes. Within a few years, 107 municipalities, 59 villages, and 14 towns were paying 180 doctors, some full-time, some part-time, to take care of their citizens.[4] This was not provincial health care, but municipal health care; still, it was a start.

There was another spasm of federal interest during the Depression, as story after story covering the misery inflicted on the ill and elderly by the moribund economy began to appear in the newspapers, and R.B. Bennett's minister of health, D.M. Sutherland, was pressed to take some action. Sutherland replied that he was awaiting the development of a plan that he understood would, in due course, be forthcoming from the Canadian Medical Association. No such plan ever appeared.[5]

A federal department of health had been established in 1919, the same year the Liberals promised a free national medical care service, but it was focussed almost entirely on two goals: preventing venereal disease and promoting physical fitness. In 1943, the total health expenditures of all levels of government in Canada came to $11.2 million; of this, the federal government spent less than 10 per cent.[6]

---

[4] J. Harvey Perry, *A Fiscal History of Canada — The Postwar Years* (Toronto: Canadian Tax Foundation, 1989), 624.
[5] Alvin Finkel, *Business and Social Reform in the Thirties* (Toronto: Lorimer, 1979), 97.
[6] Perry, *Fiscal History of Canada*, 456.

The first time Tommy pronounced clearly what he had in mind was on May 14, 1944, when he spoke at a rally in Biggar (part of M.J. Coldwell's federal riding) in support of the young CCF candidate there. He promised that, if elected, his government would set up "medical, dental and hospital services, available to all, without counting the ability of the individual to pay."[7] When Tommy came to power in 1944, he was working with a province full of people who had a strong background in co-operative effort and some acquaintance with health insurance. He knew that a broad plan was bound to meet with federal indifference and medical obstruction, but his party's directive and his own inclination made him determined to push ahead.

During the 1944 election, the Saskatchewan College of Physicians and Surgeons pronounced that the CCF was a "dangerous element."[8] No matter. The Regina Manifesto called for a health insurance plan, and the CCF repeated the pledge, promising, in words that echoed Tommy's first statement, "medical, dental, and hospital services irrespective of the ability to pay."[9]

This pledge, which was broader than any coverage ever put in place in that it included the costs of dental insurance, was the fourth of nine key promises in the program (the first was "security in your home"). But Tommy emphasized its importance to him when he made himself minister of health, although most governments assigned the portfolio to a doctor in order to ward off hostility from the medical community at the appointment of a non-professional. (In any event, the only doctor in Tommy's cabinet was a veterinarian; the College might not have liked that much better.) Tommy made an effort to get along with the doctors, but never at the expense of policy.

Hospital Insurance
The CCF program did not promise to have the system in place within its first four-year mandate. From the beginning, Tommy believed the way had to be prepared carefully, first by offering coverage to the most needy in the province as soon as possible, then by extending hospital

---

[7] Dianne Lloyd, *Woodrow: A Biography of W.S. Lloyd* (Regina: Woodrow Lloyd Memorial Fund, 1979), 116.

[8] Quoted in McLeod and McLeod, *Road to Jerusalem*, 149.

[9] These were the words used on a small, wallet-sized card distributed during the election.

insurance as a universal benefit, and finally by bringing doctors into the scheme with medicare.

Within months of his first election victory, Tommy had hired Dr. Henry Sigerist, a professor of social and preventive medicine at Johns Hopkins University in Baltimore, to examine the Saskatchewan health care system. Sigerist was told that, as it was his duty to come, he would of course not be receiving any pay. Tommy remembered: "I think he was so astonished that anyone would have the gall to ask him, and then to tell him that we couldn't pay anything except his expenses, that he came."[10] It took Sigerist exactly one month — all the time he could spare — to produce an admirably brief report. Saskatchewan's course of action would be, in the words of an old union song, to "take it easy, boys, but take it":

> The goal is clear, it must be to provide complete medical services to all the people of the Province, irrespective of their economic status, and irrespective of whether they live in town or country.[11]

To achieve this goal, the province would have to build the system gradually, at a pace to be determined by the number of people and the amount of equipment and money that could be devoted to the task. Before the province could offer hospital insurance, much less a full-scale medicare system, a good deal of preliminary work needed to be done.

At that time, Saskatchewan had fewer hospital beds per thousand residents than any other province in Canada. If you want to have hospital insurance, Sigerist said, you had better build some more hospitals.[12] The Health Services Planning Commission was quickly established to get the process underway. It would implement the plan, oversee the progress, and research what should be done next. Tommy brought in two Winnipeg doctors, Cecil and Mindel Sheps, to help. Cecil would serve as chairman of the commission, and his wife, Mindel, as secretary.

By the end of 1944, cancer victims, the mentally ill, and those suffering from venereal disease were receiving both medical care and hospitalization

---

[10] McLeod and McLeod, *Road to Jerusalem,* 147.
[11] *Sigerist Report,* 1944, Saskatchewan Archives, Regina.
[12] Douglas, *The Making of a Socialist,* 227.

at the expense of the state. Early in 1945, the same benefits were extended to old-age pensioners, blind pensioners, mother's allowance recipients, and wards of the state.

The Shepses helped with negotiations to get the College of Physicians and Surgeons, if not onside, at least in a mood to give grudging co-operation. Tommy made a major concession by agreeing that the province would pay doctors on a fee-per-service basis rather than with a flat salary, as many in the CCF felt they should be. This concession built into the system an inflationary element that would later threaten the whole structure. But Tommy felt he needed to ease the concerns of the College, whose members suspected darkly (but correctly) that they were being nudged towards a full-blown state medical system. While the concession did not do much to ease the doctors' fears, they did agree to provide service to the 25,000 patients whose bills were being paid by the province. At the same time, the College put pressure on doctors, making it well-nigh impossible for any doctor who did not want to be ostracized within his or her own profession to accept a salaried post with any clinic or municipality.

While negotiations with the College were being worked out, the construction of hospitals and clinics went ahead. The province was divided into fourteen health regions, each with its own board. Responsibility for building — or renovating, since the province contained thirty-three hospitals that could be restored at a fraction of the cost of building a new one — maintaining, and running the hospitals would remain in the communities, rather than in the hands of bureaucrats in Regina. The province would provide financial support and would try, in turn, to get some money out of the federal government.

In 1948, Ottawa finally agreed to contribute $1,000 per hospital bed, to be matched by the province, for each new bed under the program. No provision was made for expenditures between 1944 and 1948, during which the province spent $1 million on grants to the boards to aid hospital construction, a sum Tommy called, "the price you pay for being too progressive." But he was "glad we didn't wait."[13] So were many patients.

Bake Sales, Yes, Bedpans, No

The first area in Canada to establish a full medicare plan was "Health Region No.1," centred on Swift Current. Full medical care, along with preventive medicine in the form of water-testing and immunization, was paid for by a region-wide special tax. This plan was so successful in providing effective service that it might have been copied right across the province, except that the doctors' union instantly ruled against any other such aberrations.

Dr. Sigerist and the Health Services Planning Commission advised Tommy to introduce a province-wide hospital insurance scheme only gradually (they suggested starting with maternity cases). They argued persuasively that the province lacked the personnel, skill, and experience to undertake such a massive program in one leap. But Tommy worried that the longer he delayed, the more opposition would build up against him.

Early in 1946, Tommy promised to have province-wide hospital insurance in place by January 1, 1947. It was a calculated gamble that his own experts were sure was a blunder. To help his distraught commissioners, he flew to Washington and hired Dr. Fred Mott, the deputy Surgeon General of the United States, to oversee the implementation. Mott was married to a Canadian and had once lived in Montreal. That was enough of an edge for Tommy. Before long, wondering exactly how it had happened, Mott found himself on the way from Foggy Bottom to Pile O' Bones, bringing with him Dr. Len Rosenfeld, another expert in public health administration.

Mott and Rosenfeld agreed with the rest of the commission that the plan could not possibly be implemented on January 1, 1947, as the premier had promised. Showing absolutely none of the charm he could exude when he wanted to, Tommy told them that they would bring in the plan on time, or he would replace them with others who could.[14]

In early December, the entire executive of the Saskatchewan Hospital

---

[13] Ibid.

[14] McLeod and McLeod, *Road to Jerusalem,* 157. Tom McLeod was one of the key figures in promoting and implementing the health care program.

Association marched into Tommy's office to say that their organization would not co-operate with the state's plan to take over their hospitals — hospitals that, in many cases, had been built with community funds raised through churches, private donors, and bake sales. Tommy told them he had no plans, and no time, to handle bedpans. Under the legislation, financing would be centralized and administration decentralized. If they didn't like it, the province would take them over; how would they like that? Since, at this time, unpaid bills amounted to between 30 and 60 per cent of total receipts at various Saskatchewan hospitals, the association's objections vanished like a bedpan sliding under a bed. The hospitals became the plan's biggest boosters.

Despite all the worries, the plan did begin on time, and it succeeded admirably. Within seven years, Saskatchewan was the province with the *most* hospital beds per 1,000 residents.[15] That was a bold beginning; however, everyone (not only the health professionals, but their political masters, too) agreed that to establish a full medicare plan the province needed federal help.

Ottawa Stirs

In 1945, while Saskatchewan was moving its hospital insurance program onto the drawing boards, a Reconstruction Conference of federal and provincial delegates was convened to establish ground rules for the post-war period. As part of this exercise in Grand Thinking, Ottawa laid on the table a plan, adapted from schemes already in place in England and Sweden, for a national health care system, to be implemented in two stages.

The first stage would introduce hospital insurance, general practitioner care, and visiting nurses. The second, once the first was established, would bring in specialist care, dental care, pharmaceutical coverage, and laboratory services. When both stages were in place in three years, the estimated cost would be $250 million a year, of which Ottawa would pay two-thirds and the provinces one-third. Ottawa would also provide health grants and low-cost loans to the provinces to aid in hospital construction.

---

[15] Perry, *Fiscal History of Canada*, 624.

This program was laid out in five pages.[16] It had no detailed plan for implementation, and its estimates of the cost were simply crude guesses. Nobody took it seriously, but Mackenzie King could say, "Well, I tried, didn't I?"

At the conference, Saskatchewan produced the only serious proposal to come from any province, outlining a national hospital insurance scheme based on the plan it was about to implement. The reactions of the other provinces ranged from indifference to outrage. Ontario explained that its health care facilities were already overburdened, and it could not possibly take on anything new for some time to come. In the meantime, poor folk who were not covered by private insurance plans could expire in peace; the system was not yet ready for them. Quebec said health was a provincial matter, and it would look after its people in its own way, in its own time, and thank you very much, *merci beaucoup.* Everybody else yawned.

Disgruntled, but not surprised, Tommy and the Saskatchewan delegation went back to Regina and got on with the job. By the end of 1947, 93 per cent of the provincial population was covered by hospital insurance.

It was not free. The cost was covered by a per capita tax of five dollars per annum, to a maximum of thirty dollars. In addition, a new sales tax of 1 per cent was added to most commodities (upping the 2 per cent sales tax the Liberals had already installed), with the money going directly to the insurance program. While it was never intended that the whole cost of the program should be borne by individuals, Tommy felt that individuals should pay part of the cost because:

> I think people appreciate something if they've paid for it. If you give people a card from Santa Claus entitling them to free hospital services, it is not good psychology. But the amount should be sufficiently small that it doesn't impose financial burdens on anybody.[17]

This was certainly not a particularly socialist view; just common sense. (Recent data suggest that any form of deterrent fee, which is what

---

[16] Canada, Dominion-Provincial Conference, *Report* (Ottawa: King's Printer, 1946), 89–94.

[17] Douglas, *The Making of a Socialist,* 228.

Tommy was advocating, tends to backfire. Doctors, finding that some patients are reluctant to visit them because they are required to come up with a small sum of money, ensure that they face no decline of income by adding new treatments to the patients who will pay the fee. The deterrent does not lower the cost of providing health care; it just shifts more care to fee-payers. When user fees were applied in Saskatchewan in 1968, by a Liberal government, the poor and the elderly cut back their visits by 18 per cent. But doctors simply filled up the available time by seeing more of their other patients. Overall, higher-income patients increased their visits.[18])

In the end, the sales tax covered about one-fifth of the cost of hospital insurance; the per capita tax about two-fifths; and the public purse the other two-fifths, which came, in effect, from the resources royalties brought in by the development of this sector of the economy.

The plan was a success from the start, not only in providing care for thousands who had had none before, but in setting the pace for Canada. Every other province sent officials to Regina to see how the plan worked. British Columbia introduced a parallel plan in 1948, although it bogged down for four years in arguments about how to pay for it; in the end, annual premiums were rejected and replaced by an increase in the sales tax from 3 to 5 per cent. Then Alberta set up its own plan, followed by Nova Scotia.

Ottawa was finally persuaded to act by the examples of Saskatchewan and Alberta, where plans had proven not only effective, but popular; by an extensive study in Ontario that recommended public health coverage; and by a Dominion Bureau of Statistics study, released in 1953, that underlined both the widespread incidence of illness across the nation and the uneven burden of health costs on its people.[19]

Once there was a national clamour for hospital insurance, the federal Liberals decided to follow in front, and began working on a way to help the provinces — which had the jurisdiction, but not the funds — along the way. The subject was raised at a federal–provincial conference in October 1955. At this conference, Prime Minister Louis St. Laurent

---

[18] Linda McQuaig, "User fees are back; but why?" *National Post*, 19 November 2001.
[19] Perry, *Fiscal History of Canada*, 636.

made it clear that federal participation would require the agreement of "a substantial majority of provincial governments representing a substantial majority of the Canadian people."[20] Either Ontario or Quebec had to clamber aboard, or there would be no deal.

This led to meetings of all the health ministers in 1956 and a long-drawn-out series of negotiations to decide who would pay for what. Ontario, where private insurance plans were well established, was finally persuaded to participate by its own research into the sufferings of its citizens who were not covered by the private insurers, and by the argument that Ontario citizens ought not to be deprived of benefits available in the scorned province of Saskatchewan. Ottawa offered to pay each province an amount based on two calculations: 25 per cent of the average cost per capita of hospital services in Canada as a whole, and 25 per cent of the average cost per capita in each province that signed on to the plan. Together, these amounts meant that the federal government would pay about half the cost of provincial health insurance.

In practical terms, this meant that any province that didn't sign on would find that its citizens were paying, through their income taxes, for about half the cost of an important benefit to which they were not entitled, although their neighbours were. This was the leverage that made it impossible to hold out; the same leverage would later be used on behalf of medicare.

The Hospital Insurance and Diagnostic Services Act, passed in April 1957, came into effect on January 1, 1958, and spread across the nation. The last province to join, Quebec, signed up on January 1, 1961. Fourteen years after Saskatchewan had covered its population, the rest of the nation caught up. By this time, the comparatively civilized jockeying of the various parties, including governments, bureaucrats, and the medical profession, had been replaced by the all-out war that attended the introduction of medicare.

Medicare
In 1949, while still premier, Tommy left the health portfolio to take over

---

[20] Ibid., 637.

as minister of co-operative development, but he kept pressing ahead with plans to expand the hospital insurance scheme into medicare. This was part of the CCF platform in every election Tommy fought. By 1959, the finances of the province had been shored up by diversification on the one hand and Clarence Fines's sharp red pencil on the other. Ottawa was now paying half the tab for hospitalization — more than 20 per cent of the provincial budget — and that helped, too.

The late 1950s, besides being chequered with multiple elections at the federal level, saw an increasing acceptance by people everywhere — based on experience and common sense, not ideology — of intervention by the government in the affairs of the people. The welfare state was in gestation, if not actually born, and Saskatchewan was being viewed with anything from grudging acceptance to enthusiasm as the herald and forerunner of that development.

On the other hand, the CCF government that had initiated so many reforms was suffering from tired blood. Tommy had been premier now for fifteen years; he was still popular, but some of the zip had gone. He told Allan Blakeney that he thought the party needed to be re-energized.[21] What better way to bring this about than to introduce medicare?

The CCF was still in power, but its share of the vote had slipped from a comfortable 52 to an uncomfortable 45 per cent of the vote — not the right direction in which to travel. Moreover, there was no longer any point in waiting for the federal Liberals to live up to their promises of four decades earlier; they were no longer in power. After twenty-two years of government, they had been dumped out of office — first tentatively, in 1957, then thoroughly, in 1958. John Diefenbaker, the Conservative leader, showed very little inclination to tackle medicare. While the Liberals would later claim credit for introducing the nation-wide plan, the record shows that, year after year, Tommy asked Ottawa to consider contributing to a pilot program in Saskatchewan, since the other provinces seemed to be uninterested, and time after time, he was ignored. The Tories held to that proud tradition.

Tommy announced his government's intention to proceed in April 1959

---

[21] Allan Blakeney, interview by author, Saskatoon, 24 October 2000.

and spelled out the proposal in the legislature on December 16, 1959. The details of the plan, including how it was to be financed, would have to be worked out by a special committee, but the basic principles were not open to negotiation. They were:

- Patients would not be billed; medical care would be prepaid by the state.
- The plan would be universal; everyone would be covered, regardless of age, income, or physical disability.
- Medicare would not be financed by siphoning funds away from other areas of health service.
- The plan would be operated under government control, not private insurance companies.
- The legislation would have to be acceptable to both the public and the medical profession before it came into effect.[22]

Tommy expected, and announced that he expected, the Saskatchewan program to become the model for Canada:

> If we can do this — and I feel sure we can — then I would like to hazard the prophecy that before 1970 almost every other province in Canada will have followed the lead of Saskatchewan.[23]

The fourth of Tommy's conditions went directly against the stated policy of the Canadian Medical Association that their members would accept only a scheme operating through existing organizations, that is, private insurers. There were to be no state plans.[24] Government-run medicine was communism at worst, socialism at best, the CMA said, and would lead us all to dusty ruin. Bureaucrats would tell physicians how to practise, and their freedom would vanish.

The injuries heaped on the heads of the profession by this controversial fourth point in the Saskatchewan proposal were to be assuaged by

[22] Edwin A. Tollefson, *Politics in Saskatchewan* (Don Mills, ON: Longmans, 1968), 238.
[23] Quoted in McLeod and McLeod, *Road to Jerusalem,* 195.
[24] Perry, *Fiscal History of Canada,* 607.

the provision that they would have to approve the plan before it came into being. This was based on Tommy's supposition that he could, as in the case of hospitalization, get around the entrenched opposition of the doctors. He failed to realize that, fired by a constant drum roll of propaganda, not only from the CMA, but also from its elder and more belligerent brother, the American Medical Association, the doctors were more determined than ever to block state medicine. He would soon find out. (Woodrow Lloyd, then his education minister, warned him that the doctors would not give way, but Tommy, while he had a great respect for Lloyd, simply thought he was wrong.)

The CCF had called elections every four years; it was clear that this initiative would be tested by the voters in the spring of 1960, and it was.

The Beautiful Balloon — Fee for Service

In the meantime, the College of Physicians and Surgeons had made clear its continued opposition to a plan that, it stated, would turn doctors into salaried employees of the state, like teachers, instead of proud professionals, like lawyers. Tommy had already accepted fee for service when hospital insurance was introduced, and he repeated this. Too bad. The doctors simply didn't believe him, or wouldn't listen to him.

He gained nothing by this concession. It might have been better for him to have faced this problem at once. Fee for service is the fastest known way to balloon costs, whether it is your doctor deciding that he needs to see that arm of yours again, or your auto mechanic tapping your engine block mournfully and pronouncing, "I don't like the sound of that." He isn't going to charge you for the time worked on your car; instead, he has a chart that tells him that it takes two hours to put air in a tire, or whatever, and he is going to charge you two hours, whether it takes two hours or five minutes. That is how medicine works, too, which is why doctors go to Florida, and garage owners join them on the golf course.

There was, of course, a battle over the composition of the special committee that would be assigned the task of designing medicare, and again, Tommy gave way. The Advisory Planning Committee on Medical Care was expanded to include three nominees from the College of Physicians and Surgeons, who went to work to delay the committee report past the deadline of December 1960 that had been given when the committee was set up. They succeeded, with the result that the medicare battle spilled over into another imbroglio. Tommy by this time was very much involved with the creation of the New Democratic Party, and he had hoped to have medicare in place before he left Saskatchewan to take up that challenge. It was not to be.

The 1960 election was fought on the clear issue of medicare. The CMA helped the doctors raise more than $100,000, a very considerable election war chest at that time, to convince Saskatchewan voters that they were being led into the swamps of socialism. The doctors contributed more than $65,000 of this sum by way of a "voluntary levy" arranged by the College. Actually, the propaganda this produced probably worked against the doctors. Saskatchewan citizens, who had seen the health insurance plan working so well for thirteen years, simply didn't believe the preposterous claims that the government was getting ready to bring in "the garbage of Europe" to tend patients in Saskatchewan, or that women might be confined to insane asylums when they suffered from nothing more than menopausal problems, because of the wickedness of the bureaucrats.[25]

Tommy described the campaign as "abominable, despicable and scurrilous."[26] That was about right.

Ross Thatcher, the new Liberal leader, who had started his political life as a CCFer (although no one who interviewed him in those early days saw him as anything but a maverick, and a free enterprise maverick at that), trotted out his own medicare plan, which might or might not be universal in its coverage, but which would be "free enterprise" in its organization, and would be acceptable to the doctors. His government would hold a special plebiscite before adopting medicare, Thatcher asserted. Apparently the election didn't count.

The CCF won that election handily, but the government was unable

[25] Tollefson, *Politics in Saskatchewan*, 243.
[26] Quoted in *Leader-Post* (Regina), 27 May 1960.

to move ahead on the mandate thus conferred because the advisory committee was still embroiled in argument. By November 1960, it had still not held any public hearings, and showed no signs whatever of getting on with the job.

One of the problems in dealing with the doctors was that Tommy had appointed as his health minister a man whom Tom McLeod described as "the most incompetent minister in the history of the CCF."[27] J. Walter Erb kept telling the doctors what they wanted to hear, rather than what the cabinet had decided, a process that led to increasing bitterness and misunderstanding on both sides. Other ministers repeatedly asked Tommy to get rid of Erb and replace him with either Allan Blakeney, who by this time was a rising star in cabinet, or Woodrow Lloyd. But Tommy, ever loyal to his subordinates, would not be moved.

In June 1961, Tommy announced that he was going to leave Saskatchewan once more to run for the position of leader of the NDP at the new party's August convention, but he was determined to do his best to bring in a medicare bill before he resigned as premier. He asked the committee to produce at least an interim report, and over the stonewalling and objections of the three doctor members, it did so, in September 1961. This report, produced without any support from the doctors, recommended a medicare system that would be universal but would be financed by personal premiums and based on fee-for-service payments to doctors. The patient would be responsible for paying part of this fee at the time of service.[28]

This proposal did not violate any of the original five conditions laid down, and it appeared to be the best compromise the committee could achieve. Tommy immediately called a special session of the legislature to introduce the Medical Care Insurance Act, which differed from the report in one important way: the entire cost of the program would be borne by general revenues; there would be no premiums and no deterrent fees. Tommy had not changed his mind that something for nothing was a bad idea; rather, he gave way to the opinions of his colleagues in cabinet.

---

[27] McLeod and McLeod, *Road to Jerusalem*, 199.
[28] Advisory Planning Committee on Medical Care, *Interim Report*, Regina, 1962, 118–21.

The bill was not clear on how the doctors should be paid; fee for service was not at that time part of the deal. The cabinet could not make up its mind on this point and passed the issue back to the committee to deal with in a final report.

The Liberals voted in favour of the bill on second reading, approval in principle, and then voted against it on third and final reading. This would allow them to claim credit for any virtues of the legislation while condemning any shortcomings.

Royal assent was given on November 17, 1961, by which time Tommy was no longer premier. He had been elected NDP leader in August, and resigned as premier on November 1, 1961. The task of implementing his dream was passed to his successor, Woodrow Lloyd. Lloyd, a schoolteacher, and a long, bald, serious man, was at least as tenacious as Tommy, but no match for him — who was? — in the rough and tumble of political debate.

Lloyd was not as loyal as Tommy and ousted Erb from the health portfolio, although he kept him in the cabinet, as minister of public works. Dissatisfied at his demotion, Erb jumped to the Liberals.

In the meantime, the new health minister, W.G. Davies, wrote to the president of the College of Physicians and Surgeons, requesting a meeting to talk about implementing the legislation, only to receive a straight-arm. The College would not co-operate in any way.

A new commission, the Medical Care Insurance Commission, was established, but only two physicians of any stature in the province would agree to serve on it. This meant more delays while another attempt to sweeten the College was undertaken; the implementation of the act, originally set for April 1, 1962, was pushed back to July 1. The stall allowed the government more time to prepare administration; it allowed the doctors more time to prepare for a strike.

The Regina *Leader-Post* weighed in with a "survey" purporting to show that 60 per cent of the doctors they contacted were prepared to leave the province to practise elsewhere if the government did not withdraw the plan. It turned out that, in fact, the newspaper had surveyed sixty-three doctors. Actually, they had surveyed a number of doctors who represented groups of doctors, they said, that added up to a total of sixty-three. Exactly seven of the doctors the newspaper spoke to were prepared to leave.[29]

Woodrow Lloyd responded with a telegram to the province's agent general in England: "Get some British doctors. Fly them in."[30]

Keep Our Doctors

In the middle of the hubbub, on June 18, in an atmosphere of fear, tension, and concern, Tommy ran in a Regina riding in a federal general election. He lost to a Conservative, Ken More, by nearly 10,000 votes. His party won only 19 seats nationally, on less than 14 per cent of the vote. (Tommy had to wait, until Erhart Regier resigned to make way for him in British Columbia, to win a seat in a by-election in November.)

Thirteen days after Tommy's humiliation, on July 1 — a date that served the striking physicians well; many of them were going on holidays then — the strike began. News reporters from all over Canada, as well as from the United States, the U.K., and other parts of Europe, turned up to cover the work stoppage, and their reports were much more even-handed than those of the Saskatchewan dailies. Very quickly, the doctors went from picked-on medicos to bullies in the eyes of most Canadians outside Saskatchewan. Premier Lloyd used the press to repeat his willingness to modify the medicare scheme in any way that would not violate its basic principles. The College of Physicians and Surgeons insisted that the legislation must be withdrawn entirely and at once, before the province was denuded of doctors.

An outfit called Keep Our Doctors, which had sprung up some months before, organized a huge cavalcade from all parts of the province to converge on the legislature, "to impress on the government the will of the people of Saskatchewan."[31] (Apparently, once more, the election didn't count as an expression of that will.)

The *Leader-Post* strongly supported the idea that the legislature should not be allowed to make the law. A blistering editorial denounced the

[29] C.H. Higginbotham, *Off the Record in Saskatchewan* (Toronto: McClelland & Stewart, 1968), 124.

[30] Patrick MacFadden, *The Media Game*, quoted in John Robert Colombo's *New Canadian Quotations* (Edmonton: Hurtig, 1987).

[31] Quoted in Higginbotham, *Off the Record*, 126.

government for trying to proceed with legislation on the flimsy grounds that it had just won an election based on that legislation. Its praise was unstinting for those heroes who

> devoted an immense amount of energy in fighting the tyranny of determined men who are obsessed with the notion that the support of the majority of members of the legislature justifies the use of this power in the name of allegedly democratic majority rule to foist their own will on the people.[32]

If you read this three times, it makes a sort of weird logic. Governments do not have the right to pass laws just because people vote for them.

The organizers of the cavalcade that would make this dictum known to the legislators promised a mammoth gathering, with advance estimates putting the crowds expected at anywhere upwards from 20,000. Fewer than 5,000 turned up, and the most notable of these was Liberal leader Ross Thatcher, who enlivened the day by demanding a special sitting of the legislature to meet the emergency. For the cameras, he stomped up the legislative steps and kicked on the door several times. (On due consideration, somebody at the Regina *Leader-Post* decided that this photograph ought not to be published, because it made Thatcher look like an idiot, and it was stashed in a special file for "sensitive" pictures in the office.[33])

The strike lasted for twenty-three days, with only emergency services available. Nobody died as a result.[34]

The doctors were losing the propaganda war, but it wasn't doing the province any good, either. To sort the whole mess out, Lord Robert Taylor, who had been instrumental in establishing the British medicare system, was brought in as a referee, and a twenty-nine-point compromise

---

[32] Editorial, *Leader-Post* (Regina), 15 June 1962.

[33] Which is where I saw it. The same file contained a picture of Thatcher beneath the wing of an airplane with Prairie Farm Rehabilitation Act markings. He used this federal transport for campaigning, which was a no-no. The markings were painted out on the photo the newspaper ran, but the original remained on file. Concealing the photo did no good. *Time* magazine had its own picture and ran it, and Thatcher was made to appear like a — how shall I say this? — petulant fathead.

[34] Actually, deaths went down as a ratio of the general population during this period, and I got ready to write a story about this, until I discovered that this was probably due to the fact that patients *in extremis* were moved out of province just before the strike began. Another good story lost.

was reached, which, among other things, allowed doctors to practise outside the plan if they chose. Very few chose to: the doctors soon found that, for the first time, they were paid in full and on time, and they could order necessary treatments for their patients with the assurance that they would be provided, even if the patient had no money.

Dr. Efstahios Barootes, the Regina urologist who led had the strike against "state medicine," became a staunch defender of the system. He explained, "I have changed my mind."[35]

To pay for the new system, which allowed doctors 85 per cent of the schedule of fees approved by the College, Saskatchewan increased the sales tax from 3 to 5 per cent, raised corporate and personal income taxes by 22 per cent, and charged an annual premium of $12 for individuals or $24 for a family (this was later dropped).

This sum represented an increase in expenditures, and therefore of taxes, of one-fifth. However — and this is the part of the argument that seems to get lost — individual taxpayers were being relieved of much higher costs. Financially, they were ahead of the game[36] — and enjoyed a much higher standard of medical practice, in most cases.

For the first time, illness or accident was not the inevitable precursor of ruin for the average Canadian.

The Hall Report

The immediate success of the Saskatchewan plan put a good deal of pressure on the minority government of John Diefenbaker. In the June 1962 election, the Tories won 116 seats and the Liberals 100. Diefenbaker had to keep putting together a majority with the help of the Socreds, who held 30 seats, and the NDP. The NDP kept pressing for a national scheme to match that in Saskatchewan, and Diefenbaker put off the evil day in the usual way by appointing a royal commission.

To head it, he named an old friend and fellow Conservative, Emmett Hall of Saskatoon, by now one of Her Majesty's ermine-robed justices of the Supreme Court of Canada. Hall had no particular views about

[35] Quoted in *Maclean's*, 22 December 1996.
[36] Perry, *Fiscal History of Canada*, 641.

medicare when he began his exhaustive study, but, by the time he brought back a report in 1964, he was sure of one thing: Canada needed a system like Saskatchewan's. Private enterprise could never do the job well; only a government plan would serve. Canada could afford, and must afford, a national medicare program, because there was something fundamentally unfair about a system that gave health care only to those who could pay for it:

> Economic growth is not the sole aim of our society and, given the growing wealth of Canada, economic considerations should not solely be used to deny to individuals the health services needed to alleviate illness and disability and to extend life expectancy. Although we recognize that resources are limited, and individuals cannot expect to receive unlimited amounts of health care, the value of a human life must be decided without regard to whether the person is a producer or not. Health services must not be denied to certain individuals simply because the latter make no contribution to the economic development of Canada or because he cannot pay for such services. Important as economics is we must also take into account the human and spiritual aspects involved.[37]

The report recommended that the government "should make the fruits of all health sciences available to all our residents without hindrance of any kind."[38]

The Hall Report was the beginning, not the end, of the final struggle at the federal level. In his book on the inner operations of government, Tom Kent, who was Prime Minister Lester Pearson's policy adviser at the time of this struggle, and a fervent believer in medicare, writes that the Hall Report "took much of the wind out of the opponents of medicare."[39] But grave problems remained. "It did not, however, help to

---

[37] Chapter 12 of *Report of the Royal Commission on Health Services* (Ottawa: Queen's Printer, 1964).
[38] "Conclusions and Recommendations," *Report of the Royal Commission on Health Services* (Ottawa: Queen's Printer, 1964), 1.
[39] Tom Kent, *A Public Purpose* (Kingston and Montreal: McGill–Queen's University Press, 1988), 364.

solve the main problem faced by a Pearson government already committed to medicare."[40]

The interesting point in this very clear account of what was going on was how the Pearson government became committed to medicare. At least in part, this was because Tom Kent kept hammering it over the head with the arguments that were unrolling as the Hall Commission gathered evidence. And in part it was because a number of cabinet ministers, including Paul Martin, the secretary of state for external affairs, Walter Gordon, at this time a minister without portfolio, and Judy LaMarsh, the health minister, were in favour. But a great many other cabinet ministers of at least equal power, such as Mitchell Sharp and Robert Winter, were adamantly opposed, and the prime minister, as usual, just wanted peace in the family.

The Liberals espoused medicare in the 1965 election because it desperately needed to patch together a majority government, after two minority governments in a row. The 1965 election was called, in fact, for no other reason than to produce a majority (Walter Gordon, who had advised this election, resigned when it returned, instead, yet another minority). One obvious way to gain a majority was to cash in votes that would otherwise be deposited on the Liberals' left, in the NDP. During the past year, Hall, in an extraordinary departure from custom, instead of leaving his report to gather dust, had gone out on the hustings to battle for its implementation, and quickly. Canadian newspapers were now full of stories of the appalling consequences for families devastated by illness. One of those families was that of Judy LaMarsh, whose father's lifetime savings had been "swiftly swallowed" by her mother's cancer.[41] That helped the argument.

Pearson presented Canada with two main arguments for his re-election. One (very hard to sell in view of the internal battles that shook the general air from time to time) was that only a united Liberal government could preserve the nation at a time of rising separatist sentiment. The other was that, if elected, his government would have a national medicare scheme in place by July 1, 1967, the Canadian centennial.

---

[40] Ibid.

[41] Judy LaMarsh, *Memoirs of a Bird in a Gilded Cage* (Toronto: McClelland & Stewart, 1969), 121.

Tommy argued during the campaign that to give the Liberals a majority would be "just like giving them a tranquilizer" and another opportunity "to push things under the rug."[42]

When the din died, the Liberals had 131 seats, the Tories 97, the NDP 21, the Socreds 5, and the new Ralliement Créditiste 9. If the Liberals had dumped, or even delayed, the promise to bring in medicare, their hold on power would not have lasted long.

Now that the Pearson government was "committed to medicare" by the fullness of time and the exigencies of necessity, the sticker was that most of the provinces were still opposed. How could a universal plan, financed at least in part by the provinces, be imposed on them against their will?

The solution was offered by Al Johnson, who had been deputy provincial secretary of Saskatchewan when medicare was introduced there and was now assistant deputy minister of finance:

> The federal government did not need to legislate the details of a shared-cost program; it needed only to define, clearly, the principles of what was meant by medicare. Then it would contribute to the costs of any provincial program that satisfied those principles.[43]

Ottawa would pay an amount equal to half the average national per capita costs of any provincial scheme that met the guidelines. This approach not only got around the constitutional hurdle of provincial control of health services, but attempted to control the eventual cost, since any province that spent more than the national average would not get anything more than half that average out of Ottawa.

The guidelines that the provincial regimes had to meet were mostly familiar from the Saskatchewan plan, with one additional element brought about by the fact that this plan was to apply across the country:

- All services provided by medical doctors under the plan must be covered (dental care and pharmacare were discarded as too expensive).

[42] Quoted in Beck, *Pendulum of Power,* 384.
[43] Kent, *Public Purpose,* 367.

- The plan must be universal, covering everyone in the province on the same terms (deterrent fees and extra billing were possible under this point, but minimum coverage on a universal basis was guaranteed).
- The plan had to be publicly administered; it did not have to be run by provincial bureaucrats, but the province had to establish and maintain full responsibility.
- Benefits had to be transferable between provinces,

It was the Saskatchewan plan writ large.

Although the plan had to be universal, as in Saskatchewan, not all doctors in a province had to join (although most did at once). The Liberals did not, in fact, implement this plan on July 1, 1967, as promised; because of continuing opposition within the cabinet, mostly on the grounds of expense, it was delayed until the NDP made it clear that more delays might bring the government down. It came into effect on July 1, 1968, not quite half a century after the Liberals had first put it into their platform.

A number of provinces — especially those who had developed plans of their own more along the lines of projects approved by the Canadian Medical Association — were outraged. The Ontario Medical Services Insurance Plan, for example, left medical care in the hands of private insurers and simply paid the bills for those who were not already covered by employer plans (the American model). It was not universal, it was not publicly administered, and it was not transferable.

Ontario Premier John Robarts fumed:

> Medicare is a glowing example of a Machiavellian scheme that is in my humble opinion one of the greatest political frauds that has ever been perpetrated on this country.[44]

The constitution assigned health to the provinces; now Ottawa was taking over, and any province that didn't go along would be helping to foot the bill for the rest. No wonder he was sore.

---

[44] Perry, *Fiscal History of Canada*, 645.

But, vowing she would ne'er consent, Ontario consented, signing on to medicare on October 1, 1969.

Quebec passed its own Health Insurance Act in March 1970, limiting the number of doctors who could opt out of the scheme to 3 per cent. This led to a brief doctors' strike, but by the end of 1970, every province in the nation had signed on. Medicare was a national phenomenon and quickly became so popular, especially with the vast majority of doctors, that Canadians took to calling it one of the most important elements that define this nation as distinct from the United States.

The Liberals, of course, swiped the credit. Judy LaMarsh called it "the last great stone in a buttress against life's natural hazards," and "one of the crowning achievements of the Pearson administration."[45]

Well, okay. But the crown was designed by, fashioned by, paid for by, worn by, and handed on by Tommy Douglas. The battles were nearly all fought on Saskatchewan soil, and the constant bickering and controversy led to not only Tommy's personal defeat in the federal election of 1962, but the defeat of the Lloyd government in 1964. Woodrow Lloyd was often asked if he thought Tommy had deserted the province when he went to the NDP as national leader (he was asked three times by me, to come right down to it); he always said no. Tommy had stayed on to fight as hard as he could, and indeed, one of his outstanding public speeches was delivered in the legislature on October 13, 1961, when he was already the NDP leader and was on the verge of retiring from provincial politics forever.[46]

In the circumstances, the Liberal claim to having established medicare seems depressingly like a man being marched off the gangplank at sword-point pausing before the plunge to announce that he is so glad he decided to take this swim.

---

[45] LaMarsh, *Memoirs*, 122.
[46] In Lovick, *Tommy Douglas Speaks*.

Chapter FOURTEEN

Wilderness Empire

This man Douglas is — well, how'll I put it? He's a good deed in a naughty world. He's a breath of clean prairie air in a stifling climate of payola and chicanery and double-talk and pretense, global and local . . . He was and is a dreamer and a humanitarian, incorruptible, genuine and intellectually honest.
— Jack Scott, *Vancouver Sun*, 1962

While the medicare battle was first looming and then blooming, Tommy was distracted by the formation of what was to become the New Democratic Party. Like his mentor and friend, M.J. Coldwell, Tommy had some doubts about the new party, but, again like M.J., once he overcame these doubts, he went ahead with his usual drive and enthusiasm to help construct a political entity that would at last sweep the old parties to one side and launch the nation in a new direction. The trouble is, it never happened. When the New Democrats made breakthroughs, they were in provincial legislatures, not in Ottawa.

Something had to be done. Frank Scott, who had played such a crucial role in founding the party in the first place, was now the national president of the CCF. In his annual address in 1950, he suggested that it was time to come up with a new statement of objectives. In the mere flick of an eye (six years later), the party brought forth the Winnipeg Declaration, notable for its sanity and disappointing for its sanity. All the party's enemies, and even its friends, agreed it was a shame that the CCF had given up the bold and ringing rhetoric of the Regina Manifesto, beside which the Winnipeg Declaration sounded, well, wimpy. Some talk of "political realignment" was in the air, but nothing immediate came of it.

Negotiating a Settlement

While the CCF was running hard to stay in one place, its labour affiliation was growing more muscular by the year. David Lewis, who had
been the national secretary of the CCF for fifteen years, stepped down
from that post at the 1950 convention, to be succeeded by Lorne Ingle.
Lewis went back to being a labour lawyer so he could make some
money to support his family. But he was made a vice-chairman, along
with Thérèse Casgrain ("chairperson" was not in vogue yet), at the same
convention, and became the national chairman in 1954. Whatever his
title, he remained a potent force within the party, and worked ceaselessly
to make it as much like the British Labour party as possible in a different
milieu.

Lewis was the key liaison between the party and the labour movement; thus when Local 649 of the Oil Workers International Union
threatened to go on strike in the spring of 1955, and Premier Douglas of
Saskatchewan, the only socialist government in the nation, threatened to
impose arbitration, Lewis was placed in a considerable bind. On the one
hand, the union was entitled to strike to gain its ends; on the other, the
premier was certainly right when he told the union he was not going to
allow it to shut down this vital industry in a province where temperatures
of twenty-five below Fahrenheit were common:

> Much as we would dislike making arbitration compul-
> sory, I think you will agree that it would be an act of
> complete irresponsibility for us to stand idly by and
> permit a strike in an industry which affects the lives and
> welfare of thousands of our people.[1]

To make things worse, at this time two giant Canadian labour groups,
the Canadian Congress of Labour and the Trades and Labor Congress,
were moving towards their union, in 1956, as the Canadian Labour
Congress. Lewis hoped to swing this united body behind the CCF, and
Tommy was threatening to enrage them. (In his memoirs, though, Lewis

---

[1] Quoted in Lewis, *The Good Fight*, 407.

makes it clear that "I felt the Saskatchewan government was right, and I admired Douglas's firmness."[2])

The solution was ingenious. Tommy phoned Lewis with the suggestion (which amused him, although it did not amuse Lewis) that he should come out to Regina to negotiate a settlement. And that is what happened. This incident proved to Lewis, if it needed any proving, that Tommy was both principled and clever. It also proved that he was a politician first and a union man second. Everybody seemed to forget that.

Political Realignment

In January 1956, at a meeting of the National Council, Tommy mused that the party was not, all in all, rushing towards victory, and suggested "a new type of federation or the same type of federation enlarged for a genuine farmer-labour-socialist movement in Canada. I think that ought to be our aim."[3] (In 2001, the successor party would be engaged in the same sort of daydreaming.) Tommy got a good round of applause for this suggestion of realignment, whether the delegates believed it would work or not.

The 1957 general federal election brought in another minority government, but this time a Conservative one, and encouraged many in the CCF, including Tommy, to think that the Liberals were at last on the downward slope, clearing the way for the nation to divide on natural left–right lines, with the CCF on the left and the Conservatives on the right. The CCF won 25 seats, 3 of them in Ontario. Tommy told the provincial convention five weeks after the election to remember that, in the 1930s, Labour had replaced the Liberals in Britain to offset the Conservative party there: "I am confident that the same political realignment will eventually take place in Canada. As a matter of fact it is already taking place."[4] Actually, the Liberal Party of Canada was more like the cat who came back the very next day: "they thought he was a goner, but he just wouldn't stay away."

The national CCF party was not in good shape; its finances, as usual, were desperate. Its budget for the 1957 election was $20,000, a risible

---

[2] Ibid.

[3] National Council Minutes, 15–17 January 1956, CCF Papers, National Archives of Canada.

[4] Speech to the convention, 17 July 1957, Douglas Collection, Saskatchewan Archives, Regina.

figure even then. M.J. Coldwell had suffered a mild heart attack, and Stanley Knowles and Tommy had taken over making the major election speeches for him in much of the west. The thought must have crossed Tommy's mind that M.J., who was then sixty-nine, would have to be replaced before long, and that, as the only elected head of government in his party, he was bound to be considered as a candidate. But if so, he kept his views strictly to himself.

Then came the 1958 vote, which saw the Diefenbaker Tories sweep to a massive majority — 208 seats in a house of 265 (a majority that, it turned out, Diefenbaker could never control). In that election, the CCF was whacked back down to 8 seats. Moreover, both Coldwell and Stanley Knowles lost their seats, costing the party the most (perhaps the only) level-headed members of the caucus.

The party was ahead of its initial position in 1935 by only one seat (and, of course, the 1935 House had contained only 245 seats). In 1958, the CCF was attracting one out of every ten voters, a mere sliver more than it had in 1935. It was time to regroup.

Stanley Knowles, having been defeated in Winnipeg North Centre, was promptly elected as an executive vice-president of the new Canadian Labour Congress, and as promptly was put to work to bring a new party into being. The CLC convention that elected him at Winnipeg in April 1958 passed a resolution introduced by Eamon Park of the Steelworkers, calling on labour to "take part in the formation of a new political instrument."[5] Park told the delegates that the time had come for the trade union movement to depart from its traditional policy of merely supporting the CCF and to take the lead in establishing a new political voice in Canada: "CCF-plus" we would call it today.

Labour Unrest
A great many things were said at the 1958 CLC convention, though a couple of them were merely whispered. This new body was, delegates were told repeatedly, not a labour party, but a grouping of farm, labour, and other voices interested in the same goals.[6] What was not said was

---

[5] Stanley Knowles, *The New Party* (Toronto: McClelland & Stewart, 1961), 35.
[6] The wording of the resolution embraced "the CCF, interested farm organizations and other like-minded individuals and groups." Canadian Labour Congress Convention, 21–25 April 1958, *Report*, CCF Papers, National Archives of Canada.

that Canada was now an urban nation; the farm vote was not nearly as important as it had been when the CCF was launched (Canada's farm population was just over 31 per cent in the 1931 census, just over 11 per cent in 1961). In fact, the new party would be dependent on labour for much of its financing, manpower, and expertise. This aspect concerned many of the CCF's stalwarts, including its leader, M.J. Coldwell, who, in a private letter to a friend, wrote: "I've never been enthusiastic about a CCF-Labour alliance. It may work out, but labour has been for us a weak reed."[7]

A labour-linked party would go at the business of attaining office in a more energetic way than had the CCF, which had never been able to advance beyond the role of national conscience and nag, except in Saskatchewan. Organized labour had something more muscular in mind that meant a softening of some of the old policy stances. In particular, the new party would place much less emphasis on socialism, public ownership, and national economic planning and more emphasis on practical reforms.

David Lewis, in his memoirs, argued that the CCF had always aimed for power:

> There was never any doubt that the considerable educational efforts, the literature, and the meetings were intended to win support for the CCF as the political instrument of the people. From the first, the CCF was intended to be an electoral political party.[8]

But Tommy, as we have seen, had a different approach. He believed the CCF should strive for power, but not at any price. In trying to balance the need to attain power to promote good policy, and the need to trim policy to gain some lift towards power, Tommy believed the party should form and stick to sound policies and spend most of its efforts trying to get the public to catch up. He felt that the CCF, in changing its name and emphasis, would be turning its back on its own history and on the farm roots that had been so important in the beginning. This might make sense in Ontario, but not in Saskatchewan.

---

[7] Quoted in Smith, *Love & Solidarity*, 152.
[8] Lewis, *The Good Fight,* 447.

Tommy received a good deal of concerned opinions as the new party was being formed. Doug Fisher, one of the most outspoken critics of the change, wanted to know, "What are we cutting ourselves off from J.S. Woodsworth for?"[9]

Jack Corman, Tommy's attorney general, put his views in more general terms:

> The CCF, despite its inability to poll the votes to form a national government, has won the esteem and respect of Canadians for its inspired unselfishness, progressive leadership and its dogged advocacy of humanitarian reform ... the CCF has not been a failure, but a glorious success.[10]

The enthusiasts for change, led by Lewis and Knowles, were not at all sure that a glorious success was the right term to describe a national party sitting at 10 per cent in the polls and invisible in Quebec. They easily persuaded most of the party that sentiment was not as important as electability.

Knowles produced a book, *The New Party*, that laid out the argument clearly: with a new organization, the CCF would rise like the phoenix from the dead ashes of its former self, propelled by labour muscle, labour moxie, and labour money:

> To appreciate the extent to which Canadian labour has struggled with the whole question of political action, the many ways it has tried to achieve the implementation of its legislative aims, is to realize that the decision to join with others in forming the New Party is one that is soundly based. It signifies labour's sense of mission, labour's determination to win a better life, not only for its own members, but for all the people of this country.[11]

---

[9] Quoted in McLeod and McLeod, *Road to Jerusalem,* 208.
[10] Ibid.
[11] Knowles, *New Party*, 20.

If by "labour" Knowles meant the current leadership of the CLC and most of its larger member unions, this was a shrewd summary; if he meant the rank and file, he ran up against the fact that most of them still voted either Liberal or Conservative. What would now be tested was whether most of them would vote for the new party (pardon, New Party).

CCF Outvoted

Tommy was a key member of the National Council and the National Committee to Form the New Party. It was his task to promote the new party once the decision to go ahead had been accepted by the council. To what extent he was influenced by the fact that he had been premier for close to two decades and needed a new challenge is unclear.

His private vacillations about the new party appeared in letters to friends and colleagues such as Carl Hamilton, who had replaced Lorne Ingle as the national secretary: "I am not prepared to submerge the identity of the CCF unless I know what we are joining and with whom."[12] Far from shedding the CCF's affiliation with farmers, he suggested that the new group should clasp them to its union-label long johns: "My own feeling is that if prairie farmers are going to get their fair share of the national income, they must seek allies in their fight for economic justice."[13]

Tommy was disturbed that the CCF and CLC were pushing ahead with their wedding without consulting, as it were, the father of the bride: not a single farm group of any importance was in the mix. To address this problem, Tommy — along with Donald MacDonald, the CCF leader in Ontario, and Hazen Argue, the CCF MP for Assiniboia and the House Leader in the new, M.J.-less caucus — set out to invite the farmers to the wedding. They all declined, including the farm organizations in Saskatchewan, which were, in the main, fans of the CCF government (although many of them were also fans of John Diefenbaker and his Tories, especially when his government concluded massive grain deals with the Russians). They saw the new party as one likely to be dominated by eastern labour, and they were content to sit tight and await developments.

---

[12] Douglas to Hamilton, 26 August 1959, Douglas Collection, Saskatchewan Archives, Regina.
[13] Quoted in McLeod and McLeod, *Road to Jerusalem,* 209.

Tommy wanted the process of launching the new venture slowed down. In his view, the new party was not yet ready to emerge; it was not clear what it stood for, or whom it would represent. And when his suggestion that the founding convention be held in Winnipeg was rejected, his misgivings were compounded. He argued that such a venue would help to ease fears that all the shots were being called by easterners bent on winning the support of the labour movement at any price. But in February 1960, David Lewis, by now the national president of the CCF, and Stanley Knowles, who was both a CCF vice-president and a CLC executive vice-president, came to Regina to tell the Douglas cabinet that the convention would be held in Ottawa in July 1961.

Tommy had also wanted the voting at the convention to be evenly split between CCF delegates and labour delegates. Again Knowles and Lewis said no. As part of the change, New Party clubs, made up of CCFers and anyone else who cared to join, had been formed to raise money, enthusiasm, and energy, and these clubs would have to be represented. The CCF would, in the end, select 45 per cent of the delegates, the New Party clubs 25 per cent, and the labour groups 30 per cent.

Tommy argued that the party stalwarts who had worked for so many years would not be pleased by the way things were working out: "CCFers . . . will be hurt and offended if they get the impression that the CCF has been tricked into a founding convention at which they can be outnumbered and outvoted."[14] When this plea fell on deaf ears, Tommy came very close to repudiating the new party in a statement to the Saskatchewan legislature on March 9, 1960:

> Any new national party will not in any way affect the
> status of the Saskatchewan CCF . . . If it decides to affiliate
> with the new party, the position of the Saskatchewan
> CCF will remain unaltered. This will not affect the
> provincial autonomy we now enjoy under our constitu-
> tion, and our policy will continue to be set by our
> annual constituency and provincial conventions.[15]

---

[14] He wrote this opinion in a letter on 24 February 1960, to Hazen Argue, who would shortly become his rival for the leadership, and shortly after that, his bitter enemy.
[15] Quoted in McLeod and McLeod, *Road to Jerusalem,* 211.

Tommy's position was made even more difficult by a nasty internal battle that had developed around the federal leadership of the CCF party.

More Negotiating

After his defeat in the 1958 Diefenbaker sweep, M.J. Coldwell intended to retire as national leader of the CCF. However, with a new party forming, it was convenient for the party to have Coldwell as interim leader. If he stepped down, whoever became national leader in his place would be a strong contender for a similar post in the new party. Many influential CCFers, including David Lewis, were determined that Tommy Douglas should fill the role of national leader of the new party. Since Tommy wasn't in the federal house, he could not take over the leadership of the CCF from Coldwell, and Lewis was determined that no one else would step in. (Lewis had been asked by a number of party bureaucrats[16] to run himself, but he was shrewd enough to see that his election would reinforce the notion that eastern labour had taken over the party.[17])

Thus, when M.J. submitted his resignation, rather sadly, to the national executive two weeks after the election, it was tabled.[18] He repeated the request to step down in his report to the national convention in Montreal. The executive instructed Lewis to form a committee "to approach Mr. Coldwell and urge him seriously to consider continuing in the role of National Leader." M.J. agreed, reluctantly, and was re-elected by acclamation.

Now the gloves came off. Coldwell was the national leader, but the House leader was Hazen Argue. The former boy wonder from Assiniboia (he was first elected in 1945, when he was only 24) was now anxious to reach beyond the status of mere MP. As the only Saskatchewan survivor of the Diefenbaker sweep, Argue felt he was owed something. Under his urging, the parliamentary caucus began to push for his election as party leader at the 1960 convention, the one that was to act on the maturing plans for the new party.

---

[16] Including my mother, Margaret Stewart, then the Ontario provincial secretary, who liked Tommy better than Lewis, but felt that his ignorance of French, and indeed of most aspects of Quebec politics, were insuperable obstacles. She turned out to be right.

[17] His memoirs, of which only the first volume was completed before his death, do not go into the leadership issue at all. The explanation given here is one he gave me himself.

[18] Stewart, *M.J*, 205ff.

As usual, there were complications involved in the pushing and shoving. David Lewis, who was then the national president, but who always held what could only be called the David Lewis Office in the CCF, had made it clear that he did not want anyone to run against Tommy Douglas for the leadership of the new party. Douglas, in turn, would not say openly whether he wanted the job or not. This is hardly surprising: in the middle of the medicare wars, he was not going to give any sign that he was about to bolt for Ottawa. And he was having misgivings about the new party that played a role in his reluctance to commit.

The leadership issue became further muddied by a split that developed between the parliamentary group and the party executive, with the former backing Hazen Argue, and the latter bitterly opposed. Carl Hamilton, the national secretary, who had begun as a friend of Argue's, had, on further acquaintance, changed his mind. "Simply put," he said later, "Argue was a totally conscienceless man."[19] At caucus meetings, which Hamilton attended in an ad hoc role, he made his distaste known. Not surprisingly, the caucus resented what they regarded as high-handed interference by the party bureaucracy, and made it clear that unless Argue was named party leader, they would not have him back as House leader.

Coldwell, alarmed and upset, said he could not possibly remain as national leader until the official launch of the new party unless the 1960 convention was unanimously in favour of such a role for him. When Argue made it clear that there would be no such unanimous vote, Coldwell would not allow his name to be entered in the nomination at all.

The executive proposed a solution: Argue could be named "parliamentary leader," something less than national leader but greater than house leader. But Argue, with the caucus behind him, persuaded the 1960 national convention to bolt from the executive recommendation — a fairly frequent occurrence in the CCF. Argue became national leader (House leader) on the books. But no one could make the party hierarchy like it.

The whole thing was a petty squabble, the main result of which was

---

[19] Ibid., 213.

to belittle Coldwell, who deserved better from the party he had served so long. Later — much too late — Lewis would admit that much of the bitterness that developed was his fault:

> I as president of the CCF was very much in the wrong in trying to get a unanimous vote for Tommy. It arose out of the tradition we had had — no one had opposed Woodsworth, no one had opposed Coldwell. They were the Chosen.
>
> I met with Hazen and tried to dissuade him from being a candidate. It was wrong. This attitude produced a bitterness around the Hazen-Douglas contest.[20]

Arguing with Argue

Tommy did not agree to run for the leadership of the NDP until June 28, 1961, one month before the founding convention, and did not resign as premier of Saskatchewan until November 7. He later made it clear that the person who influenced him most in his decision to run was not David Lewis, but M.J. Coldwell:

> Ever since 1941 he has said he hoped I would succeed him some day. And he felt very strongly that all the work he and Woodsworth had done would come to naught unless someone could bring the various factions together in the new party and weld them into a fighting force.
>
> It's not going to be easy.[21]

The convention took place at the time and in the place decreed by the Joint Committee (as part of the play to Quebec, the National Committee to Form the New Party had been renamed the Joint Committee, as "National" meant "Quebec" in Quebec). It was by far the liveliest, as well as the largest, political convention in Canada to date.

---

[20] Ibid., 256–57.
[21] Shackleton, *Tommy Douglas,* 253.

This was before politics became the handmaiden of television; national conventions were able to get by with a minimum of pompoms, cheerleaders, bands, and photo ops — they were there, but not in indecent array. It was the first national convention to have simultaneous translation, part of the party's program to embrace and promote bilingualism; a noble effort, but doomed (the party's embrace of Quebec won it no votes there, but cost it votes in the west).

The Ottawa Coliseum sweltered in the grip of a heat wave, and some of the discussions, especially the debate on whether Canada should or should not withdraw from the North Atlantic Treaty Organization (those in favour of NATO won), added to the sweatbox.

There was a battle over the party name, as well. Many of the delegates wanted to stick to the New Party; many wanted some version of the CCF kept alive, perhaps as the "Social Democratic Party"; and others, while they didn't mind the "New Democratic Party," pointed out that NDP might sound a little sinister to many European immigrants at a time when DP was generally understood to stand for "Displaced Person." Happily, the vote went in favour of the New Democratic Party, the name already approved in the higher enclaves, or quite a lot of signs and stationery would have gone into the garbage.

The platform endorsed by the convention was based on the Winnipeg Declaration and owed only a distant kinship to the Regina Manifesto. The words "socialism," "socialist," and even "democratic socialist" were not used once.

This compelled the *Ottawa Journal* to break into verse:

> Oh no! We never mention it;
> Its name is never heard.
> Our lips are forbid to speak
> That once familiar word,
> Socialism.[22]

Tommy put the same point in another way: the new party, he explained

---

[22] Smith, *Love & Solidarity*, 154.

to reporters, no longer wanted to take the cream separator away from its owners; "All we want is some of the cream."[23]

Pemrose Whelan, in her description of the convention, refers to the "almost palpable tension"[24] on the leadership issue, which came to a vote on Friday, the fourth day of the convention. Well, memories differ. For most of the press corps in attendance, the only question around the leadership was how badly Tommy would whip Hazen, and how mad Hazen would be when he was whipped. The answer to both questions was "plenty."

The vote was a walkover for Tommy, who won by 1,391 to 380 over Argue on the first ballot. John Courtney, a Saskatchewan political scientist, described the tussle as

> a contest between a small, belligerent, but quite power-less caucus, most of whose members supported their leader, and the extra-parliamentary party professionals in support of an extraordinarily successful provincial premier. There was never any doubt who would win.[25]

After the vote, Argue had his picture taken with his arm around Tommy, while he told the party, "No matter what my role in the years ahead, I shall speak for you, I shall work for you, I shall never let you down." Six months later, he indicated the depth of his commitment by bolting to the Liberals, and, at a press conference in Regina — after an uneventful meeting with the Saskatchewan Provincial Council and a friendly visit to Tommy Douglas at his home on Angus Crescent — he tore up his party card. The NDP, he declared, was "under the heel of the unions," which made it, rather than a democratic party of reform, "a dark and sinister threat to democratic government in Canada."[26]

The party had no notion this thunderbolt was coming; Carl Hamilton was tipped off by Norman DePoe, a CBC-TV reporter who had spoken to Argue just before he called the press conference. Tommy's only public comment was to issue a statement saying that Hazen apparently had

---

[23] Quoted in *Maclean's*, 29 July 1961, 5.

[24] Whelan and Whelan, *Touched by Tommy*, 84.

[25] John C. Courtney, *The Selection of National Leaders in Canada* (Toronto: Macmillan, 1973), 177.

[26] Ibid., 257.

found his spiritual home among the Liberals, and "We wish the party well of him."[27]

(To the immense satisfaction of Carl Hamilton, among others, Hazen Argue's career came to a very sticky end. Re-elected in Assiniboia in 1962, he was defeated a year later, then was transmogrified into a senator by Lester Pearson in 1966. He was so unpopular in Saskatchewan that news of his appointment had to be held up until after a by-election because of reports that the Liberals would lose if it were known.[28] He became secretary of state for agriculture, and then, in 1989, he was charged with misuse of Senate funds, which he had diverted from various accounts into a boodle bag to support the (unsuccessful) bid of his wife, Jean, for a Liberal nomination. The charges were eventually withdrawn on compassionate grounds when it was discovered that he was dying of cancer. He died on October 2, 1991.[29] In a rather strange exorcism, the NDP national office banned any photographs of Argue from its walls, so that, while every other person who has held the post of national leader is on display, Argue is not.)

Back to Ottawa

Once more Tommy moved back to Ottawa, and Irma began looking for an apartment there. Their daughters were both grown up by now. Shirley had married the son of an Alberta beer baron, Tom Sick, and they had moved to England, where she was combining motherhood with acting. Tommy's first grandchild, Tad, was born of this marriage (which ended in divorce). Joan was at the University of Saskatchewan, studying nursing.

The transition must have been difficult, for both Irma and Tommy. He had been premier for seventeen years, had had a large staff, an adequate budget, and — something no one likes to say aloud, but that is vastly important to any politician — a good deal of direct power (not quite of the "I say come, and he cometh; I say go, and he goeth" variety, but power nonetheless). He always lived modestly and never put on airs, but he had, inevitably, developed a certain self-assurance of the kind that caused

---

[27] Shackleton, *Tommy Douglas*, 259.

[28] Peter C. Newman, *The Distemper of Our Times: Canadian Politics in Transition, 1963–1968* (Toronto: McClelland & Stewart, 1968), 74–75.

[29] *Canadian News Facts*, 23:4088 and 25:4393.

one of those who worked closely with him to comment, "If you want me to be absolutely frank, he was an arrogant little son-of-a-bitch."

He didn't display much arrogance at 125 Metcalfe Street, the new party headquarters, where help was scarce and money scarcer, nor after he was defeated in his bid to be MP for Regina in the June 18, 1962, federal election. The Diefenbaker party benefited across the west, and especially in Saskatchewan, as much due to a bumper wheat crop, combined with higher prices, as to a suspicion that the NDP was some sort of labour cabal.

Why did Tommy run in Regina? The only explanation he gave was that "It was a complete misreading of the political situation to think we could go in there and win."[30] When the campaign began, Tommy expected that the rejuvenated party would return to Ottawa with somewhere between 40 and 45 seats. But as the campaign wound on, Diefenbaker, with his rumbling tones and perfect oratorical timing, played everyone else off the stage. His speeches often made no sense, but they sounded wonderful. One of his favourite phrases, for example (accompanied by shaking jowls and an accusative index finger), was "It's a long road that has no ashcans." (The more you think about it, the less it makes sense.)

The television cameras loved Diefenbaker, and this was a television election, from start to finish. The NDP did not have enough money to buy air time, nor enough pull to get much free air time. That went, as always, mainly to the old parties.

As the national party leader, Tommy spent most of his time outside his riding, but it would not have made any difference if he had had more time to spend in Regina. The opponents of medicare had orchestrated a campaign of dislike and disinformation that included painting the hammer and sickle on the doors of known CCFers and assuring the voters that, because of Tommy, the province would soon be bereft of physicians.

Allan Blakeney later recalled the bitter result:

> I remember riding in a car caravan — that's how we
> conducted elections in those days, great long car caravans

---

[30] McLeod and McLeod, *Road to Jerusalem,* 226.

starting at the airport and going down through the city. I rode in that caravan with Tommy. Thousands of people were lining the route, most of them staring coldly at the man who worked so hard for them.

And on election night when Tommy went down to a crushing defeat, I remember the message of hope he gave to his tired and grieving workers. No words of reproach or recrimination, just the words of the old Scottish poem:

> Fight on, my men, said Sir Andrew Barton,
> I am hurt, but I am not slain.
> I will lay me down and bleed awhile,
> And then I'll rise and fight again.[31]

After delivering himself of this dramatic stuff, Tommy went home to Angus Crescent and buried his sorrows in a cup of tea. With raisin toast. He lost by 9,428 votes to a Conservative, Ken More. "Well," he said, "I saved my deposit."[32] (That is, he earned more than 15 per cent of the votes cast in the riding; he earned, in fact, 29 per cent.)

Of the 19 seats the NDP won in this election, only 2 were in Saskatchewan. British Columbia's urban- and labour-oriented ridings produced 10. The NDP was the fourth party in the House, behind the Conservatives (116 seats), Liberals (99), and Social Credit (30, of whom 26 were Quebec Créditistes).

The good news was that the NDP had gathered more than a million votes, although its proportion of the popular vote, 13.4 per cent, was pretty much what the CCF's had been in 1949.[33] But exit polls indicated that more members of organized labour had voted for the Conservatives and the Liberals than for the NDP. (The proportions were 37 per cent Liberal, 37 per cent Conservative, 13 per cent NDP, 12 per cent Socred; as usual, it was the electoral system, not the voter, that did some of the harm. The Socreds won 30 seats with fewer votes than the NDP.) In

---

[31] A Tribute to Tommy, April 1986, Douglas Collection, Saskatchewan Archives, Regina. It probably doesn't matter much, but both Tommy and Diefenbaker, who used the same tagline, slightly misquoted it. The original went, "I am wounded, but I am not yet slain / I'll but lie down and bleed a while/ And then I'll rise and fight again."

[32] Ed Whelan, in Whelan and Whelan, Touched by Tommy, 91.

[33] Beck, Pendulum of Power, 343.

Quebec, despite its efforts to promote bilingualism and what was then called "the French fact," the NDP won 4 per cent.

The great labour alliance had yielded only modest results, and a great many former CCFers wondered if they had sold their birthright for a mess of pottage. What had the party bent itself all out of shape for?

Another election on April 8, 1963, did not improve things much for the NDP. This time, the Liberals formed a minority government with 129 seats, while the Tories got 95 and the Socreds 24. The NDP lost 2 seats, coming back with 17, although its share of the popular vote was the same: 13 per cent.[34]

Tommy was the leader of the party, but the NDP was still wandering around in the wilderness. The leadership of it was not a promotion from being premier of a province.

---

[34] Ibid., 370–71.

Chapter FIFTEEN

Ottawa Again

In Toronto, party organizers and publicity men were brain-storming about how to get attention and give the NDP a "with-it image." It was the 1960s and Toronto had opened up, with Yonge Street featuring strippers and topless go-go. One of the publicity types, only half in jest, suggested that an NDP rally should be led by a naked lady riding a horse down Yonge Street. Douglas considered this proposal carefully and finally said: "I think that would be a very good idea; it must be years since the people of Toronto have seen a horse."
— Michael Bradley, *Crisis of Clarity*, 1985

Tommy was the federal leader of the NDP from August 2, 1961, until April 27, 1971. During that time, he fought in six elections — four general elections, in 1962, 1963, 1965, and 1968, and two by-elections, each after a stunning defeat. After his loss in Regina in 1962, he was elected in a by-election in Burnaby, British Columbia, where he was re-elected in 1963 and 1965. In 1968, the year Trudeaumania swept the land, he was defeated in Burnaby and announced his retirement. However, a month after that defeat, Colin Cameron, the NDP MP for Nanaimo-Cowichan-The Islands, died of a heart attack. Tommy was persuaded to step in, and won a by-election in February 1969. By this time, he was waiting for a chance to slip out of the leadership, leaving it to David Lewis. That happened in 1971, although it was quite a tussle. Tommy continued as the MP for Nanaimo until his real retirement in 1976.

During the decade when he led the NDP, its share of the popular vote went from 13.5 per cent in the 1962 federal vote to 17.0 per cent in the 1968 campaign, and its share of House of Commons seats went from

7.2 per cent in 1962 — 19 seats — to 8.3 per cent — 22 seats — in 1968. These were disappointing advances for both the former Saskatchewan premier and the NDP party. They had had grander goals in mind.

The Downing of Dief
Tommy's second go as an MP encompassed a number of incidents that shed light both on that time and on his character. One of these was his part in bringing down the Diefenbaker government and paving the way for sixteen straight years of Liberal rule, until the Tories, under Joe Clark, scrambled out for their brief moment in the sun in 1979.

The speed with which the Diefenbaker government dissolved into warring factions after its massive victory in 1958 was a wonder to behold. Diefenbaker, long on charisma, short on policy, managed by dint of unrelenting effort to alienate almost all of the key pressure groups within his party (except the farmers, who forgave him much for his wheat sales and Roads to Resources programs). Peter C. Newman, in his devastating portrait, *Renegade in Power*, summarized Diefenbaker neatly: "The right instincts were in him, but throughout his stormy stewardship, they languished in the cupboard of his soul. He gave the people a leadership cult without leadership."[1] (Ironically, Tommy was able to generate the leadership, but never the cult.)

The U.S. president, John F. Kennedy, was accused of calling Diefenbaker a son-of-a-bitch in a marginal note to one of his aides, but he denied the charge, saying that he didn't know enough about the Canadian prime minister to make such a remark until much later. But he did admit to thinking that the Conservative leader was "a platitudinous bore."[2] And he was driven to rage by Diefenbaker's attempt in the 1962 election to use a planning document Kennedy had left behind during a presidential visit to Ottawa in 1961. Diefenbaker claimed that the working paper, which listed the items Kennedy was to "push for" in Ottawa, constituted interference in Canadian affairs. (The list included Canadian membership in the Organization of American States and "Stricter control measures against the Communists in Laos and South Vietnam.")[3]

[1] Peter C. Newman, *Renegade in Power: The Diefenbaker Years* (Toronto: McClelland & Stewart, 1963), xi.
[2] J.K. Nesbitt, in *Vancouver Sun*, 9 January 1964.
[3] Newman, *Renegade in Power*, 265.

Diefenbaker's threat to release the working paper, which the Americans regarded as blackmail, was withdrawn after an exchange of insults, public and private, that left Canada–U.S. relations in tatters and the Diefenbaker cabinet in deadly disarray.

Tommy rather admired the prime minister's willingness to tangle with the Americans, but he did not and could not admire the disarray, nor the shifts in Tory strategy (if that is not too strong a phrase for the prime minister's mood swings, which caused the shifts).

In 1957, Canada and the United States had formed NORAD, the integrated North American Aerospace Defence Command, and in 1959, the Diefenbaker government, the same fellas who had plunged into NORAD, cancelled the Avro Arrow interceptor, which was to have been Canada's main contribution to the defence pact. Instead, Canada would stand on guard with two squadrons of Bomarc-B anti-aircraft missiles and five squadrons of Voodoo interceptors. The problem was, Canada had never accepted the stationing of nuclear arms in this country, and neither the Voodoo nor the Bomarc was rigged for nuclear war-heads. Diefenbaker's defence minister, Douglas Harkness, argued early and often that Canada had committed itself to nuclear arms when it signed on to NATO; the secretary of state for external affairs, Howard Green, said he would resign if Canada adopted nuclear arms. So, Canada took the missiles and the Voodoos, but left them unarmed.

The prime minister, invited to address this dilemma on a number of occasions, smothered it in a fog of words that eluded the best efforts of any translator to turn it into sense in either of Canada's official languages.[4] Canada had spent $685 million to acquire armaments from the Americans which, without their warheads, were well-nigh useless. Hard to explain.

Until January 1963, this was just another Canadian cock-up; the NDP and Liberals were both opposed to nuclear arms, the Socreds were for, and the Tories were, well, for and against. On January 4, 1963, General Lauris Norstad, the retiring supreme commander of NATO, said in a speech in Ottawa that Canada had committed itself to accepting nuclear

---

[4] I covered these events as the Ottawa correspondent for the *Star Weekly Magazine*, and this account is from my reports at that time.

weapons when it cancelled the Arrow. This was an extraordinary and improper claim for a military man to make, and it put the cat fairly among the Tory pigeons. On January 12, Liberal party leader Lester B. Pearson did one of his famous about turns, embracing nuclear arms for Canada, although he had been "completely opposed" up to this time. His new stance came about, he explained, not because he was in favour of nuclear arms, but because Canada had agreed to them when it joined NATO. Everything he had said before on this subject was now inoperative.

On January 30, the American State Department waded into what was now a catfight in the cabinet with a statement that largely agreed with Pearson and made the prime minister look like a liar (not hard to do, actually). The statement said that, indeed, Canada had accepted nuclear warheads, and this was understood at the time the NATO documents were signed. However, Canadians need not trouble their tender consciences about the warheads, because "custody of the United States nuclear weapons would remain with the United States." Somehow, it was not comforting to Canadians to hear that they were being lumbered with nuclear arms, but that the Americans retained the right to explode them wherever and whenever they felt inclined.

Tommy attacked the State Department's missive as "an unwarranted and unprecedented intrusion" into Canada's affairs.[5] On the other hand, he condemned the vacillations of the cabinet:

> The government has to come down on the side of Mr. Green, who is against nuclear weapons, or Mr. Harkness, who is for nuclear weapons. Any government which tries to ride two horses going in different directions is going to find itself sitting in a most undignified position.[6]

On Monday, February 4, 1963, Lester Pearson moved a general non-confidence motion in the government, citing "the lack of leadership, the breakdown in unity in the cabinet, and confusion and indecision in

---

[5] It may have been unwarranted; it was certainly not unprecedented. The Americans had already passed laws under which Canadian corporations with U.S. links were banned from trading with Cuba.

[6] *Globe and Mail*, 1 February 1963.

dealing with national and international problems."[7] The Conservatives, with 116 members, could have survived this motion (assuming that all its troops came on board) with the help of the 30 Social Credit MPs, and might have survived with the help of the NDP, whose 19 seats, added to those of the Tories, would just squeak out a majority in the 265-seat House if the government could attract even two Socred votes.

On the morning of February 5, with the non-confidence vote looming in the Commons that afternoon, Wallace McCutcheon, a Tory senator and minister without portfolio (he was usually referred to as "the Senator from Bay Street" because of his financial background) telephoned Tommy in his fifth-floor office of the House of Commons to ask for NDP support in the upcoming vote. Not to worry about Diefenbaker, McCutcheon said; within a few days of a successful vote, the Tories would shove him off onto the Supreme Court.

Tommy's refusal was flat:

> We're not interested in getting rid of Mr. Diefenbaker, and least of all in replacing him with you and your friends from Toronto. We're not voting against Mr. Diefenbaker. We're voting against the fact that the government has been unable to govern.[8]

The NDP caucus was not by any means all of one mind on the non-confidence vote. Toppling the government would no doubt let in the Liberals, so nothing would be gained on the nuclear issue and the NDP would probably be squashed in the vote. Bert Herridge and Colin Cameron, two of the party's left-wing western MPs, made it clear that they would vote with the government if Tommy was fool enough to back Pearson's motion. (It is ironic that Tommy would go on to occupy Cameron's seat; the two men were seldom in agreement.)

Robert Thompson, the leader of the western Socreds (which encompassed only 4 seats; the other 26 were under the firm control of Réal Caouette in Quebec), sent in a list of demands to Diefenbaker, including

---

[7] House of Commons, *Debates,* 4 February 1963.
[8] McLeod and McLeod, *Road to Jerusalem,* 236.

the demand of a promise to make a clear statement on defence policy, and went into the House to declare that "an election at this time . . . would be a tragedy to Canada."[9] Then he reversed himself, in part because the prime minister did not bother to reply to his demands (although Gordon Churchill, his deputy, accepted them all), and in part because Réal Caouette told Thompson that he, Caouette, could bring back 60 seats in Quebec if the non-confidence vote provoked an election. That sounded nice.

Tommy had no illusions about what would happen if the Liberals won the vote: "It (the non-confidence motion) was like a bee sting. It would be effective, all right, but it would kill the bee."[10]

On the floor of the House, 109 Tories and 2 NDP members voted with the government; the rest of the NDP caucus and all of the Liberals backed the Pearson motion, and it carried 142–111.

The subsequent election was described by Mark Gayn of the *Toronto Star* as a "strange, rowdy, expensive, emotional, bruising campaign,"[11] while George Bain of the *Globe and Mail* characterized it as "Abraham Lincoln vs. John F. Kennedy." Pearson, an uninspiring orator and weak television personality, managed to squander a huge lead in the public opinion polls and snatch defeat from the jaws of victory, while Diefenbaker, unencumbered by any need to stick to facts, very nearly survived.

Tommy was encumbered, not only by a regrettable tendency to level with the voter, but by a lack of funds. But he did what he could. He castigated the Tories for procrastination and indecision and the Liberals for the nuclear flip-flop and for seeming to want a majority government for its own sake, and not because they knew what to do. The Liberal slogan, "Paralysis or Pearson," was eerily reminiscent of "King or Chaos," and the argument for stable government was not persuasive. Tommy said: "For twenty-two years we had stable government under the Liberals, so stable it never moved . . . When you remember how a stable smells, I don't think you'll want stable government."[12]

Tommy came out clearly against nuclear arms, whether under

[9] Newman, *Renegade in Power*, 369.
[10] Peter Stursberg, in *Saturday Night* (May 1963).
[11] Quoted in Beck, *Pendulum of Power*, 349.
[12] Quoted in *Ottawa Journal*, 4 March 1963.

Canadian or U.S. control, took a strong stand for Canadian independence, and deplored the Liberal proposal to postpone improvements in the Canadian welfare system until later, because of "economic difficulties": "Why, in a country so richly endowed as Canada and so far behind already in the field of public welfare, should we get even further behind?"[13]

For one brief moment, the NDP dreamed of a breakthrough in Quebec, where both the Quebec Federation of Labour and the National Trade Unions had come out against Caouette, and union leader Gérard Picard had agreed to lead the NDP campaign.

But when the votes were counted, the NDP had dropped 2 seats and the Socreds 6, and there was no Quebec breakthrough. Canada still had a minority government, although it was Liberal instead of Conservative. Again, the NDP held not a single seat in Saskatchewan, and Tommy held his Burnaby-Coquitlam seat against a parachuted candidate, Liberal policy guru Tom Kent, with a much-reduced majority.

Kent claimed in his memoirs that the NDP ran a rough and dirty campaign:

> The organizers clearly put all the pressure they could on union members to vote for Douglas. Their most visible techniques, however, were to tear down opponents' signs and create as much disruptive noise as possible at their meetings. I could not believe that Tommy Douglas relished these proceedings on his behalf, but if he tried to prevent them he failed.[14]

The NDP, needless to say, saw it as merely a pretty tough election in the riding, which was won more on Tommy's behalf than by him. He spent most of the campaign elsewhere, as national leader.

After the election, the NDP flirted briefly with the Liberals, meeting one Sunday afternoon to explore possibilities. Tommy, David Lewis, and MP Douglas Fisher went to the Ottawa apartment of Walter Gordon,

---

[13] Quoted in *Ottawa Citizen*, 9 March 1963.
[14] Kent, *A Public Purpose*, 203.

the newly-minted Liberal finance minister, for a general discussion with
Gordon and Keith Davey, the Liberal national director. Pearson was supposed to attend this little coffee klatch, but never made it.[15] Tommy
talked about a number of measures his party favoured, including
increases in the old-age pension, implementation of a contributory pension plan, tax reforms to benefit the less well-off, and a development
corporation to protect the economy. (All of these reforms came about,
but the NDP got little credit for any of them.)

As Gordon remembered, "It was a friendly meeting, but nothing
came of it."[16] David Lewis made it clear that he was opposed to any kind
of working arrangement with the Liberals. However, word of this dal-
liance spread quickly in Toronto and Ottawa. Tommy, who had seen
firsthand that the Liberals were not interested in reforms as much as
they were in a coalition that would keep them in power, announced that
he would never sanction a merger; he would resign first.

The 1963 election did very little to advance the NDP; it was, obviously, much more useful to the Liberals. Even so, it is hard to see how
Tommy could have voted with the Diefenbaker government in the
teeth of its manifest incompetence. Tommy's decision to back the non-
confidence motion turned out to be politically expensive, but principled. It would have been shrewder, surely, to keep the Tories in power
until they fractured so badly that not even a cunning campaigner like
Diefenbaker could bring in seats.

The Nationalist

Over the next five years, the Pearson Liberals were racked by scandals
like the Rivard Affair; missteps like the first Walter Gordon budget,
which had to be withdrawn and recast; and divisions like the barely
concealed hostility of both its left wing, led by Walter Gordon and Tom
Kent, and its right, led by Robert Winter and Mitchell Sharp. Even so,
they managed to introduce, and implement, many of the reforms that
had been on the NDP list, or some version thereof.

We have already seen how medicare was floated onstage. The Canada

---

[15] Walter Gordon, *Walter Gordon: A Political Memoir* (Toronto: McClelland &
Stewart, 1977), 178. In his memoirs, Walter Gordon wrote that both Pearson and
Allan MacEachen were to have attended, but "it transpired that neither . . . was
able to come at the last moment." He speculated that this unexplained absence
"may have raised suspicions in the minds of the visiting NDPers."
[16] Ibid.

Pension Plan, the contributory pension scheme Tommy had mentioned to Walter Gordon (and which had been propounded by social democratic governments decades earlier and put into place in the United Kingdom and Sweden in 1959), was introduced into Parliament in June 1963. It was immediately attacked by the provinces, especially Ontario and Quebec, as an invasion of their turf. Which, of course, it was. Quebec produced its own plan, to be self-financed by a pool of funds made up of contributions from individuals and their employers. This would produce a massive investment fund and was a distinct improvement over the federal plan, which would have seen the money paid into and out of general revenues every year. The end result was a merger of ideas, and the creation of two plans — the Canada Pension Plan and the Quebec Pension Plan — that irritated everybody and worked wonderfully.[17] It came into force on January 1, 1967, and was a fine way to begin Canada's centennial celebration.

Still, from the point of view of the Canadian voter, the NDP was steadily outflanked by the Liberals, even if the Liberal version of NDP ideas was somewhat, or even extensively, watered down. The notion that Canada ought to do something to protect its economy, especially against the aggressive intrusions of the United States, certainly got watered down.

Tommy had always been an advocate of independence, had even been, in a mild way, a nationalist, although that was not the proper attitude of a socialist. (Woodsworth had frowned on nationalism as outmoded and likely to interfere with the brotherhood — or, now, the brotherhood and sisterhood — of labour, which ought to be exempt from parochial thought.) While the government of Saskatchewan under Tommy welcomed foreign firms, particularly in the oil sector, that was because there were no Canadian firms to take on the developments the province needed. When the TransCanada Pipeline was being built, Tommy argued that it ought to be a publicly owned utility: "The control of a vital natural resource is destined to fall into the hands of financial interests outside Canada."[18] Which is, of course, exactly what happened.

---

[17] There is a detailed description of the evolution of the plans in Eric Kierans with Walter Stewart, *Remembering* (Toronto: Stoddart, 2001), 93–95.

[18] McLeod and McLeod, *Road to Jerusalem*, 246.

The unions that were becoming so central to the NDP's finances were badly divided on the nationalist issue. Most of the giant unions were international (mainly American) in their origins, policies, and strike funds. While stoutly maintaining their independence on all important matters, they were, during these years, more inclined to strike the gong for international brotherhood than for nationalism. The same union leaders who deplored the dominance of corporations whose decisions were made in New York and Chicago denied that the same forces were at play in their own organizations. As Tennyson said, simple faith is more than Norman blood.

The founding convention of the NDP had recommended the establishment of a development corporation, which would create new enterprises by using pension funds and other pools of capital, enterprises that would be in Canadian hands. At the same time, this new corporation would buy back some of the manufacturing concerns that were already in foreign hands. At the time of the NDP founding, just under 30 per cent of Canadian manufacturing was foreign-owned, mostly by American companies, and a number of studies had already shown that the value-added jobs were flowing across the border. Canadians, in the classic phrase, were "hewers of wood and drawers of water," which the Americans turned into furniture and whiskey and sold back to us. When he spoke on the subject in 1966, Tommy used examples that are just as valid today:

> In western Canada, and particularly in B.C., they stand every day and watch the logs with bark still on being put onto ocean ships . . . and then go down and watch the plywood coming back. They see pulp going out, and us buying back paper. They see iron ore and moly and coal going out and we buy back steel. They see copper ore going out and we buy back wire and cable and electrical appliances. And it has dawned on them over the past ten or twenty years that what we're exporting are jobs.[19]

---

[19] T.C. Douglas, interview by Richard Allway, 1966, National Archives of Canada.

Tommy was not alone in his concern; some Canadian economists and politicians were on his side. Kari Levitt, an economist at McGill, produced a book called *Silent Surrender* that became part of the ammunition for every nationalist. In it, Levitt showed that the Americans were (and are) buying us out with our own money. In the period from 1957 to 1964, 85 per cent of what showed up on our figures as "U.S. direct investment" in Canadian mining, manufacturing, and petroleum was raised here, mostly by way of reinvested earnings. By 1968, the figure for U.S. investment in out-of-Canada funds was less than 5 per cent. At the same time, Canadian subsidiaries of U.S. firms were sending back more in profits than they received in new capital.[20]

Walter Gordon, who had become a nationalist when he led a royal commission into Canada's economic prospects between 1955 and 1958 (he described a scene that echoed Tommy's examples, but in eastern Canada: pulpwood slurry being pumped across the river in New Brunswick to U.S. factories that sent it back as fine paper), argued for the establishment of a Canadian Development Corporation and got it injected into the Liberal platform in 1963. This proposal served the Liberals for three elections, 1963, 1965, and 1968. If you wanted a CDC, there was no need to vote for the NDP; the Liberals were offering the same model, with whitewalls and automatic steering.

The CDC that eventually emerged, however, was somewhat retooled. Walter Gordon was gone, done in by the 1965 election (in which he promised the prime minister that one more election would bring the Holy Grail of majority government). And even Pearson — who was no nationalist, but who could be chivvied — was gone. Pierre Elliott Trudeau was in charge, and Pierre Elliott Trudeau had no time for nationalists.

The Liberals, at Gordon's urging, had produced an Economic Council of Canada to provide independent studies on the shape and direction of the Canadian economy. It was emasculated. The CDC finally produced by Trudeau's finance minister, Edgar Benson, had as its first priority "to make a profit."[21] It would begin with a pool of public money — $250 million

---

[20] Kari Levitt, *Silent Surrender* (Toronto: Macmillan, 1970), 64ff.

[21] Walter Stewart, *Shrug: Trudeau in Power* (Toronto: New Press, 1971), 132.

— and would sell shares to raise the cash it needed to invest in profitable enterprises — its investors shied away from Canadian firms whose margins were slim. It would not interfere in the foreign takeover of Canadian firms that were not making money, no matter how worthy or important the work they were doing. Only if there was a buck to be made would the CDC come alive.

Tommy described the CDC produced by the Trudeau government as "a complete sellout to private enterprise."[22] No matter; whatever political kudos were to be gained from nationalism had been captured by the Liberals.

The Moralist

Canada's silent complicity in the horrors of the Vietnam War was part of the price we paid for our lack of independence. Lacking a foreign policy of our own, we could do no more than agree with whatever the Americans decided to do. In the case of Vietnam, this meant that, as one of the three members of the International Control Commission, we were charged with the duty of keeping arms out of Vietnam, while, as partners in the Canada–U.S. Defence Production Sharing Agreement, we sold more than $3 billion worth of war materials to the Americans. Green berets worn so proudly through many a smashed hamlet in Vietnam were sewn in a loft in Toronto, and a dynamite plant in Valleyfield, Quebec, shipped explosives to plants in the United States, where they were made into bombs to drop on the people we were supposed to be helping through the ICC.

When Prime Minister Pearson timidly suggested, in a speech at Temple University, that perhaps the Americans should stop dropping bombs — whether of Canadian or other extraction — long enough to talk, he was browbeaten and humiliated by U.S. president Lyndon B. Johnson, and there wasn't a damn thing he could do about it. To quarrel with the Americans, even to question the Americans, could invoke economic penalties, he admitted; better to hope for some softening of U.S. policy, to be brought about either by elves or via "quiet diplomacy."

---

[22] Ibid.

From the beginning, Tommy made his distaste for the American intervention in Vietnam known, saying:

> The United States is seeking to foist on the people of South Vietnam a government of rapacious landlords, military dictators, and former collaborators of a military regime . . . We are not masters in our own house. We are becoming an economic colony of the United States, and our capacity for independent action in world affairs is being reduced to zero.[23]

This stance no doubt did him a good deal of harm in the polls.

The subject was seldom debated in Parliament. When it was, in May 1965, Tommy called for American withdrawal from Vietnam and/or the immediate opening of peace talks with the North, along with the establishment of an international peacekeeping force in Southeast Asia. For this, he was ignored by the Liberals and castigated by the Tories.

The next time a full debate took place, in February 1967, Paul Martin presented Tommy's proposals as government policy — without credit, of course — while insisting that Canada must, because of her position on the ICC, remain neutral. Tommy was enraged:

> We witnessed today the Secretary of State for External Affairs, like Pontius Pilate of old, publicly washing his hands of all responsibility . . .
>
> The fact that we are a neutral and a member of the International Control Commission, it seems to me, does not justify for one moment the minister's contention that Canada must be silent . . . We are discussing the greatest moral issue of our time. As I have said before, in the opinion of the members of this party, the bombing of North Vietnam is legally indefensible and morally inexcusable. What is happening in Vietnam is shocking

---

[23] T.C. Douglas, speech to the British Columbia NDP, 3 July 1967.

the conscience of the world more than anything that has happened since Hitler tried to exterminate the Jews in Europe.[24]

His final stinging crack was: "In Washington they have their hawks and doves and in Ottawa we have our parrots."

On Vietnam, Tommy made the demarcation between the NDP and any other party clear, and whether it won him votes or lost them was the least of his concerns (it certainly won him some votes from Liberals who were disgusted with their own party; it probably cost him some votes from the right wing of his own party).

Tommy was by this time a superb parliamentary performer, an able administrator, and a man who was admired more than he was feared by his opponents. He had never been tainted by serious personal scandal, never done anything underhanded or mean. But he was not possessed of the one immeasurable quality for which Canadians would soon be clamouring: charisma.

---

[24] House of Commons, *Debates*, 13 February 1967.

Chapter SIXTEEN

His Finest Hour

> *It was Tommy Douglas of the NDP who stood in the House, day after day, and hammered the government for suspending civil liberties, and if you ask me today why I wasn't up there beside him, I can only say, Damned if I know. He showed political courage of the highest order.*
>
> — Eric Kierans, *Remembering*, 2001

In February 1968, Stephen Lewis, the elder son of David Lewis and at this time an Ontario MPP (he would oust Donald MacDonald, the provincial leader, in October 1970), flew out to Vancouver to talk to Tommy in his Burnaby riding office. Accounts differ as to whether, as he insists, he flew at the behest of the Ontario NDP caucus or on his own initiative (Donald MacDonald could not recall any discussion in the caucus on the matter). His purpose was to suggest to Tommy that the time had come for him to step down as the NDP's national leader.

Tommy was sixty-three years old; he had been the federal NDP leader for nearly seven years, and, as far as anyone could tell, the task of building the New Jerusalem had advanced only slightly from where it had been when the party was founded. The NDP had been doing better in public opinion polls, but that was mostly because the Liberals were in their usual state of disarray. New Democrats held 21 seats, more than the CCF had held in 1958 (8), but less than the CCF had held in 1957 (25). The party had advanced from fourth to third place in the House of Commons as the Ralliement Créditiste sank slowly into the sunset, but it was still a long way from gaining, or even threatening to gain, power.

The NDP had finally established a foothold in Ontario, probably a reflection of the activity of the trade union movement, but in Quebec, the provincial NDP was taking a position that had nothing to do with the national party's view of federalism. Quebec NDPers were "near" separatists, in the same way that brewers concoct near beer. The central office dealt with this phenomenon by ignoring it, while the Liberals gloated. Every time one of the party's Quebec offspring unlimbered a statement that smacked of heresy, the federal brass, emulating Nelson, would lift the telescope to a blind eye. And the sacrifice of principle was not followed by a shift in votes.

Meanwhile, the old-line parties were making leadership changes and reaping the benefits in public opinion. When Robert Stanfield, the former premier of Nova Scotia, replaced an aging and crotchety John Diefenbaker as Progressive Conservative leader in September 1967, the public responded by thrusting the Tories to the top of the polls. Dalton Camp, the Tory president and a close friend of Stanfield's — and always a shrewd observer of the political scene — concluded that "the party has triumphed over its trauma [the unseating of Diefenbaker, in which Camp himself played no small part] and seems headed for electoral victory."[1] That idea faded with the coming of winter and the solitary walk in Westmount that, as we were told, led Pierre Elliott Trudeau, then minister of justice in the Pearson cabinet, to enter the Liberal leadership race. (The stroll-in-the-snow story was slightly marred by the fact that press kits for his run were already in the works, but nobody noticed that.)

Gordon Donaldson, in his collective biography of Canada's prime ministers, wrote that Trudeau burst onto the Canadian political scene "like a stone through a stained glass window."[2] An evocative phrase, if you allow the stone a few years to get through the glass. Trudeau had been a CCFer and, as an editor of *Cité libre* magazine, a bitter critic of the Liberals and their embrace of nuclear warheads for the Bomarc missile.[3] He had been in the House of Commons for three years before being launched at that stained glass window; but it is true that, once aloft, he made quite a hit. Liberals were in transports of joy, and uncommitted

---

[1] Quoted in Beck, *Pendulum of Power*, 399.

[2] Gordon Donaldson, *Seventeen Men* (Toronto: Doubleday, 1969).

[3] Trudeau wrote: "I would have to point out in strongest terms the autocracy of the Liberal structure and the cowardice of its members. I have never seen in all my examination of politics so degrading a spectacle as that of all these Liberals turning their coats in unison with their Chief, when they saw a chance to take power." *Cité libre* (April 1963).

voters, especially female uncommitted voters, were signing membership cards by the thousand. His popularity was helped along by a series of kissing episodes captured on television, which showed the new star being embraced, as it were, from coast to coast. "If it puckers," wrote George Bain of the *Globe and Mail*, "he's there."[4]

Possibly the only eight people in Canada who did not know, early in 1968, that Trudeau would be chosen as the next leader of the Liberal party at the convention in April were the eight men who were running against him. And even they had their suspicions.

Thus, at the time Stephen Lewis went out to Vancouver, the most likely candidates for Canada's next prime minister were Tommy, Robert Stanfield, who was a decade younger than Tommy[5] and a new face in Ottawa, and Pierre Elliott Trudeau, a brilliant young (well, youngish[5]) lawyer from Quebec. The argument that it was time for a change made a certain amount of sense. Still, Tommy was wounded that the case had been put to him so bluntly; put, moreover, by the son of the man poised to succeed him as national leader. David Lewis was only five years younger than Tommy and represented essentially the same, slightly dog-eared strain of socialism in the public mind.

The relationship between Tommy and David was complex. Each admired the other, and said so — in exactly the tone used by two top students who always say they like each other, but really don't. David, even when he was actively persuading Tommy to leap from Saskatchewan to Ottawa, wanted to be asked to take on the job himself. Tommy thought that David, while undoubtedly brilliant, was also undoubtedly autocratic, and while he might help the party in Ontario, he certainly wouldn't do it much good west of the Lakehead.

Tommy had intended to prepare the way for a successor from the next generation — someone like Allan Blakeney, perhaps. But however much Stephen Lewis protested that he was not there on behalf of his father, that, indeed, his father would be "horror struck"[7] when he found out about the trip, Tommy knew when he was being given the elbow.

---

[4] Quoted in Stewart, *Shrug*, 11.
[5] He was born on 11 April 1914.
[6] Not as young as he said he was, though. His 1968 *Parliamentary Guide* entry, which he prepared, showed him to have been born in 1921. It was only much later that his sister ratted to the press that he had actually been born in 1919. He was closing in on fifty. (See Stewart, *Shrug*, 8.)
[7] Quoted in McLeod and McLeod, *Road to Jerusalem*, 271.

Accordingly, he told party insiders he was prepared to step down at the next federal convention, in 1969.

He was, therefore, no more than a caretaker leader in the eyes of many insiders when, not many weeks after he spoke to Stephen Lewis, Prime Minister Pearson stepped down, Pierre Trudeau stepped up, and the nation was in the throes of another election.

Roses and Rhetoric

The 1968 election was unlike anything Canadians had seen before. It was almost entirely given over to television, a medium in which neither Stanfield nor Tommy shone particularly, but which suited Trudeau to a T. He capered and danced and waved; he kissed the girls and made them sigh; he came out with a motto, "the Just Society," that sounded exactly right and could be made to mean anything.

Television is at once the most powerful and the most deceptive of media because it depends so much on the accident of appearance. Had there been television in Mackenzie King's time, he could never have been elected; had there been television in Sir Wilfrid Laurier's time, he could never have been defeated. The camera can make a wise man appear a fool, a bumpkin appear weighty; it may unmask one man as a liar and transmit another as the very soul of integrity. The results may have nothing to do with the real qualities of a candidate, only with his or her apparent qualities.

Trudeau was quick, cool, articulate, shrewd, witty, a man whose drifting past seemed romantic, whose apparent detachment appealed to a nation sick to death of the screams and whines of its politicians. He made it look as if he were being dragged into the leadership race almost against his will, while others scrambled, schemed, and begged for power. Above all, he *looked* superb; whatever quality it is that makes TV work for one person and not for another, Trudeau had it.

Trudeau flitted across the nation in a DC-9 jet, visited three or four provinces a day, held rallies at shopping malls (where he was surrounded by pompom girls in miniskirts of orange and white), and made no promises that could come back to haunt him, or even be tested against common sense. He was bright, and quotable in both official languages. At the same time, he was a bitter foe of nationalism, whether in Israel or Quebec. Western voters who wanted to "put Quebec in its place," a lamentably populous lot, could do so best, ironically enough, by voting for a Quebecker.

Vague statements like "If Canadians want to take a bit of a risk, if they want to take a chance on the future, then we're asking them to vote for us"[8] made Trudeau sound like a bit of a radical, and, indeed, he made some of his own party nervous on this score. But his vagueness concealed the fact that he was, in the end, deeply conservative in his approach to economic issues.

Beside Trudeau, Stanfield seemed lumpish, and Tommy petulant. Stanfield flew in a propeller-driven plane and made laconic, dull, and sensible speeches. Tommy flew economy on Air Canada and made lively, provocative speeches that, in most cases, he might as well have shouted into the closet back in his Burnaby apartment. Both Tommy and Stanfield tried to make economic issues the heart of the campaign, and both failed utterly. At a time when the nation suffered from high inflation, high unemployment, and a massive shortage of affordable housing, the Liberal cabinet ministers, who had been in charge of the nation for the last five years, asked the people to elect them so that they could help Trudeau "get the country moving again."[9] And the electors obliged.

Stanfield came out with a proposal for a guaranteed annual income — which startled everyone, including his own party — and then seemed to back away from it to propose some sort of negative income tax. He could not say what level of income would trigger whichever mechanism became the policy, or how much it would cost. Trudeau dismissed the whole thing in one devastating sentence: "I would not buy a set of long underwear if I didn't know how much it would cost."[10] He could talk this way; he hadn't made any proposals clear enough to attract a price tag at all. Even Peter Newman, who was, and would remain, one of Trudeau's biggest fans, wrote that, when Trudeau made a speech to

---

[8] Quoted in *Globe and Mail*, 15 June 1968.
[9] Beck, *Pendulum of Power*, 404.
[10] Geoffrey Stevens, *Stanfield* (Toronto: McClelland & Stewart, 1973), 217.

50,000 screaming spectators in Toronto, "The kid holding up a lonely sign that read 'Fifty to One He Says Nothing' turned out to be right."[11]

For most of the campaign, Tommy was out of sorts: his old knee injury flared up again; the NDP was short of funds, as usual; and to make matters worse, he was not at all sure that the party was even behind him. David Lewis was running in York South in Toronto, making all the right noises, but getting ready, day by day, to step forward into the leadership at the earliest decent moment.

The only time Tommy managed to hold his own with Trudeau was during a nationally televised leaders' debate on June 9, two weeks before the election. He very nearly didn't appear in that debate: both CTV and the CBC wanted only Stanfield and Trudeau before the cameras. But James Renwick, the NDP national president, shouted and shamed them into including Tommy. Once he got before a little pulpit-like podium, Tommy did very well, using the Carter Commission Report, a massive document that underlined the inequity of Canada's tax system (and which was about as popular in Liberal circles as a polecat at a garden party), to challenge Trudeau's "Just Society" slogan: "I can say to Mr. Trudeau that he cannot talk about the just society until he first commits himself to a just tax structure."[12]

Trudeau, typically, ignored the main point — the Carter Commission argued that every dollar of income, however earned, should be treated as income and taxed fully — and replied as if the only issue were capital gains taxes: "There is nothing moral or immoral about the absence or presence of a capital gains tax; it is a matter of knowing whether you will raise enough money to make it worthwhile."[13]

Tommy got no further when he cited the Watkins Report, a study done by a young Liberal economist, Mel Watkins of the University of Toronto, that concluded that Canada was being rapidly taken over, not by American dollars, but, just as Kari Levitt had argued, by Canadian dollars siphoned out of the economy and shipped across the border. Trudeau, in response, cited the Liberal promise to form a Canada Development Corporation. Since this had been promised back in 1963,

---

[11] Peter C. Newman, in *Toronto Star*, 20 June 1968.

[12] Transcript of the debate, 9 June 1968, National Archives of Canada.

[13] Ibid.

Tommy replied that Liberal promises tended to resemble a Chinese proverb: "There is a large noise on the stairs, but no one comes into the room."[14]

The NDP campaign was energized by Tommy's performance in the debate — a number of commentators not known for being partial to the NDP thought Tommy had won it — but it made little difference in the end. The NDP won 5 seats in Saskatchewan, in part because the Diefenbaker magic had turned sour and Stanfield was a Maritimer, and in part because Dalton Camp, who was now a Tory candidate in Toronto, had pronounced that the promised national medicare program was doomed to failure. But the party's overall vote slipped slightly, from 18 to 17 per cent, and it wound up with only one more seat in Parliament.

Much more devastating was the fact that Tommy had been defeated in Burnaby (the riding was now called Burnaby-Seymour; it had been redistributed, which didn't help). Ray Perrault, the Liberal victor, won by only 138 votes (Tommy had won by nearly 10,000 votes in 1965), but however the spin doctors massaged the result (they pointed out, correctly, that Perrault had obtained a plurality due in part to the collapse of the Social Credit vote), two facts remained: Tommy had been beaten, and Canada had a new prime minister, who looked likely to be in place for quite a time.

Tommy announced that he would not allow anyone to step aside so that he could find a place in the Commons by way of a by-election. He flew back to Ottawa, where he announced, this time publicly, that he would resign as NDP national leader at the next federal convention.

In July, David Lewis, who had won in York South, was named the NDP's parliamentary leader, and he told reporters that he was not "at present" planning to run for the party leadership. He hoped the new leader would come from a younger generation. This sentiment was received with wise winks inside the party and snorts of derision outside.[15]

Then Colin Cameron, the left-wing gadfly from Nanaimo-Cowichan-The Islands, died suddenly of a heart attack, a month after the federal vote. The local riding association promptly asked Tommy to fill the vacancy, and in September he agreed to do so. With Irma, he moved into

---

[14] Ibid.

[15] Allan Blakeney told the *Globe and Mail* later, "There was a fair amount of speculation at that time as to whether anyone believed that. I said, 'Oh, come on, David wants to be leader of the party, if even for a brief time.'" Quoted in McLeod and McLeod, *Road to Jerusalem*, 273.

an apartment at 1 Chapel Street, on Nanaimo's attractive waterfront, and began organizing for the by-election, which Trudeau delayed and delayed until February 1969. The NDP ran a formidable campaign, flying in full-time organizers from the Canadian Auto Workers and public service unions, and Tommy won the by-election handily, with 57 per cent of the vote. He then flew back to Ottawa to re-occupy the leader's chair.

David Lewis welcomed him cordially, while preparing to bid him an equally cordial farewell when the time came. The *Globe and Mail*'s Ottawa bureau reported that Lewis was organizing the caucus and running much of the parliamentary business: "He runs the show and is preaching for a call even now."[16]

The Father
Not long before the party's federal convention in October 1969, Tommy was caught up in another, much more personal drama.

His daughter Shirley, now divorced from Tom Sick, had moved to California with her second husband, Canadian actor Donald Sutherland, whom she had met in Rome while she was dubbing voiceovers for spaghetti Westerns. Shirley had always been active in politics, and she didn't change with the arrival of twins Kiefer and Rachel, born in 1967. In 1969, she joined a group called "The Friends of Black Panthers," to raise money for the Panthers' legal expenses and for a breakfast-for-children program they ran in Los Angeles. The Black Panthers were, to put it mildly, a motley crew, ranging from liberal to anarchist and containing some rather nasty customers, but all Shirley Douglas wanted was to help feed some kids.

At 5:30 a.m. on October 2, 1969, a scene like one you would see in an old movie about Nazi Germany was enacted at the Sutherlands' Beverly Hills home. A squad of ten officers burst through the door and began to ransack the place. They later claimed that they had information that Shirley and a friend of hers, playwright Donald Freed, were holding hand grenades for the Black Panthers.[17] Tad, Shirley's ten-year old son,

---

[16] *Globe and Mail*, 20 March 1969.
[17] This account is from the Associated Press coverage carried in the *Leader-Post* (Regina), 4 October 1969.

stood against one wall, terrified. Rachel and Kiefer were in a bedroom, crying.

The raiders found nothing, but charged Shirley anyway, with "conspiracy to obtain a destructive device" — the hand grenades that they couldn't find. The U.S. attorney responsible for the case claimed that Shirley and Freed had purchased them from an undercover cop. Later, the prosecution claimed to have found the grenades at Freed's apartment, and still later, it came out that they had been planted.

When Tommy heard about the arrest, he called a press conference in Ottawa, not merely to protest his daughter's innocence, but to boast about her: "I am proud that my daughter believes, as I do, that hungry children should be fed whether they are Black Panthers or White Republicans."[18] The next day, October 5, he flew down to Los Angeles, where he was met by a crowd of reporters anxious to interview the leader of what they described as "the Canadian Communist Party." They told him his daughter wasn't at the airport to meet him and asked, "Are you disappointed?"

"Who says she's not?" Douglas shot back; and there she was, making her way politely through the throng of journalists.[19]

The charges did not get to court until 1970, when they were thrown out for lack of any shred of evidence to support them. Even so, U.S. immigration officials mounted a campaign to deport her, and in 1978 she returned to Canada. By this time, her marriage to Sutherland had dissolved.

The Waffle Heats Things Up

Tommy returned to Ottawa to prepare for the federal convention in Winnipeg at the end of October. This was where, David Lewis supposed, Tommy would hand on the baton. But it was not to be.

Most of the agitation for a new leader came from the younger members of the party; and they were not entranced at the notion of replacing a man born in 1904 with one born in 1909 as representative of new thought. However, the stars-to-be were still not visible. The philosophy

---

[18] Quoted in *Ottawa Journal*, 5 October 1969.

[19] The scene was caught on camera, and appeared in a documentary on Tommy called *Keeper of the Flame*.

professor Charles Taylor, undoubtedly young, impeccably bilingual, thoroughly modern, and unquenchably a Quebecker, had been shellacked in the 1968 vote. Ed Broadbent, a brilliant young academic from Ontario, was untried, and no one else with anything like national stature was visible. The youngsters could nudge Tommy and point to the door — they had already done so — but no one stood on the other side but Lewis.

The Ontario Provincial Council, where most of the earlier agitation to nudge Tommy out the door had started, wrote him a letter, begging him not to retire. He might have been tempted to fire back a short, rude reply, but he was too good a party man to indulge himself. Instead, he issued a press release announcing that he would stay on until the 1971 convention, but "under no circumstances" would he stay after that.[20] He emphasized that he was remaining in place for reasons of political strategy, while the party scoured the countryside for a less age-challenged successor.

Lewis was furious, but never betrayed his anger in public. Indeed, he signed the nominating papers, along with Broadbent, Manitoba premier Ed Schreyer, and Charles Taylor, and Tommy was re-elected as leader without opposition. However, he was no longer the man in charge; as the party became bogged down in internal strife over the Waffle, it was hard to detect whether anyone was in charge.

It's hard to explain to outsiders about the Waffle. It was such an NDP kind of thing. The Waffle was a group of angry young men — they were overwhelmingly, though not exclusively, men — who seemed determined to wreck the party to which they belonged because it had "abandoned the principles for which it once stood."

That's what they said. Actually, neither the NDP nor its parent, the CCF, stood for the kind and degree of nationalization that the Waffle wanted. Perhaps while the words of the Regina Manifesto were still echoing around the Calgary meeting of the CCF in 1933, the party was dedicated to the proposition that the state should be the owner of all of the nation's major means of production. After that, a semblance of proportion crept in until, by the time of the Winnipeg Declaration, most

---

[20] Press release, 5 May 1969, Douglas Papers, National Archives of Canada.

party members understood that they lived in a mixed economy. They wanted a fairer distribution of society's wealth; if state ownership was the only solution in some sectors of the economy, then that solution should be applied. Otherwise, not.

The young men of the Waffle didn't see it that way. They believed that Marxist economic principles (not politics) explained the way things worked, and they believed that if the party went back to its roots, those fifteen minutes in Calgary, it would be purified. This might, or might not, lead to electoral success. They didn't care. Purity is what they were after, and if the upper councils of the party weren't prepared to bring out the incense and swing the censer on behalf of purity, to hell with them.

The solution for the Waffle, you might have thought, would be to launch a new party, closer to their heart's desire, rather than to shove a spoke in the wheels of the only vehicle in sight that seemed, at least, to be going in the right direction. But no, the Waffle were going to bring the NDP to heel. And the NDP, trapped in the politesse of party mechanics, never seemed to know what to do about it.

The term "Waffle" came from Ed Broadbent. In 1969, when the newly minted MP from Oshawa-Whitby was trying out his wings, he was accused of waffling on the answer to a question, and retorted, "I'd rather waffle to the left than waffle to the right." Not exactly up there with "*L'état, c'est moi,*" but it caught on. The younger, more restless, and more frustrated members of the party began to form a coalition around Broadbent: James Laxer, a professor at the University of Toronto; Mel Watkins, who had bolted from the Liberals when his report was filed in the Ottawa recycling bin; Gerald Caplan, an associate professor at the Ontario Institute for Studies in Education; John Harney, another teacher; and a handful of others. They were overwhelmingly academics, learned rather than experienced, filled to the brim with a kind of cunning innocence that had them stacking NDP meetings to shove through resolutions of socialist purity and undiluted sappiness, just as the Communists used to do, then fading off into the night, leaving the wreckage behind.

As a reporter for the *Toronto Star*, I spent several days with the Waffle, and found it exhilarating, but not enlightening. At a meeting in Brantford, Ontario, for example, after a strong and pointed speech by Mel Watkins, a resolution was propounded to solve the nation's housing problems. Briefly, the solution was to expropriate houses from their present owners and turn them over to the state, which would redistribute them to others who needed them more. During these massive expropriations, fair prices would be paid to the owners, but "This, of course, does not include landlords."

After the meeting, a man came up to question Watkins. He had built a couple of houses that he was renting until he could sell them. "Doesn't this resolution mean the government could take away my place and pay me nothing?" he asked.

Watkins had to admit that it did.

"Well, do you think that's fair?"

Watkins allowed that, no, when you came to think about it, it wasn't fair.

The man went on, "How about a guy who's moved by his company and rents his house until he can sell. He's a landlord, too, isn't he?"

Well, yes, he is, and no, he wouldn't get any compensation either. But the resolution stood, and remained the model resolution the Waffle kept trying to sneak past riding associations.[21]

The Waffle were able to indulge themselves with the confidence of a group that knows it has no chance of ever having to carry out any of its proposals. The federal structure of the NDP, like that of the CCF, conferred advantages on any upstart group; the federal party could not move against them, because they belonged to associations affiliated with the provincial party organizations. About all the central office could do when confronted with one of these resolutions, which were played vigorously in the press (the media, by and large, treated the NDP like a suspicious odour in a back room, but they loved the Waffle and gave their activities prominent play), was to whine that the Waffle did not represent official party policy with whatever inanity it was currently peddling. David Lewis, and Stephen, once he caught on to what was happening, dismissed the

---

[21] Stewart, *Shrug*, 194–95.

group as self-righteous, doctrinaire, and anti-democratic, because of the way they operated.

But Tommy seemed to get a certain enjoyment out of the Waffle and the stir they caused. He appeared on a television panel with Cy Gonick, a Winnipeg academic who became a prominent Waffler, and appeared to support Gonick's argument that the old parties had already whipped off most of the NDP's garments and it was time for a new suit. He became alarmed, however, when the Waffle issued its own policy manifesto, called Towards an Independent Socialist Canada, about a month before the federal convention in 1969. The manifesto set forth a bold new approach in which all major industry in the country would be held by a combination of state ownership and worker control. It embodied a good deal of Marxist rhetoric, which the main body of the party was not anxious to defend at the polls.

Tommy congratulated the Waffle on their effort to provoke a "spirited convention," but told them he could not embrace their economics:

> I think while there's a place for public ownership, that widespread public ownership can be a very blunt instrument that can lead to a greater bureaucracy without necessarily solving the economic problem that you're trying to solve.[22]

This just proved to the Waffle that Douglas was an old hack, as they had thought all along.

He returned the insult when the 1969 convention turned on a plenary debate of the Waffle manifesto. Tommy described that paper's proposals rudely: "It's like a man who wants to burn down his house because he's got rats in the basement."[23]

The Waffle resolution went down to defeat, but many of its members were elected to seats on the National Council, and Mel Watkins was elected vice-president. He then wrote a letter to the *Globe and Mail*, apologizing for accepting this position.

---

[22] *Question Period*, CTV television program, 17 October 1969.
[23] Quoted in McLeod and McLeod, *Road to Jerusalem,* 279.

The battle continued in the provinces when the Waffle attacked Premier Woodrow Lloyd, in Saskatchewan, for being "too soft." Lloyd, who was in ill health, and worn out with the medicare battle, resigned soon after this and went to work for the United Nations. (He died in Korea in 1972, at the age of fifty-eight.) In Ontario, the rebels persisted in agitating for reform and pushing for power, and in Quebec, they lined up with the Parti Québecois; on one notable occasion, Wafflers trooped out of a Montreal NDP meeting and adjourned to a PQ gathering nearby.

By the time of the 1971 convention, when Tommy was stepping down, the main body of the party was ready to move against the Waffle, and a Waffle resolution to nationalize all resource industries was beaten back by a three-to-one margin. Soon after, James Laxer, the Waffle candidate for leader, was defeated handily by David Lewis, who finally got his hands on the leadership when it was, arguably, about a decade too late; he was sixty-three, the same age Tommy had been when Stephen Lewis went out to Vancouver.

The Waffle was eventually done in by the labour movement in Ontario. The Waffle organized a caucus within the Ontario Federation of Labour and began issuing press releases condemning the "rightists" then in command of the unions. Labour was not as polite, or as democratic, as the NDP. Union leaders, like Dennis McDermott of the Canadian Auto Workers and Murray Cotterill of the Steelworkers, began to say bluntly and out loud that if the party did not rid itself of the Waffle, it could forget about union support, either at the polls or at the bank.

In June 1972, by a massive majority, the Ontario Provincial Council passed a resolution that amounted to an ejection of the Waffle; they were told to get rid of the name and stop behaving like a party within the party, or get out. They got out. Within a few months of the Ontario showdown, the Waffle had disappeared; the academics who gave it most of its fire went back to their classrooms (except for Broadbent, who quickly eschewed the Waffle's radicalism, established himself as an aggressive and active MP, and prepared himself for the party leadership, which became his in 1975).

Tommy, meanwhile, was hard at work as the NDP's energy critic. He had not been directly involved in the confrontation, both because it was an Ontario scrap and because he was no longer the federal leader. But while this turmoil was going on, Tommy Douglas, in a kind of unrehearsed and unscheduled Last Hurrah, showed the party and the nation the true quality of his leadership.

War Measures

Tommy won the highest regard among his colleagues and opponents in Parliament through a stance that brought him nothing but abuse at the time: his instant, unshakeable opposition to the imposition of the War Measures Act, and its successor Public Order Act, by Prime Minister Trudeau in October 1970. It was, said Donald Brittain, in his documentary on Tommy, "his finest hour."

On Monday, October 5, 1970, at 8:15 a.m., two men gained access to the home of British trade commissioner James Cross, in Westmount, Quebec, on the pretext that they were delivering a birthday gift. What they carried, however, was not a gift, but revolvers. They handcuffed Cross and bundled him into a waiting taxi. A bystander heard one of the men say, "We're the FLQ."

Soon afterwards, the police received a ransom note containing a list of seven demands, which included publication of a manifesto from the Front de libération du Québec. The ransom note also demanded the release of twenty-three "political prisoners" — whose numbers included convicted terrorists — $500,000 in gold, and the re-hiring of *les gars de Lapalme,* workers who had been hired to move the mail in Montreal and then discharged. They also wanted a plane to fly them to either Cuba or Algeria with their gold. The FLQ had written out a list of "enemies of the people," for the edification of the general public.

The next morning, at a meeting of the Cabinet Committee on Priorities and Planning, Trudeau made it clear that Canada would not give in to these demands, but would keep negotiations open to save the life of James Cross. A message went back to the FLQ (these messages were always left in a telephone booth indicated to one of two Montreal radio stations by the kidnappers, with the location passed on to the RCMP), rejecting the demands but asking to speak to the kidnappers. They replied that Cross would be killed if their demands were not met by 8:30 a.m. on Wednesday. A series of pre-dawn raids that day resulted in thirty arrests, but no clues as to the whereabouts of the trade commissioner. The 8:30 deadline was ignored.

On Wednesday afternoon, the kidnappers sent along a handwritten note from Cross to prove that he was still alive. That evening, external affairs minister Mitchell Sharp, at a news conference, asked that a mediator be named by the FLQ to deal with the federal authorities. The man named was Robert Lemieux, a Montreal lawyer.

On Thursday, October 8, at 10 p.m., Radio-Canada met one of the key demands, broadcasting the FLQ manifesto in French. It was also printed in major newspapers the next day. It turned out to be a near-illiterate hodgepodge of demands, complaints, and threats.

On Saturday, October 10, Pierre Laporte, the labour minister in Robert Bourassa's Quebec cabinet, was seized at machine-gunpoint from outside his home on the south shore of the St. Lawrence River, near Montreal. This crime came shortly after Jérôme Choquette, Bourassa's justice minister, had refused to release the prisoners demanded by the FLQ and offered instead to trade safe conduct to Cuba for the release of Cross. The abduction was described as an "instant response" to Choquette's statement, but it could not have been; the abductors were driving around Laporte's home while the justice minister was speaking.

This was the work of an entirely different group of FLQ supporters who had decided that the seizure of Cross was a mistake; what was needed was a French-Canadian hostage. However, the accidental timing made it appear that the terrorists were a highly organized, incredibly swift-moving organization.

That night, Premier Robert Bourassa moved into a guarded suite on the twentieth floor of the Queen Elizabeth Hotel in downtown Montreal. On Sunday, October 11, while senior officials from Ottawa and Quebec held a series of meetings to plot strategy, Robert Lemieux, the lawyer who was acting as a go-between, was arrested, charged with "obstructing justice," and thrown into jail. That night, Premier Bourassa made a speech that seemed to indicate he was willing to negotiate with the kidnappers. Lemieux was then released from jail and was asked to act as their spokesman.

Because this was the Thanksgiving weekend, there was a pause of two days while the police scrambled around, senior bureaucrats met, and not much happened. Then, on the Tuesday after the long weekend, John Diefenbaker, the leader of the official opposition and, before this, ever the defender of civil rights, asked pointedly in the House whether the government was willing to impose the War Measures Act. On Thursday, the cabinet, or rather the prime minister, decided to do just that. It came into effect the next day, October 16.

Under the regulations that came into effect with the imposition of this legislation, Canadians could be arrested and held without recourse to a lawyer, without charge, without bail, merely on suspicion. It became illegal ever to have belonged to the FLQ, a party that had been legal for seven years in Canada. Retroactive crimes were manufactured, and citizens were jailed on these uncharged offences. The curbs to liberty and the rule of law that were imposed in 1970 were much the same as those imposed in 2001 after the tragedy of the World Trade Center in New York; and both times it was the leader of the NDP who stood in the House to challenge them.

However, it was not at all clear that the NDP in 1970 formed anything like a united front on the subject. Frank Scott, the party stalwart and a stalwart civil libertarian, declared his support of War Measures from the start, but David Lewis, who was not only the heir-all-too-apparent, but the practical leader in questions of parliamentary strategy, was uncertain. Even as the caucus moved into the House chamber for a recorded vote,

Lewis asked Tommy if he thought what they were doing was wise.
Tommy replied, "I am going to vote against this if I am the only person
who does."[24] As it happened, sixteen MPs voted against the government,
Tommy and fifteen NDP colleagues. Four other NDPers voted with the
government.

The case for imposition was supported by almost no concrete evidence. What follows is an edited version of the account given by Eric
Kierans, who was Trudeau's minister for communications at the time, in
his memoirs.

> When ministers ask questions, they are answered by
> Lalonde [Marc Lalonde, then principal secretary to the
> prime minister], not the Prime Minister, and what he
> tells us is that Quebec is ready to explode. If swift and
> stern action is not taken at once, the best information
> from the best experts informs us that there will be riots,
> political assassinations, chaos.
>
> . . . There was no secret knowledge that explained the
> imposition of War Measures. Everything we were told
> in Cabinet came from the streets outside. Turner [John
> Turner, then minister of justice] also argued that "under
> the present law, the prosecution of this type of violent,
> criminal conspiracy is rendered difficult, if not impossible,
> under the present provisions of the Criminal Code."
>
> . . . When the War Measures Act was proclaimed on
> October 16, 1970, two reasons were given. The first was
> that there was an apprehended insurrection, the evi-
> dence for which Canadians were to take on faith. The
> second was that Quebec had asked for the imposition of
> the Act, which was undoubtedly true, but might have
> been more frankly explained by announcing that the
> Quebec police and the RCMP were agreed on the suspen-
> sion of civil liberties, and everybody else went along.[25]

---

[24] Shackleton, *Tommy Douglas*, 303.

[25] Kierans, *Remembering*, 181.

What the Kierans account does not convey is the degree of hostility Tommy encountered from fellow parliamentarians for daring to suggest that two kidnappings and a great deal of public hysteria did not make the case for setting aside the civil liberties of ordinary Canadians. In the following excerpt from Hansard, the reader needs to be aware that when the official recorder sets down the words "Oh, oh!" or "Hear, hear!" the phrases actually uttered on the floor of the House were a good deal stronger, and sometimes unprintable:

> Mr. DOUGLAS (Nanaimo-Cowichan-The Islands):
> We are prepared to support the government in taking whatever measures are necessary to safeguard life and maintain order in this country. But, Mr. Speaker, we are not prepared to use the preservation of law and order as a smokescreen to destroy the liberties and the freedom of the people of Canada.
> Some hon. MEMBERS: Oh, oh!
> Some hon. MEMBERS: Hear, hear!
> Some hon. MEMBERS: Shame!
> An hon. MEMBER: There is no shame.
> Mr. DOUGLAS (Nanaimo-Cowichan-The Islands):
> I wonder if the Liberal members who are shouting "Shame" have read the regulations.
> An hon. MEMBER: Yes.
> Mr. LANGLOIS: The hon. member should go to Quebec and find out about the situation.
> Mr. DOUGLAS (Nanaimo-Cowichan-The Islands):
> The government, I submit, is using a sledgehammer to crack a peanut.
> Some hon. MEMBERS: Oh, oh![26]

When Tommy argued that the violence of FLQ supporters did not justify the suspension of civil liberties, he was accused of being afraid or

---

[26] House of Commons, *Debates*, 16 October 1970.

of being a closet separatist (that was Trudeau's contribution to the debate at this point); when he argued that the arrests of so many Quebeckers, all francophones, would buttress rather than weaken support for the separatist cause, he was drowned out by shouts from the government side. (He turned out to be quite right.)

He stood beside his desk — with one hand stretched out, fingers down, to support him — and spoke calmly, never once losing his temper or responding to the taunts with a smart crack (it was not a time for smart cracks), and tore the government's arguments to shreds.

Not that anyone paid any attention at the time. In the aftermath, Prime Minister Trudeau's approval ratings shot up, and the NDP standings in the polls sagged to 13 per cent. It appeared that the leader of the NDP, by leading wisely and well, was doing his party no good at all.

Perhaps Stephen Lewis had it right after all; perhaps it was more than time to step down. And so, while Tommy remained leader until his formal resignation at the federal party convention in April 1971 (it took four ballots for Lewis to gain the leadership), he was something of a spent force after the events of October 1970 — events that showed Canadians, who didn't want to know, how impressive a leader he really was. Still, he would prove to be, as always, an effective and energetic member of Parliament.

Chapter SEVENTEEN

Do Not Go Gentle . . .

He never despaired, no matter what the obstacle. That exuberant and hopeful spirit, based on the deep conviction that society should be organized for the benefit of all the people and not for a privileged few, is what took him through all of the obstacles in his long and remarkable life. That is his legacy to us today.
— Ed Broadbent, Hansard, February 24, 1986

Tommy, at sixty-seven, was an active and energetic member of Parliament, even if he was no longer the party leader. As an MP, his most important contribution was his role in helping to establish a national energy company, which came about, as so many advances have done in Canadian politics, because the NDP was able to demand reform of a minority government.

Trudeau's spell of enchantment on the general public had begun to pale a little when the economy turned sour at the beginning of the 1970s and Canadians were introduced to a new word, "stagflation," to describe the combination of high interest rates and high unemployment. Trudeau had married the beautiful but somewhat disconnected Margaret Sinclair, had alienated much of his own party by his arrogance, and had enraged western Canadians by first his neglect and then his scorn of them ("Why should I sell your wheat?"). By the time he had to go to the electorate again, on October 30, 1972, he was very nearly defeated. Not by the NDP — which improved to 31 seats, but was still a long way from mounting a serious threat to take over power — but by Stanfield's Tories.

However, Trudeau once more campaigned with twice the panache and energy with which he governed and managed to squeak out a narrow victory. The end result saw the Liberals with 109 seats, the Tories with 107, the NDP with 31, the Socreds with 11, and Others with 2.

The Liberals, as a result, could retain power only by cutting a deal with the New Democrats. As part of this deal, the NDP were able to demand a Foreign Investment Review Agency (FIRA), charged with ensuring that, in the foreign takeover of any Canadian corporation with assets of more than $250,000 or annual sales of more than $3 million, there would be a "significant benefit" to Canada. With the passage of time, FIRA was effectively emasculated by the hang-up over what constituted a "significant benefit," but at the beginning it seemed like a bold step. The NDP also managed to force on the government a crown corporation that would give it an inside position in the energy sector.

The Royal Canadian Oil Farce

The NDP advocated a government-owned oil company early and often (it was part of the founding convention's bundle of policies), and Tommy, who took on the energy critic's job in 1969 while he was still the leader of the party, argued that Canada must have self-sufficiency in energy, which could only be obtained by increasing domestic supplies and control over energy policy. This meant that Canada would have to have a corporation of its own in the oil business, or it would never know which policies made sense — oil is anything but a smooth ride.

Cost has never had anything to do with the price of oil; it has always been an artificially priced commodity. During the 1950s and '60s, international oil firms produced Arabian light crude — the bellwether grade — for ten cents a barrel and sold it for a "posted" price of $1.75 to $1.98. They were able to do this because the world oil market was dominated by seven major oil companies, the "Seven Sisters," which moved 98 per cent of the oil on the international stage.[1] Their artificially high prices created massive royalties for exporters and profits for themselves, which they collected, mainly, in foreign lands where the taxes were few and low.

The first revolution in this cosy system occurred when the Middle Eastern states began to cut themselves in by nationalizing their own

---

[1] Five of the Seven Sisters were U.S. firms: Exxon, Texaco, Gulf, Mobil, and Standard Oil of California. The others were British Petroleum and Royal Dutch Shell. Their tangled history is given in Christopher T. Rand, *Making Democracy Safe for Oil* (New York: Little, Brown, 1975).

resources in the 1950s. Then, when Exxon, the world's largest oil company, abruptly cut its posted price twice, in 1959 and 1960, without even consulting the Arabian oil-producing nations, the Middle Eastern states were so furious that they formed a body, the Organization of Petroleum Exporting Countries (OPEC), to try to assert control over their own commodity. The cartel owes its creation not so much to the Arab sheiks who are so often blamed for it, as to the crude and grasping ways of the Seven Sisters.

Canada's oil policy was formulated by the oil firms themselves, and they decided, in their wisdom, that it was best for them to import oil from Venezuela to serve eastern Canadian markets and to use western Canadian oil for western markets and for export to the United States. Venezuelan oil cost the Maritimes more than the eastern United States paid for Middle Eastern supplies, but there was no danger that a pipeline would be built to ship western oil east. The oil firms didn't want that, and a Royal Commission on Energy explained candidly that such a pipeline could not be built because the multinationals would not support such a policy.[2]

Canada's "national oil policy" was not made in Canada; it was made in the oil company boardrooms of the United States. The nub of that policy became a determination to export more and more oil to the United States. At first, Tommy favoured this idea, until his own research began to suggest that we might be running out of oil, despite the reassurances of the oil firms that we had the stuff up to our navels. In the summer of 1973, he addressed an NDP summer convention on this subject, condemning "the economic insanity of selling our cheap supplies of oil and gas to the United States," and the convention adopted a resolution calling for a change in policy.

The Liberals paid no attention. They had been assuring Canadians for years that, just as the fuel firms insisted, we had so much oil and gas we should sell it as fast as possible, while we could. In 1971, energy minister J.J. Greene, using figures supplied by the oil companies (there were no other figures available), had announced that Canada had "923 years

---

[2] Lawrence Solomon, *Energy Shock* (Toronto: Doubleday, 1980), 93

supply for oil and 392 years for gas." The exactness of the numbers sounded impressive. And trade minister Jean-Luc Pepin had made a speech in which he said:

> In maybe twenty-five to fifty years, we'll be heating ourselves with the rays of the sun and then we'll kick ourselves in the pants for not capitalizing on what we had when oil and gas were current commodities.[3]

Then the OPEC nations began to send oil prices up through their operating arm, Aramco (the Arab-American Oil Company, which was effectively controlled by the Seven Sisters; they were delighted to comply with orders to increase their own profits along with the OPEC take).

In May 1973, Tommy suggested a freeze on domestic oil prices as a way to keep the oil companies from reaping a windfall profit. There should also be a tax on the export of oil, he said, so that Canada could collect the difference between a lower domestic price and the new and higher world price as the oil crossed the border. This would later become the approach of Trudeau's National Energy Programme, and it raised hackles in every household west of the Lakehead. The effect would be to keep prices lower in eastern Canada at the expense of the western exporting provinces, especially Alberta and Saskatchewan.

Tommy later amended the proposal to suggest that the export tax would be paid to the producing provinces, but he still found himself in a battle with Allan Blakeney, who by this time was premier of Saskatchewan. "We had a meeting in Toronto," Blakeney recalled, "and while nobody shouted at anybody, I was pretty upset."[4]

The meeting, at the Royal York Hotel, saw representatives of the NDP federal caucus, led by David Lewis and Tommy, trying to explain to Blakeney why oil prices should be controlled. "I couldn't see it," Blakeney recalls. "Under our constitution, it is the provinces who have the job of managing natural resources."[5] If the oil companies were making a windfall profit, he argued, it was up to the provinces to get it

---

[3] Rand, *Making Democracy Safe*, 150.
[4] Allan Blakeney, interview by author, Saskatoon, 24 October 2000.
[5] Ibid.

back by way of royalties. In any event, it was manifestly unfair to ask the western provinces to turn what would amount to billions of dollars of lost revenue over to the consumers of the rest of Canada, who had never shown the slightest inclination to cut the prices of goods flowing *into* Saskatchewan to below the world price for the benefit of the people there.

Tommy was uncomfortable with the position forced on him by his own logic and left much of the argument at that Toronto meeting up to David Lewis. Blakeney was not entirely comfortable, either. He could see that he might be perceived as lining up with the "blue-eyed sheiks" of Alberta, the staunchest defenders of the oil companies.

The argument was still raging within the NDP when the roof fell in, as a result of Egypt's attack on Israeli forces along the Suez Canal on October 3, 1973. Two weeks later, the Arab oil ministers met to discuss an embargo against "unfriendly nations," and on October 19, when King Faisal of Saudi Arabia learned that the United States had agreed to provide $2.5 billion worth of arms to Israel, an embargo was declared against all oil shipments to the Americans.

Although the amount of oil actually blocked was small, the psychological effect was not. Oil prices on the international market went from $2.41 a barrel to $17.34 in just a few weeks. North American producers, despite warnings that had been echoing around the world for months, had done nothing to guard against an embargo — why would they? All it meant for them was higher prices — and now announced that due to circumstances beyond their control, they had to quadruple their prices (and later double them again) because of the shortage.

In reality, there was no shortage. During the crisis — which lasted from October 19, 1973, until the embargo was lifted on March 18, 1974 — oil imports were actually higher than they had been before the embargo. There was more gasoline on hand than ever, but the oil companies were not even running at capacity.[6]

The OPEC nations and the oil companies made a killing; but as people began to become aware of the massive fraud being perpetrated, a certain restiveness arose. Canadians had been told by the oil companies

---

[6] Stewart, *Uneasy Lies the Head*, 145ff.

that we had the stuff coming out of our ears; now, suddenly, we were running out and, if we didn't act soon, we'd be freezing in the dark. Canada's National Energy Board, which had overseen the quadrupling of Canadian petroleum exports to the United States, suddenly discovered that "Canadian oil supplies would be inadequate to serve Canadian markets . . . by 1982."[7]

In the middle of the crisis, the federal government decided to dust off a study it had commissioned in 1971 on the possibility of creating a national energy company. This study had been performed by an American firm, of course, and the Arthur D. Little Company of Cambridge, Massachusetts, had turned most of the work over to a Canadian geologist, Wilbert H. Hopper. Because he didn't like crown corporations, he told the Arthur D. Little Company to forget about the idea, and the Arthur D. Little Company told the government, and the government forgot about it.

But there is nothing like an election to open a government to new approaches, and the 1972 election meant that the Liberals were now dependent on the NDP. And so it came to pass that the same cabinet that had given the notion of an oil crown the heave-ho in 1971 suddenly discovered that it mightn't be such a bad idea, after all, in 1973. They commissioned another study, *An Energy Policy for Canada — Phase I,* which was dropped on ministerial desks in October 1973, just when the ministers were hearing from the folks lined up at gas stations that things were not going too well on the we've-got-lots-of-oil front.

Now it was clear to everyone who had even a modest grasp of the subject that Canada had allowed itself to become absolutely dependent on foreign oil companies, who were responsible to their own stockholders and to nobody else. It was also clear that Canada could not trust the foreign firms who operated our oil industry to level with us. Yet, even at this late date, there were many in the Liberal cabinet who opposed the idea of a national oil company, and if Trudeau had owned a majority, the government might well have ignored Tommy's repeated suggestions to get on with it. However, Trudeau did not have a majority, and David Lewis,

[7] Ibid., 151.

as the NDP leader, made it clear that unless legislation establishing such a company appeared forthwith, his party would back a non-confidence motion against the government. He instructed Cliff Scotton, the national secretary of the party, to prepare for an election and warned the caucus that there could be no turning back.

On December 6, 1973, Prime Minister Pierre Trudeau, with something of the air of Jack Horner producing a plum, announced that his government had just had a terrific idea: to form a national oil corporation; "The objective of that policy, to be reached before the end of this decade, is Canadian self-sufficiency in oil and oil products."[8]

While Trudeau was speaking, David Lewis was in Edmonton to make a series of pre-election speeches. Tommy, who was in the House, walked out to the lobby and telephoned Lewis to tell him that the government had capitulated completely. He then committed the party to supporting the government in the non-confidence vote.

However, the drama was not yet over. Bill C-8, An Act to Establish a National Petroleum Company, was introduced in May 1974, just before the Liberals lost another non-confidence vote, this time based on their budget. The NDP, although it was not at all anxious to face yet another election, balked at that budget because it seemed to do nothing for the unemployed and too much for corporations.

Thus, the oil-company-in-waiting became part of the 1974 election campaign; the Liberals were for it; the NDP claimed parenthood; and the Tories were against it. To reward the NDP for its prescience, the voters cut the party's parliamentary representation almost in half; it went from 31 seats down to 16.[9]

Trudeau managed to make it look as if his party had been responding to public opinion in reversing itself on a national oil corporation. The NDP, he said, were like a flock of seagulls; because they squawked a lot, "they thought they were actually running the ship."[10]

Tommy replied by noting that all of the major steps taken by the government over the past year had been first proposed by the NDP, then rejected by the Liberals, and then put in place by the Liberals, with NDP help:

---

[8] House of Commons, *Debates,* 6 October 1973.
[9] The Liberals came back with 141 seats in a House of 264; the Tories won 95 seats and Social Credit 11, and there was one "Other."
[10] House of Commons, *Debates,* 24 February 1974.

It was the members of this party who, in January of last year, advocated putting domestic controls on the export of oil. The government said there was no need to do that, and then imposed them on March 1.

It was the members of this party who advocated export controls on gasoline in April. And the government finally implemented them later in June. It was the members of this party who, in May, advocated a price freeze on domestically produced oil, a two-price system, and an export tax to pick up the windfall profits. And the government put those into effect on September 6. It was this party which first proposed, and for years had been proposing, a pipeline to Montreal, which the government's energy report tabled in this House last June rejected, but which the government accepted and the Prime Minister announced on September 6. It was this party [which] first put forward the proposal for a one-price system across the country, which the Minister of Energy, Mines and Resources said was completely impractical, and which the government has now adopted.

I think when the people of Canada review the steps that have been taken with respect to the oil crisis during the past twelve months, they will be inclined to say, "Thank God for the seagulls."[11]

But the people of Canada did not review the steps that had been taken; they believed the prime minister and rewarded him accordingly. Petro-Canada, the company established by new legislation given royal assent on July 10, 1975, had, as its president, Wilbert Hopper, the same man who had decried the whole idea of a state-owned firm. The chairman was a former business executive and prominent Liberal, Maurice Strong, but he soon departed for a job with the United Nations, and Hopper became chairman and chief executive officer. However, since

---

[11] House of Commons, *Debates*, 5 March 1974.

he ran the company exactly as if it were a private concern, the irony of his position was not apparent.

Today, Petro-Canada is in the final stages of being sold to private stockholders — the Canadian taxpayer owns only about 18 per cent of the issued shares — and it has never been the company Tommy envisioned, because it has been run like a private firm, not a government one. It followed tamely behind the foreign firms in their marketing gimmicks and pricing policies; it joined in behaviour towards the Lubicon Cree of Alberta that the World Council of Churches condemned as "cultural genocide."[12] It attracted the attention of the Auditor General of Canada for its secretive policies.[13] Although Canada was officially opposed to commercial dealings with the apartheid regime of South Africa, Petro-Canada continued to ship large quantities of sulphur to that rogue state. It expanded not so much by exploration, although it was an oil explorer, as by buying up its competition. By 1985, it had spent $5 billion of taxpayers' funds, and it was hard to see what the taxpayer had gained, beyond a modicum of exploration (paid for, mostly, by government exploration grants). We had set up a corporation to protect us from Big Oil, and it became Big Oil. Then it went private.

Once again, Tommy had produced a policy that had been adopted, reluctantly and under duress, by a Liberal government; once again, the policy had been twisted into something quite different from the original proposal; and once again, whatever votes were attracted by a new initiative were delivered elsewhere. He continued to support Petro-Canada to the end of his days, and to pay little attention to the way it actually operated.

Tommy showed no signs of bitterness or regret over the fact that another NDP policy had been plundered by the Liberals; he got on with the job of criticizing the government's energy policy. His days were now somewhat shorter and less stressful, although he still worked long hours.

Uproar over the Atom

Tommy's next battle was over atomic energy. As premier of Saskatchewan, he had been a fan of nuclear power, and in his early days

---

[12] Quoted in McLeod and McLeod, *Road to Jerusalem*, 298.
[13] Stewart, *Uneasy Lies the Head*, 159.

as energy critic his only concern was to see that Uranium City, in northern Saskatchewan, got the same amount of funds for development as similar cities in northern Ontario. However, as time went on, "the friendly atom" (which, we had been told, would produce energy so cheaply that there would be no point in having meters to measure the stuff in our homes) was becoming a serious safety concern, both in the mining of the uranium that fuelled CANDU reactors[14] and the disposal of the spent fuel from the reactors.

When India exploded a nuclear device on May 18, 1974, using plutonium that had been extracted from a reactor called CIR (for Canada-India Reactor), which we had given to the Indians, alarm bells went off. External affairs minister Mitchell Sharp called the incident "most regrettable"; then his department went back to helping Atomic Energy of Canada Limited (AECL) peddle more reactors, first to Pakistan (which used its CANDU to extract plutonium for its own atomic explosion), then to South Korea, and then to Argentina. What made the sales interesting was that we ladled out massive low-interest or no-interest loans to support them; the more we sold, the more it cost us. We unloaded a CANDU on Romania with a $2 billion price tag, and Romania paid us by dumping trade goods on us. Then we sold one to Turkey, again for $2 billion, under a contract that had Canada building and paying for the reactor, and then endeavouring to sell the power to the Turks to recover our investment.[15]

None of these sales was accompanied by strictures against misuse of the plutonium or, indeed, any strictures regarding safety. When I asked a senior official of Atomic Energy of Canada what precautions would be taken to ensure that the Turkish reactor would not be used to make a bomb, he replied that he didn't know and wouldn't find out.[16]

Tommy began asking questions about nuclear safety in 1974 and 1975, arguing that no CANDU should be sold to any nation that had not first signed the international Nuclear Non-Proliferation Treaty.[17]

---

[14] CANDU stands for Canadian Deuterium Uranium, which describes the operative system of the reactor. As reactors go, it is probably the best, and safest, if there can be such a thing, in the world.

[15] Stewart, *Uneasy Lies the Head*, 104ff.

[16] Ibid.

[17] Neither India nor Pakistan would sign the treaty, or ever has. They argue that the western nations, having secured nuclear weapons for themselves, are trying to discriminate against Third World countries. They have a point.

In later sales, some safeguards were put on the use of spent fuels, but no provision whatever was made in case the safeguards were ignored. Tommy warned that this policy could bring international calamity:

> The fact is that the world is living on the edge of Armageddon. It may be that the contribution we have made to that situation up until now has been made unknowingly, but the step now being taken by the government is being taken deliberately and the government has a very heavy burden on its conscience.[18]

The government bore that burden with remarkable ease, and only became slightly concerned when the Auditor General reported that Atomic Energy of Canada had paid bribes and kickbacks of at least $15 million to promote CANDU sales in South Korea and Argentina. At least $8 million of that was paid in "expenses" to two mysterious companies that never reported what the funds were used for, nor ever supplied any receipts. In the case of the Argentine deal, $2.5 million was paid directly into two Swiss bank accounts; when the Public Accounts Committee invited representatives of the receiving firms to journey to Ottawa to chat about the deal, they shyly declined to come.[19] Oh yes, and Canada lost $130 million on the Argentine sale. Tommy lashed out at AECL's managers: "They go on spending public funds, carrying out policies and introducing programs not only without any reference to Parliament but in many cases with no reference to the minister to whom they are supposed to report."[20]

Tommy's role in the debate was essentially an educational one. He was a good researcher, and his speeches, packed with information and insights, provided fodder for many articles and speeches made by others. He had begun to be treated by the media as something of an icon, which had its good and bad points. He was no longer regarded as a bogeyman; on the other hand, he was no longer regarded as a serious threat, either. Accordingly, his views on energy matters got better play

---

[18] House of Commons, *Debates*, 30 January 1976.
[19] Stewart, *Uneasy Lies the Head*, 36, 37.
[20] House of Commons, *Debates*, 7 July 1977.

than many of his earlier views, and certainly much better play than the ordinary critic of a government portfolio might be expected to get when his party stood third, and a wobbly third at that, in the federal house. He had become that underrated but invaluable personage, a first-rate member of Parliament listened to with care, if not always agreement, by members on all sides of the House.

Not a Man You Got to Know

Tommy had also become a little testy. Well, he had always been a little testy, as an NDP loyalist, Barbara Wallace, told Ed and Pemrose Whelan:

> Tommy arrived from Ottawa and we had a meeting in somebody's house. He came in with his charming, affable greetings. Then Tommy said, "What have you been doing? Have you got signs?" Well, no, we didn't have any signs. "Have you got anybody canvassing?" Well, no, we didn't have anybody canvassing. "Well, have you got committee rooms?" Well, no we didn't have committee rooms. "What have you been doing all this time? We have to get this thing going." He blew his top at all of us. Then we got going.[21]

Dale Lovick, who worked on Tommy's campaigns in Nanaimo (and went on to hold two cabinet portfolios in the provincial NDP government and then to edit *Tommy Douglas Speaks*), found him "very hard-nosed about wanting things done — on the verge of being abusive."[22] Lovick thought this might have come from "seventeen years of being a premier; you get to expect people to jump":

> He would come to an association meeting and begin making big plans for campaigns, and when we would say we didn't have any money, he would say, "Don't you worry about the money; we'll get the money. You just

[21] Whelan and Whelan, *Touched by Tommy*, 113.
[22] Dale Lovick, interview by author, Nanaimo, 3 May 2001.

do your job." Of course, in many cases, he would get the money.[23]

Lovick admired Tommy tremendously — "A lot of us were drawn into the party almost entirely by his reputation and his speeches" — but like many of Tommy's admirers, never felt he really knew him: "He was not a man you could get to know, really. There was always this private part of himself that never got revealed."

When Lovick said this to me over a restaurant table in Nanaimo, my mind went back fifteen years to a conversation I had with Cliff Scotton, who was both the federal secretary of the NDP and, on two federal campaigns, Tommy's minder. "You didn't get to know him, really," Scotton said then. "You just got to accept him, and admire him."

Scotton told me how, at the end of one federal campaign, when they had been together every day for months, he came to say goodbye to Tommy. They were staying at the Fort Garry Hotel in Winnipeg, and Tommy was flying back to his riding in British Columbia, while Cliff was on his way to Ottawa: "I came into his room, and he was sitting there in a chair beside the bed. I don't know what I expected, not a hug or anything like that, but at least a thank you. I said, 'Well, I'm off,' and he said, 'Well, goodbye.'"

That was Tommy. Actually, when you think about it, it was Tom, his father, as well. Remember Tom, in Winnipeg all those years ago, finally unbending far enough to say to Tommy, "You did no bad."

Tommy was even hard on Irma, from time to time. But in November 1976, when it was clear he would not be running for Parliament again and his riding association held a testimonial dinner for the Douglases, Tommy paid Irma tribute in a speech that started, as usual, with a couple of jokes:

> You know, I heard the other day about a scene in front
> of the pearly gates, and at the pearly gates they had two
> entrances. One said, "For men who are dominated by
> their wives." And the other gate said, "For men who are

---

[23] Ibid.

NOT dominated by their wives." And the first gate had a long row of men stretching as far as the eye could see, all trying to get in. And the second gate had only one man standing there. And St. Peter came along and said, "What are you standing here for?" And the fellow said, "I don't know. My wife told me to stand here." So that's what I do, just whatever my wife tells me to do.

But I want to say in all seriousness, of course, that it's not just that Irma kept the home together when I was running all over the country. Somebody once said to her, "With Tommy running all over the country, aren't you afraid he'll chase women?" And she said, "No, no. In Weyburn we used to have an old Collie dog that used to chase cars, but he never knew what to do with them when he caught them."

With the jokes out of the way, he went on to talk about what his wife really meant to him in his public life:

When I came back, Irma was always there with a cheerful word, no matter how black things were, no matter how dark it got, no matter how many lickings we'd taken. The darker it got the more cheerful she was. I remember when, in the midst of the 1948 election, Walter Tucker sued me for one hundred thousand dollars. And I was worried all the way driving back to Regina. You know, we didn't have one hundred thousand cents let alone one hundred thousand dollars. And I thought, now how is Irma going to take this? Because Irma always worries about owing ten cents to anybody. She will walk ten blocks to make sure it is paid. What's she going to think about this? And it was about one thirty in the morning when I got in, I thought, she'll be in bed, I'll sneak into bed and we'll talk about it in the morning. The moment I touched the door she opened the door and says, "Hi, come on in, coffee's ready." I said, "What about the hundred thousand dollars?" And she said, "Oh, we've been through tough times before. We'll see it through this time." That's the thing that makes it possible to carry on.[24]

When they begin to give you testimonial dinners, it is time to put out the dog and kick the fire. In early 1979, Tommy retired at the age of seventy-four, and turned his energies to promoting his political views through the Douglas-Coldwell Foundation, then headquartered in the cramped NDP building on Metcalfe Street, a brisk one-kilometre walk or a short bus ride from the apartment at 440 Laurier Avenue East, where Irma and Tommy lived. Every morning, he would go to work, just as before, but he would have lunch at the Colonnade Restaurant instead of the parliamentary cafeteria — the same lunch, a fried egg on whole wheat toast, with a pot of tea — and talk to the many people who would recognize him and want to chat about politics, current or past.

At first, he travelled a good deal, and led a trip sponsored by the foundation to the People's Republic of China. He had been the first senior Canadian politician to call for the recognition of China and its admission to the United Nations.

In the winter, Tommy and Irma would spend about six weeks in Florida, and in the summer, they spent a good deal of time at a cottage Tommy built himself in the Gatineau Hills, north of Ottawa.

He wrote a number of newspaper and magazine articles and began to peck away at a book, *A New Democracy*. This was not to be a memoir — for he mistrusted memoirs as likely to be self-serving (a pity, his own recollections would have formed an invaluable contribution to Canadian history) — but a critique of political and economic thinking. It was never completed; in fact, it was barely begun.

Eleanor McKinnon, who had been with him since he first became

[24] Quoted in Lovick, *Tommy Douglas Speaks*, 262, 263.

premier of Saskatchewan in 1944, continued to work for him, as his private secretary now, to help with the constant stream of letters, queries, and requests to make speeches (for free) that came in almost every day.

He joined the board of Husky Oil Corporation, a move that surprised some of his friends and annoyed others. Tommy on the board of an oil company? But to anyone who remembered his early days as an entrepreneur and investor in Regina, it didn't seem so odd. Robert Blair, the nationalist-minded president of the company, was a great admirer of Tommy's, and Tommy returned the favour.

In 1981, a routine visit to the doctor disclosed that he had inoperable cancer. Only a very few people close to him heard anything about it; he carried on as if nothing had changed. Drugs brought about a remission, for a time, but the last five years of his life were spent in a spirited but doomed battle against the encroaching disease.

In 1984, while out for one of his daily walks, he was hit by a bus — he was getting very hard of hearing and stepped out from the curb right into the path of the bus — and wound up in hospital. From his hospital bed, he issued the cheerful bulletin, "If you think I'm in bad shape, you should see the bus!"

He continued to be called on by his party on grand occasions and could still electrify a crowd. However, he was gradually dragged down by the cancer and saw only a few old friends over the next few years. By early 1986, it was clear that he was fading fast, but when Tom McLeod went to see him,

> . . . he was as cheerful as ever. We talked about all sorts of things, and he said, "Now, as soon as I get over this thing, you and I are going to go out on a membership drive for the foundation. We'll go right across the country, and raise a heck of a lot of money. Don't you forget."[25]

That was just a few days before he died, at home, with Irma and his daughter Shirley nearby, on February 26, 1986.

---

[25] Thomas McLeod, interview by author, Victoria, 6 May 2001.

Chapter EIGHTEEN

The Legacy

Sometimes people say to me, "Do you feel your life has been wasted? The New Democratic Party has not come to power in Ottawa." And I look back and think that a boy from a poor home on the wrong side of the tracks in Winnipeg was given the privilege of being part of a movement that has changed Canada. In my lifetime I have seen it change Canada. When you people sent me to the House of Commons in 1935, we had no universal old age pension. We have one now. It's not enough, but we have one. We had no unemployment insurance. We had no central bank of Canada, publicly owned. We didn't have a wheat board, didn't have any crop insurance, didn't have a Canada Pension Plan, didn't have family allowances.

Saskatchewan was told that it would never get hospital insurance. Yet Saskatchewan people were the first in Canada to establish this kind of insurance, and we were followed by the rest of Canada. We didn't have medicare in those days...

—Tommy Douglas, November 20, 1970

The above quote is from a speech Tommy made in Prince Albert, Saskatchewan, when his days as a party leader were drawing to a close. Doris Shackleton quoted the speech at length in her biography, with the comment that Tommy revealed himself in his speeches "as he never did in private conversation."[1]

This quote ought to be set against the fact that, on the day Tommy died, February 24, 1986, successor governments, both Liberal and Conservative, had already begun to dismantle the social safety net that Tommy had spent his entire life helping to put into place. They had even begun to corrode medicare itself, his proudest accomplishment.

---

[1] Shackleton, *Tommy Douglas*, 309.

Medicare was fully in place across the country in 1971. Mr. Justice Emmett Hall, whose report had completed the work Tommy started and moved the program to a federal level, looked at it again in 1981. In this report, he declared that extra billing by doctors, which had either begun or was contemplated in a number of provinces, should be banned.[2] This paved the way for the Canada Health Act in 1984 to clarify the rules under which federal aid to the provinces would be paid. Now there were five conditions to be met before money could flow from federal coffers: the provincial plan must cover all physicians' services, as defined in the provincial legislation; and it must be universal, portable, publicly administered, and free of other user fees or extra billing. Ottawa could hold back, dollar for dollar, an amount equal to the extra billing charges or user charges, such as the extra fees many hospitals had begun to levy.

Too late now. It was also too late for a salaried solution when Ontario doctors rebelled at this removal of extra billing, which they had been collecting at the rate of $50 million a year.[3] They staged a strike that lasted twenty-five days and earned them a reputation for pig-headedness and greed. The government stood firm and allowed no extra billing.

However, long before this amendment to make medicare complete, the scheme was under acute stress because of the fact that it was a government-funded plan without government financial controls. It was inspired in the first place, as we have seen, by a handful of people, led by one man of singular determination, and it was imposed on most of the provinces and the medical profession against their wishes. The compromises made necessary along the way, such as giving in to the insistence on fee-for-services payment to the doctors, meant that costs could not be effectively curbed.

When he first implemented medicare, as we say, Tommy was against the fee-for-services approach, but caved in on this crucial point as the necessary price of peace in the Saskatchewan struggle. Maybe he was right in the first place, and doctors should have been put on salary to begin with. To all those who complain that this would be like putting lawyers on salary when they perform legal aid, the proper response is

---

[2] Perry, *Fiscal History of Canada*, 655.
[3] Ibid., 657.

"What a good idea."

In the same way, Tommy thought there should be some sort of financial tag attached to every medical procedure, even if it was a small one, to prevent abuse of the system. In this case, he was overruled by his own backers, and gave way.

Because of the compromises that Tommy made in the beginning, we ended up with a program under which whatever the hospitals spent or the doctors prescribed would be provided, and the costs were passed along to the general taxpayer. Administrators couldn't even budget costs in any meaningful way; they could only work out what had been spent the previous year, and add a factor of inflation.

Not surprisingly, public medical expenses soared, for a number of reasons.

Costs that were once private were now public; the bills that were once paid out by individuals were paid by government cheques instead. The cost of the services was not rising, but the public expenditure on these services was, very visibly, on the increase. This was, and is, invariably reported as a jump in medical costs, when, in fact, the same dollars are being paid to doctors and hospitals out of general, rather than private, pockets. This key factor is almost never taken into account in cost comparisons: the money was always spent by individuals; now it was spent collectively. We were told that costs were soaring.

Canadians were getting a new, improved service — decent medical and hospital care for every person in the country. New treatments, drugs, and devices were constantly coming on the market, and they were usually much better than what they replaced, and they always cost more. Drugs were not even included in the original proposals; now they cost more than the fees of the physicians. And the population was aging, with, we were told, much higher costs incurred by Canadians over sixty-five.

The Geezer Factor

This last factor was used to promote near panic on the subject of medical costs. Right-wing think-tanks, one of the commodities never in short supply in Canada, "proved" by extrapolation that the old geezers and their disintegrating bodies would bankrupt the nation ere long. Tom d'Aquino, head of the Business Council on National Issues (BCNI), put it this way: "Our aging population means that health-care bills will rise sharply at the same time as the proportion of workers shrinks."[4]

The C.D. Howe Institute, funded by the same folks who fund the BCNI, astounded us all by coming up with the same conclusion, estimating that within forty years, health costs will eat up a staggering 57 per cent of provincial budgets.[5]

Even champions of medicare were impressed into a gloomy acquiescence. Unless something was done, we were told, extra spending caused by the geezer generation over the next half-century would, by itself, add $530 billion to the debts being accumulated as a legacy to our children.

However, when researchers looked at what has happened, instead of riding an extrapolation into Never-Never Land, a somewhat different pattern emerged. In the first place, over the past two decades, national productivity has pretty well kept pace with the increase in government health expenditures.[6] This is evident even in the figures used by the C.D. Howe Institute, but they dismiss them as irrelevant, because things can only get worse. (It is kind of a built-in reflex over there: things are going to get worse; the only way to make them get better is — guess what? — to cut taxes to the large corporations and rich individuals.) Canadians will continue to be able to produce a decent medicare system.

Just as importantly, the sharp rise in future costs is built on the assumption that the elderly in the future will use as much as or more of the services provided than before. So, more old people, more costs. This is true, but with some qualifications that turn out to be crucial.

---

[4] *Toronto Star*, 8 September 2001.

[5] The study was called *Will the Baby Boomers Bust the Health Budget?*, but the question mark was wasted. The C.D. Howe group knew the answer: they would.

[6] Figures from Statistics Canada show that health expenditures as a percentage of the gross domestic product increased through the 1970s from about 7 per cent in the 1970s to 10.1 per cent in 1991. Then the share declined to 9.5 per cent in the late 1990s. The trouble with these numbers is that the share of private spending on health increased from about 25 per cent to just over 30 per cent in the same time period, and private spending appears to increase faster than public spending. (Because, for one thing, it includes drug costs for most of the population.) What can be said for sure is that health costs are not, in fact, "exploding" or "rocketing"; on a per capita basis, except for drug costs, they have been declining modestly over the past five years.

The first is that providing medicare to the population seems to be doing exactly what Tommy, among others, always said it would do: producing healthier people. A number of studies in Canada (and in the U.S., where medicare is available to those over sixty-five, though not to the general population) point to the fact that when seniors have access to medication for high blood pressure, they suffer fewer heart attacks; when they have a hip replaced — now an almost routine operation — they don't have to go into a nursing home; when they live healthy lives, with regular checkups, they are much less likely to become disabled. An American study published by the U.S. National Academy of Science found that between 1982 and 1995, the proportion of seniors (that is, remember, those Americans on a medicare system) using health facilities declined significantly.[7] They were now getting decent care; in the end, looking after them cost less, not more.

In a study produced in 2001, the Saskatchewan Commission on Medicare concluded:

> The impact of aging, per se, on health utilization and costs in Canada was shown long ago to be quite small. Recent research from Canada and elsewhere strongly suggests that the elderly are healthier now than decades ago and tomorrow's elderly are likely to be even healthier. Moreover, patterns of care can change dramatically: Hospitalization rates have been declining for thirty years and long-term care institutionalization rates have been halved between 1981 and 1999. Thus, there is little reason to believe that, on its own, the aging of the population will require a massive infusion of cash into the health system.[8]

The Cost

In 1945 Canadians spent $250 million on health, of which governments spent $68 million, or just over 26 per cent.[9] Health care was costing

---

[7] Tom Walkom reported the study in the *Toronto Star*, 6 September 2001.
[8] Quoted in the *Toronto Star*, 11 June 2001.
[9] Perry, *Fiscal History of Canada*, table 22.1

Canadians just over 2.2 per cent of the gross national product. By 1962, after the introduction of hospital insurance, we were spending $2.56 billion on health, almost half of it through government — 5.9 per cent of our GNP. A decade later, governments spent 70 per cent of the health care costs of $8 billion — 7.3 per cent of GNP. By 1982, we were spending $31 billion, with the government paying the same 70 per cent; that came to 8.6 per cent of GNP. We hit the ceiling in 1992, when health costs, at $70 billion (and the government share at 74 per cent), ate up 10.2 per cent of GNP. Since then, the government share of health costs has declined to roughly 70 per cent, back where we were two decades ago.

The Romanow Report (officially, the *Report of the Commission on the Future of Health Care in Canada*, subtitled *Building on Values: The Future of Health Care in Canada*), released in late 2002, approached this subject by noting that the cuts in spending left us with a system that cost us, in public and private health care costs, 9.1 per cent of our GDP, less than we spent on health a decade ago.[10] And, significantly, less than we *ought* to be spending.

Incidentally, there has never been a year, from 1971 onwards, when the United States was not spending more, both per capita and in proportion to its GNP, than Canada, for a system that leaves 40 million people without any health insurance at all.

These numbers must be set in context from two angles. The first is that we are getting a constantly improving result. Canadian life expectancy, general health, disease control, and child mortality showed huge improvements during this time. The second is that, compared to the Americans, who have kept fooling with various combinations to avoid any government-run health plan, we did very well indeed. In 1975, our health costs consumed 7.1 per cent of GNP while theirs consumed 8.2 per cent; at the end of 1996, our figure was 9.5 per cent, theirs 14.2 per cent.

And the Americans still have a vast stratum of citizens who have no coverage whatever, while their general health statistics keep drooping.

---

[10] The report is available at www.healthcarecommission.ca.

The Romanow Report shows that in all the major categories of health measurement, including life expectancy, infant mortality, perinatal mortality, disability adjusted life expectancy, and potential years of lost life (due to illness), Canada ranks much higher than the United States. That nation, in most of these indices, is near the bottom of all countries belonging to the Organization for Economic Co-operation and Development.[11]

The issue was summarized in a recent academic study this way:

> On average, Americans spend about 75 per cent more per capita than Canadians, while Swedes spend 33 per cent less. Interestingly, American health outcomes are substantially worse than Canadian outcomes in both life expectancy and infant mortality.[12]

The Americans had, in a vain attempt to save money (administrative costs eat up as much as a quarter of health spending in the United States, compared to about 4 per cent in Canada), herded most of their people into Health Maintenance Organizations, or HMOs, to negotiate group charges for panels of incorporated doctors hired by the insurance companies. As a result, most Americans have little real choice of doctor, although it was the cry of "free choice" that led them to reject the Canadian system, where we do have free choice (although few Americans believe that for a minute).

The Savage Cuts

Unfortunately, the studies and surveys commissioned in recent years had not been done when our lords and masters, responding to the propaganda posing as research that flooded the nation in the 1970s and 1980s, took an axe to the system. The motto seemed to be Chop First, Think Later. Armed with the latest pamphlets from the wealthiest think-tanks money could buy, the federal government — whether Liberal or Conservative — and the federal bureaucracy became convinced that

---

[11] Ibid., figures 1.1 through 1.8, 12–13.

[12] Harvey S. Rosen, Paul Boothe, Bev Dahlby, and Roger S. Smith, *Public Finance in Canada* (Toronto: McGraw-Hill, 1999), 315.

only savage, across-the-board cuts imposed from above would bring spending under control. Since Ottawa was bound to pay half of whatever qualifying costs were incurred by the provinces, with no limit, the only way to impose a limit was to abrogate the deal. So that was done.

The process began when the federal government, in 1977, transferred 13.5 per cent of the income-tax points to the provinces, increasing their taxing powers and decreasing Ottawa's. At the same time, federal transfers to pay for all social services, including health, were divided into two elements: a direct cash payment to each province, plus the revenue that came from the tax points. Ottawa agreed to update the value of the tax points transferred in 1977 in line with the growth in population, and other factors.

However, there was no full correspondence with growth on the cash side of the equation. There, any growth in transfers was tied to growth in the GNP, so that it would rise with increasing national income.

This was all worked out by a federal Liberal government. Then, beginning in 1986, the Tories added their spin, limiting the increase in cash transfers to any gain in the GNP over 2 per cent annually.[13] If national income increased by 3 per cent, the payout to the provinces would go up by only 1 per cent. The effect was to cut back the federal contribution to both health and education costs, without appearing to do so. Every year, the cash transfers declined.

Ottawa was moving towards a balanced budget by cutting its help to other levels of government. Successive federal budgets claimed $14.4 billion in cost cuts between 1993 and 1998; nearly half of this — $6.8 billion — consisted of cuts to the transfer payments.[14]

Then came another savage blow. In 1995, the federal budget bundled all its transfer payments into a single block, and reduced it. Instead of separate programs, each with its own budget and regulations, all transfers for health, post-secondary education, and social assistance were stuffed into one lower block grant, known as the Canadian Health and Social Transfer, or CHST. This arrangement, worked out by the then finance minister, Paul Martin, was arrived at to persuade the provinces to go

---

[13] Perry, *Fiscal History of Canada*, 447.
[14] House of Commons, *Fifth Report of the Standing Committee on Financing* (Ottawa: 1997), 118–19.

along with a cut of $7 billion in total funding in this area. It was a devil's compact, if ever there was one; Ottawa gave up the right to make sure health care funding was spent on health care in return for permission to slash. The effect of these cuts was to justify the provinces in making similar cuts, which they did.

Then the two levels of government began a shouting match, which continues to this day, as to where the blame falls for the savagery inflicted on medicare. Obviously, it falls on both levels, but there is no doubt where it started — in Ottawa.

In all, more than 50,000 hospital beds were closed in Canada between 1985 and 1995; everywhere, hospital budgets were cut, thousands of nurses (but no doctors) were fired.

The cuts, usually made in haste against self-imposed deadlines, were always defended on the grounds that they were unavoidable, "given the financial constraints," but that was simply not true. The choice that was made, every time, was to transfer the bleeding to those who could not defend themselves as well as other groups — to patients, hospital workers, and nurses, rather than doctors and pharmaceutical firms, who continued to pull in more and more money as the system was being destroyed around them.

In Ontario in 1997, at almost the same time that nurses were told the freeze on their salaries that had been in place since 1993 would be continued, a deal was struck with the Ontario Medical Association to pay the doctors $594 million more over the next three years. That deal swallowed all the projected (and, it turned out, somewhat illusory) savings the province had gained by closing twenty-five hospitals. Ontario hoped to save $430 million by closing hospitals; it gave the doctors another $594 million.[15] The nurses can't, or won't, bring the entire medical system of a province to a halt; history has shown that the doctors can, and will.

As the waiting lists grew for everything from cancer care to cardiac operations, we began to turn back to the private sector to provide the care that had been removed from the system. In 1996, when, for the fourth

[15] *Globe and Mail*, 2 June 1997, and *National Health Expenditures in Canada, 1975–96.*

year in a row, real per capita health spending declined, private spending grew by just over 5 per cent; it has grown by more than 35 per cent since 1990, and now, once more, represents more than 30 per cent of all health spending.

To make up for some of their lost income, hospitals began treating patients privately, after hours, to earn cash on the barrelhead. This set off a great argument about "creating a two-tier system" of health care, as if we hadn't had such a system for three decades. However, the $20 billion now spent annually on private medicine is no longer money spent on nose-bobs, boob jobs, holistic medicine, and other items that the provinces do not choose to cover. A lot of it represents money paid by those who can afford to jump the queue to get preferential treatment. Preventative medicine, where the best returns for money spent are to be found, is being abandoned. The costs are incalculable, but preventative medicine has no effective lobby.

And then, as story after story broke in the media about the suffering of ordinary Canadians because of the dismantling of their health care system, governments, both federal and provincial, began to find them-selves in trouble. Nurses began to work to rule; doctors, who realized, at the last minute, that their prayers might one day be answered, and medicare done away with, began to complain; and the general public, who found that any time a member of the family was admitted to hospital, a nightmare began to unfold, raised bloody hell.

In Ontario, where hundreds of millions of dollars had been spent to pay off nurses and make them go away (and where more than a third of all Canadian nurses are employed), more hundreds of millions were spent to lure them back again. We stopped talking about the shortage of money, and began to talk about the shortage of nurses, doctors, and hospital beds. The Canadian Nurses Association released a study in 2000 that showed not only that we had fewer nurses per capita in 1999 than a decade earlier, but that we were facing a shortage that could run as high as 113,000 nurses within the next decade (there were 256,544 registered nurses in Canada in 1999).[16]

---

[16] *Supply and Distribution of Registered Nurses in Canada* (Canadian Nurses Association, 2000).

Canadians, collectively, bellowed "Enough!" and for once, they were heard. The result was an extraordinary deal worked out in the autumn of 2000 between the federal and provincial governments. Under the deal, Ottawa agreed to add at least $21 billion to the transfer payments to the provinces over five years, starting in 2002. The transfers will go from $15.5 billion in 2000–01 to a minimum of $21 billion in 2005–06.[17] The total of new money will also add to at least $21 billion. To put this in perspective, the 2001–02 payment, $18.3 billion, is still lower than the same payments made in 1994 ($18.7 billion).

Ottawa was simply putting back some of the money it had swiped from the health care system.

But it *was* putting it back, and it was coming as close as a Liberal administration has ever come in history to admitting that it had blundered. The provinces reacted in their various ways. Mike Harris, the then premier of Ontario, who had presided over the most brutal dismemberment of the health care system in the land, flew into a rage because, he said (correctly), Ottawa was still not paying what it used to pay, and ought to pay, to support medicare. He noted that where the federal share of costs was once 50 per cent, the actual share of health funding now borne by Ottawa is about 16 per cent.

This was not merely looking a gift horse in the mouth; it was kicking it in the teeth.

As the howls of rage rose, Ottawa at last responded with three major commissions into the past, present, and future of health care in this country. One of these was headed by a Conservative, Don Mazankowski, a senior member of the Mulroney government since retired back to his native Alberta. One was led by Senator Michael Kirby, a lifelong Liberal. And the third was chaired by Roy Romanow, the former NDP premier of Saskatchewan. And they all said the same thing, in different ways:

Medicare needs fixing, not dismantling. It needs more money, not less.

The Mazankowski document suggested that more private medicine might be a help, but all three reports concluded that medicare is, over all, the cheapest, most efficient, and fairest way to fund health care. And all

---

[17] *Toronto Star, Globe and Mail*, 12 September 2000.

three dismissed the notion of a parallel private system, much less the American system.

The Romanow Report, the most ambitious and heavily documented of these reports, made an unanswerable argument, in plain English (astonishing, for anyone used to royal commissions): "Medicare is a worthy national achievement, a defining aspect of our citizenship and an expression of social cohesion. Let's unite to keep it so."[18]

Romanow called for an injection, over three years, of an additional $8.5 billion in federal funding to the provinces, specifically aimed at five health areas: primary health (i.e., doctors and nurses), rural and remote health, catastrophic drug coverage, limited home care services, and diagnostic services. Then he wanted Ottawa to restore its funding of health care to previous levels, adding $6.5 billion to the monies already budgeted by Ottawa. The studies that accompanied the report argued that the additional money would not mean an additional drain on the treasury; the costs would be more than covered by even today's modest annual increases in the growth of our economy.

Romanow also dealt with the Geezer Factor, by noting that, while Canadians over sixty-five cost the health care system roughly three times as much as the national average, the increased costs in the years ahead are expected to amount to "about 1 per cent a year."[19]

> There are countries which already have significantly larger elderly populations than Canada, spend significantly less and achieve similar health outcomes in comparison to Canada.[20]

The Geezer Factor Was, and Is, a Fake

To keep medicare on the rails, Romanow called for the establishment of a new Health Council of Canada to oversee the spending, and to ensure that money allotted for health care went to health care. The CSHT should be dropped, he said, and given a decent, or even indecent, burial.

The Romanow Report naturally, inevitably, set off another round of

[18] *Report of the Commission on the Future of Health Care in Canada* (Ottawa: 2002), xxxi.
[19] Ibid., 19.
[20] Ibid., 20.

finger-pointing, name-calling, and figure-fuzzification among the provincial and federal governments. For example, the feds insist on adding all the value of the tax points granted to the provinces to their share of the payments (on the grounds that the provinces could, if they wished, spend the whole amount on health). The provinces, in turn, normally refuse to recognize these tax point as value, and only count the cash transfer. Thus, Ottawa says that it is paying more than 20 per cent of provincial health charges, while the provinces put it at less than 16 per cent.

But in the end, as even the most Conservative (and conservative) of the politicians recognized, Canadians wanted medicare, and they wanted it to deliver decent, universal services. After a series of seemingly endless meetings, the Chrétien Liberals, who had been so active in demolishing the system, committed themselves to significant reform in the federal budget of February 18, 2003.

Despite some dodgy accounting that had the provinces screaming again that Ottawa was not paying its share of costs, this document committed the federal government to spend $27.1 billion in new money over a five-year period (another $7.7 billion had already been slated under a new arrangement with the provinces that had been announced previous to the budget, and there was, remember, that previous deal to increase funding over five years).[21] While right-wing critics complained that the government was spending us into perdition, the actual increases in all federal program spending (as opposed to debt servicing, elderly benefits, and other unavoidable charges) were scheduled to come in at less than the growth in the Canadian GDP.[22]

The budget made medicare its centrepiece and reversed the pattern of slashing/neglect that had been in place for so long. Just as importantly, much of the new money was tied to specific programs, such as hospital bed shortages and home care. The budget set up a Reform Fund to pay the provinces $16 billion over five years for these purposes. If the provinces want to draw down the money, they cannot just stick it in a side pocket; it has to go where directed. At the same time, Ottawa promised

---

[21] The provinces claimed that Ottawa was double-counting existing health transfers and that the new money actually spent will not reach the $15 billion over three years that Romanow recommended. The Canadian Health Coalition contended that, because there existed no accountability mechanism, there is no way to be sure exactly what money will be spent on what. *Toronto Star*, 19 February 2003. The budget appears in full at www.fin.gc.ca.

[22] "Spending plans are actually modest," *Globe and Mail*, 19 February 2003.

to establish, someday, somehow, an oversight program like the one suggested in the Romanow Report. If it keeps its word, never a sure thing, this will reverse the deal cut in 1995 when the feds agreed to the CHST.

Tommy Was Right All Along

What Canadians learned, or should have learned, from this exercise is that Tommy had it right all along. Medicare is something that Canadians, of whatever ilk or political persuasion, recognize as something good, something to be proud of, something to defend. Even those politicians who, like Harris and Alberta's Ralph Klein, have done the system the most harm, dare not say they are taking an axe to medicare because they think it is no damn good. The wrecking ball is always preceded by an announcement that the government at the controls is doing this out of love, in order to improve the system we all love. When Klein declared in 1992 that spending on health services was "literally going through the roof," he proceeded to slash health budgets by $515 million over the next three years. Then, when an election loomed in 1997, he suddenly found that he had overdone it, and was in political danger (among other things, a retired radiologist, the brother of one of his key campaign workers, ran against Klein to protest the cuts). He then found $145 million he didn't know he had, and put it back into the system. Got away with it, too; he was re-elected.

Medicare now costs Canadians, in current dollars, about $74 billion annually. This is quite a lot less than was spent in the year 2000 on corporate mergers in Canada ($100.9 billion, much of it written off on taxes).[23] We are to believe that the Canadian economy can readily bear the costs of removing competition from the marketplace, but not the cost of keeping healthy. Seems odd. Seems unbelievable. Seems, indeed, like something most Canadians will simply not believe.

If there is anything heartening in the agony we have been going through recently, it is that no one, anymore, in any position of real authority, wants to replace medicare. It is to be improved, reformed, redeemed, and made sustainable, even by its severest critics. If they sound

---

[23] Walter Stewart, *Dismantling the State: Downsizing to Disaster* (Toronto: Stoddart, 1998), 287.

a little like the Americans who liberated villages in Vietnam by destroying them, well, that is a pity.

No doubt there will continue to be attacks on medicare. It has so many natural enemies out there in the private sector who salivate at the thought of the profits to be made by aping the American system that we will continue to be bombarded with studies proving that, in one of the richest nations in the world, at the richest time in world history, we cannot afford the kind of health service Tommy envisioned when it all began in 1944. And no doubt every attack will be met by a counter-attack, and a lot of struggle, and then, unless the Canadian character changes beyond recognition over the next few years, a successful defence of the system that, with all its faults, continues to serve us so well.

I like to think that every time one of these victories is won, some-where, Tommy smiles.

The Wit and Wisdom of T.C. DOUGLAS

The religion of tomorrow will be less concerned with the dogmas of theology and more concerned with the social welfare of humanity.

— Research review, 1934

It has been said that a country's greatness can be measured by what it does for its unfortunates. By that criterion Canada certainly does not stand in the forefront of the nations of the world although there are signs that we are becoming conscious of our deficiencies and are determined to atone for lost time.

— Comment at the Dominion-Provincial Conference, 1946

This is a democracy and in a democracy if a government is elected on a promise to cure arthritis by giving baths at Watrous, I would say it is the duty of that government if elected to send arthritic patients to Watrous, whether or not it would do them any good.

— Statement as the minister of health, Saskatchewan, 1951

We have many Saskatchewan people who go to British Columbia because of the climate and a lot of them come back because of the weather.

— Comment at a federal-provincial tax conference, 1960

Give us 70 seats and we'll turn Parliament upside down. Give us 170 seats and we'll turn the country right side up.

— Campaign speech, 1963

The Liberals talk about a stable government, but we don't know how bad the stable is going to smell.

— Election comment, 1965

I do not think that the dead hand of the past should be allowed to stay the onward march of progress. Human rights are sacred but constitutions are not.

— Quoted in the *Globe and Mail*, 1966

I don't mind someone stealing my pajamas, but he should wear all of them if he doesn't want to appear indecent.

— Complaint that NDP programs were appropriated by Liberals, 1968

A recession is when your neighbour has to tighten his belt. A depression is when you have to tighten your own belt. And a panic is when you have no belt to tighten and your pants fall down.

— Biographical essay, 1971

In the 1960s my job was to ensure that Canadians did not fall asleep on their full stomachs.

— *Time* magazine, May 3, 1971

It is good that Mr. Trudeau did not consult the cabinet. It would probably have insisted on a study session followed by a white paper about which nothing would be done.

— Comment on Prime Minister Pierre Trudeau's marriage, 1971

Index

socialism *(continued)*
  fear of, 41–42, 100–102, 106, 179–83, 213
  religion and, 55–58, 59, 60–61, 106
  Tommy Douglas and, 76, 84, 93, 209
  in United States, 75, 202
Socialist Party of Canada, 102–3
Social Planning for Canada
  (League for Social Reconstruction), 128
South Africa, 297
South Korea, 298, 299
South Saskatchewan Regiment, 143, 170
Soviet Union, 79, 95–96, 105
Spain, 136–37
Spencer, W.T., 98
Spry, Graham, 96–97
Spurgeon, Charles Hadden, 53
Standard Oil of California, 139
Stanfield, Robert, 270, 271, 273
Star Phoenix (Saskatoon), 186–87
Stephen, George, 199
Stevens, H.H., 111–13, 115, 124
Stewart, Margaret, 245(note 16)
Stewart, Walter, 68, 131 (note 1)
Stinson, Ted, 121
Stonewall, Manitoba, 52
Strachan, David, 34
Strathclair, Manitoba, 64
Strong, Maurice, 296
Student Christian Movement, 61
Sutherland, D.M., 214
Sutherland, Donald, 276, 277
Sutherland, Kiefer, 276, 277
Sutherland, Rachel, 84, 276, 277
Sweden, 158
Sweet, F.W., 53
Swift Current, Saskatchewan, 218

T
Talney, Mark (Talnicoff), 44–45, 52, 54, 67
Talney, Nan (Douglas), 14, 24, 29, 41, 48, 52
taxes, 202, 274, 292
Taylor, Charles, 277–78
Taylor, E.L., 45
Taylor, Jack, 50
Taylor, J.S., 127
Taylor, Robert, 230–31

Thatcher, Ross, 226, 230
Thomas, Jimmy, 205
Thompson, Robert, 259–60
Toronto Star, 203, 260
Trades and Labor Congress of Canada,
  50, 195, 238.
  See also Canadian Labour Congress
transfer payments, 312–13, 315, 317–18
Trotskyites, 133–35
Trudeau, Pierre Elliott
  in election campaigns, 272–75, 289–90
  and energy policies, 294–95
  and FLQ crisis, 283–84, 287–88
  and Liberal leadership, 270–71
  and nationalism, 265, 273
  NDP influence on, 289–90, 292, 294–95
  and the west, 289
Tucker, Walter, 183–91, 198–200
Turkey, 298
Turner, John, 286
Tweedsmuir, Lord. *See* Buchan, John
Tyre, Robert, 194–2

U
Underhill, Frank, 96–97, 101, 103, 129
unemployment, 70–72, 113–15, 204–5
unions, 169. *See also specific unions;*
  labour movement
United Church of Canada, 62
United Farmers of Alberta, 51, 59, 78–79,
  102–3, 115
United Farmers of Canada, 95–96, 105
  Saskatchewan Section, 86–87, 88–89
United Farmers of Manitoba, 60
United Farmers of Ontario, 127, 134–35
United States. *See also* Vietnam War
  and Canada, 256–57, 258, 266–68
  eugenics in, 78, 81
  health in, 309–11
  and oil industry, 291, 293, 294
  socialism in, 75, 202
University of Chicago, 74–75
University of Toronto, 135–36
Urich, John M., 163

V
Van Horne, Cornelius, 59

Vietnam War, 266–68
Vulcan Iron Works, 23, 48

W

Waffle movement, 278–82
Walden, David, 182
Wallace, Barbara, 300
war. *See specific wars*
Warrows, Parania, 188
Watkins, Mel, 274, 279, 280, 281
Watson, David, 32
Webb, Beatrice, 19, 76, 213
Webb, Sidney, 19, 76, 77, 213
welfare. *See* social assistance
Wells, H.G., 77
Wesley College (Winnipeg), 56
Western Conference of Labour Political
  Parties (1929), 88–89
Western Labor Conference (1919), 50
Western Labour Conference (1932), 99
Weyburn, Saskatchewan, 65, 67, 71, 74,
  85–86, 117–19
Weyburn Independent Labor Party, 95
Weyburn Independent Labour Association,
  84, 94
Whelan, Ed, 5, 64, 300
Whelan, Pemrose, 64, 249, 300
Whidden, H.P., 57
Whitehorn, Alan, 182
Whitney, James P., 176
Wilkins, W.D., 172–74
William I of Germany, 212
Williams, Charles Cromwell, 194–95
Williams, George Hara, 89, 162.
  See also elections, federal
  in CCF, 95–96, 107–8, 144–45, 155, 156
  and land-use policies, 96, 104, 105

Williams, George Hara *(continued)*
  and M.J. Coldwell, 121, 123, 144
  and Tommy Douglas, 125–26, 144,
    145–46
  and war, 137, 138, 140, 141, 143, 146
Winch, Ernest, 103
Winnipeg, 23–28
Winnipeg Citizen, 42
Winnipeg Declaration of Principles,
  179, 208–9, 237, 248, 278–79
Winnipeg Free Press, 45
Winnipeg General Strike, 38–39, 42–45,
  55, 56, 93
Winnipeg Grenadiers, 143
Winnipeg Trades and Labor Council, 42
Winter, Robert, 233, 262
Wood, Henry Wise, 59
Woodsworth, James Shaver (J.S.), 50, 84,
  94, 121
  as activist, 45–46, 56, 59
  and formation of CCF, 97–100, 101
  influence of, 29, 47
  as Member of Parliament, 47, 69, 86, 127
  and M.J. Coldwell, 87–88
  as pacifist, 137, 139–43
  as party leader, 128–29, 135, 142–43, 145
  as social worker, 25–26, 38–39
  views of, 25–26, 134
  and Winnipeg General Strike, 45–47
Woodsworth, Lucy, 45
Workers' Unity League, 91
workfare, 170
World Youth Congress, 136
Wylie Commission, 89–90

Y

Young, Edward J., 116–17, 119–21